O Lord, my God:

In reverence I thank You
for the graces and the gifts
You bestowed on Your faithful Servant,
Metropolitan Andrei,
to do Your work and pray
that through Your Fatherly Mercy
he may be glorified here on earth
to Your further praise
and to the salvation of the people
You entrusted to his care.

Amen.

WORDS

OF THE SERVANT OF GOD

Metropolitan Andrei Sheptytsky

Seniors Club
Ukrainian Catholic Brotherhood of Canada
Toronto

Preparation of this volume for publication was possible by a grant from The Horizon Program, Health and Welfare Canada and the Ukrainian Canadian Foundation of Taras Shevchenko, Winnipeg, as well as, generous donations from various organizations and individual sponsors.

ISBN 0-921537-11-5

Cover design: Claus Mohr

Printed by: The Basilian Press, 265 Bering Ave., Toronto, Ontario, M8Z 3A5

Published by the Seniors Club of UCBC
4 Bellwoods Avenue
Toronto, Ontario, M6J 2P4
Canada

CONTENTS

SERVANT OF GOD
Metropolitan Andrei Sheptytsky
1865-1944

FOREWORD

God blessed Ukrainian people with many gifts during the one thousand years of their history as a Christian nation. Perhaps the most important of these have been the spiritual and church leaders sent to guide them through the vicissitudes visited upon them by history. Of these leaders the most distinguished was Metropolitan Andrei Sheptytsky, Servant of God. In many aspects he personifies the principal values of Ukrainian Christianity.

He was a leader who instilled in his followers a willingness to endure and overcome unspeakable hardships, an eagerness for self-sacrifice, a sense of dignity and sacred duty that helped carry them through their darkest hours.

For forty-five years he was a bishop-pastor. He lived for his flock, and prayed that, if necessary, he might be granted a martyr's death for his people. When he died fifty years ago, he left his Church a remarkable legacy. Apart from the example he set through his life, suffering, and sanctity and in addition to his many apostolic initiatives, he left his Church a precious collection of writings: pastoral letters, theological treatises, reports and correspondence.

In many respects they remain as relevant today, as when they were written (some at the beginning of the twentieth century), and have assumed a rightful place in the treasury of Ukrainian Catholic thought. Two of these spiritual works make up the bulk of this publication.

The Ukrainian Catholic Brotherhood of Canada (UCBC) is the official lay organization for men of the Ukrainian Catholic Church. It is a non-political, charitable organization. Its aims are: to develop and enrich the religious and spiritual life of its members; to reinforce their identity as Ukrainian Catholics; to preserve, develop and perpetuate the Ukrainian language and culture; and, to strengthen the spiritual dimensions and moral values of Canadian life.

The Ukrainian Catholic Brotherhood of Canada has branches, in seven provinces, each affiliated with a Ukrainian Catholic parish. The Seniors Club of the UCBC, which consists of a group of founding

9

members of Toronto branches of the Brotherhood, has undertaken the publication of this book in tribute to the great Metropolitan and to mark the fiftieth anniversary of his death in 1944.

In preparing this volume, the main published works of the Metropolitan, accessible to the Publishing Committee, were reviewed. These were primarily the four volumes published in Ukrainian by different publishers and places. Volume I appeared in 1965 under the sponsorship of the Ukrainian Theological Society, Toronto. The Redeemer's Voice Press, Yorkton, Saskatchewan, published Volume II in 1969. Publication of Volume III (1978) and Volume IV (1983) was undertaken by the Ukrainian Catholic University of Pope St. Clement, Rome.

From this collection of Metropolitan Andrei's writings two important works were selected and are presented here in translation. These are *On Prayer* and *The Gift of Pentecost*. Both had originally been published in instalments by the *L'vivski Arkhieparkhial'ni Vidomosty* (The Lviv Archeparchial Bulletin).

As background for readers, two items by other authors were added. These are: a brief biographical note by Prof. Ilarion Holubowycz, who worked with the late Metropolitan, adapted from a similar piece originally published in 1961 by the Ukrainian Christian Movement in Great Britain; and, *Metropolitan Andrei Sheptytsky as Author* based on previously-published material by Dr. Anatol M. Bazylewycz.

Without the support of many individuals and institutions this work would not have appeared. Particular thanks are due to:

The New Horizons Program, Health and Welfare Canada and the Ukrainian Canadian Foundation of Taras Shevchenko, Winnipeg, which made publication of this book possible;

The Eparchial Executive of UCBC (Eastern Canada) for its encouragement throughout the project;

Individual financial contributors for their generosity which is acknowledged in another part of this volume.

The initiative for conceiving this publication project and carrying it to a successful conclusion belongs to the Seniors Club of the UCBC. The following are its current members (in alphabetical order): Stefan

Babiak, Michael Cybulsky (*Chairman*), Rev. Jaroslaw Lewycky, Lubomyr Lewyckyj, Julian Martyniuk, Teodor Perejmybida (*Treasurer*), John Piatka, Hryhorij Swerhun, Paul Szwec, Mykola Ziniak (*Secretary*). The first chairman of the Club was the late Alexander Klufas after whose passing Father Jaroslaw Lewycky participated in the work of the group.

Thanks are particularly due to Father Dimitri Pankiw, Father Boris Kyba, CSSR, Father James Sharinger, and Messrs Oleh Bych, Eugene Chorostil, Michael Cybulsky and other members of the Seniors Club, for translating individual parts of the material in this book. Father Eutimy Wolinsky, hegumen Studite Fathers, Woodstok, for cooperation and support.

A special debt of gratitude is owed to the three-member Publishing Committee into whose hands this project was entrusted by the Seniors Club. They are: Myroslav I. Diakowsky, who provided editorial services; Mykola Ziniak, who undertook to establish the sound financial base; and Michael Cybulsky, who assumed the responsibility of coordinating the project.

This book is offered to its readers in the hope that the words and spirit of Metropolitan Andrei Sheptytsky will serve to nurture their spiritual growth.

Michael Cybulsky
Toronto, 1995

TO THE READER

Biblical references in this book are based on the Revised Standard Version Common Bible (*The Holy Bible, Revised Standard Version containing the Old and New Testaments with the Apocrypha/Deuterocanonical Books, Expanded Edition*) published by Collins. This is an Ecumenical Edition endorsed for general use by His Eminence, Cardinal Koenig, Archbishop of Vienna and President of the World Catholic Federation for the Biblical Apostolate.

The references themselves (book, chapter, verse) have been included in the body of the text for convenience.

For further reading about the life, work, and thoughts of Metropolitan Andrei Sheptytsky, the following are some books that might be consulted:

Korolevsky, Cyril   *Metropolitan Andrew (1865-1944)*
                     Translated and revised by Serge Keleher
                     Stauropegion, Lviv 1993

Father Cyril Korolevsky (born Jean Francois Joseph Charon) became a priest of the Greek-Catholic Church and for many years worked closely with Metropolitan Andrei.

Magocsi, Paul R.,   *Morality and Reality. The Life and Times*
editor   *of Andrei Sheptyts'kyi*
                     Canadian Institute of Ukrainian Studies
                     University of Alberta
                     Edmonton 1989

This volume is based on scholarly papers (substantially revised) originally delivered at a conference, "Andrei Sheptyts'kyi: His Life and Work" held in Toronto in 1984, as well as original material prepared for this volume.

Husar, Lubomyr   *Ecumenical Mission of the Eastern Catholic Church*
                  in the Vision of Metropolitan Sheptytsky
                  Roma: Pontificia Universitas Urbaniana, 1975

Chirovsky, Andriy   *Pray for God's Wisdom*
                     Metropolitan Andrey Sheptytsky Institute
                     of Eastern Christian Studies
                     Ottawa, 1992

METROPOLITAN ANDREI SHEPTYTSKY AS AUTHOR

Metropolitan Andrei's written works can be classified as belonging to three major periods. The first period lasted from his enthronement as Bishop of Stanislaviv in 1899 to his exile in Russia in September, 1914. The second period extends from his exile until 1927, when he participated in the V-th Velehrad Congress and wrote *Skhidnya i zakhidnya mental'nist* (Eastern and Western Mentality). The third period extends from the conclusion of the Metropolitan's major unionistic speeches and conferences, primarily in Western Europe; that is, from 1928 until his death in 1944.

The first and third periods were the most productive.

The First Period (1899-1914)

In the first period are many epistles on various matters, pastoral letters addressed to the faithful in Ukraine, and a lengthy catechistic letter entitled *Bozha Siyba* (God's Sowing), 1913. He also codified the monastic statutes of the Sisters Servants (1905), the Basilian Sisters (1909), and the Studite Brothers (1904); the *Sknylivskyi Typikon*, written in 1905, was published in 1910. During this time he also prepared materials for the Lviv Eparchial Synod (December 28-29, 1905), delivered speeches at the Synod and also addressed the Diet (parliament) of Halychyna (Galicia).

All these letters and works are linked to the organizing of the church, the spiritual and academic life of the Stanislaviv eparchy, the Lviv archeparchy and the whole metropolia. Also to this period belong the Metropolitan's organizational activities and speeches at the I-st and II-nd Velehrad Congresses (1907 and 1909).

It should be noted that in 1903 he was ill and did not write.

Metropolitan Andrei was deeply concerned about those who, for different reasons, had left their native land for Canada, the United States, and other countries in search of a better lot in life. As head of the Mother Church he felt responsible for their well-being. The manifestation of this pastoral responsibility for Ukrainian immigrants

13

was the publication of: *Do Rusyniv osilykh u Kanadi* (To Rusyns [Ruthenians] who have settled in Canada) 1901 and 1902; and *Kanadiyskym rusynam* (To Canadian Rusyns), 1911; as well as: *Pamyatka dlya rus'kykh robitnykiv v Angliyi, Argentyni, Brazyliyi, Daniyi, Kanadi, Spol. Derzhavam, Frantsiyi, Shvaytsariyi i Shvetsiyi* (A memento for Rusyn workers in England, Argentina, Brazil, Denmark, Canada, Germany, the United States, France, Switzerland and Sweden), 1911; second edition 1914.

We might also include in this period everything that the Metropolitan wrote before he became Bishop of Stanislaviv in 1899. Thus, the beginning of this period should be pushed back to the 1890's. If more materials from this period were to be found, it might well constitute a separate period.

Three items of information from this period are known.

First, the Metropolitan together with Rev. Platonid Filyas, OSBM, founded *Misionar* (The Missionary), the most widely-circulated popular religious monthly in Halychyna. Both were its co-editors, and thus the publication must reasonably have included materials from the Metropolitan's pen.

Second, while at the Basilian Monastery at Dobromyl', the Metropolitan began a study of the works of St. Basil the Great. This was in 1893-96 and was related to his duties as Master of Novices at the monastery. It is possible that other materials were written at this time, perhaps in connection with his work as missionary and later professor of theology.

Third, while a student and before entering the Basilian monastery in 1888, he composed a profoundly ascetic prayer about the numerous members in his family who served God as priests or monks. The contents of this prayer indicate knowledge about the founders of various religious orders, both Western and Eastern. This prayer was written at his birthplace, Prylbychi, May 23, 1888.

The Second Period (1914-1927)

The second period was the least productive in terms of written works.

However, this period is replete with a number of very profound

14

speeches and reports delivered during congresses dealing with Church union. Among these are: *Pro vidnovu slovyans'koho chernetstva* (On the renewal of Slav monasticism), 1921; *Pro rolyu Zakhidnikh u dili zyedynennya Tserkov* (On the role of Westerners in the matter of Church union), 1923; *Pro rolyu monashestva dlya spravy obyednannya Tserkov* (On the role of monasticism in the matter of Church unification), 1923; *Psykholohia uniyi* (The psychology of the Union), 1925; and, *Skhidnya i zakhidnya mental'nist'* (Eastern and Western mentality), 1927. Also to this period belongs a long letter, *Rosiys'kyi Katolyts'kyi Ekzarkhat* (The Russian Catholic Exarchate), 1927.

The conferences dealing with Church union represent the culmination of the Metropolitan's unionistic thoughts. Everything that he wrote later on this subject has its roots in these conferences and related speeches, reports, and essays. They, as his other activities, awakened interest on the part of the West in the Eastern Church. The result was not only a change in the way Roman Catholics approached the Eastern Orthodox, both those not in union as well as those united with the Apostolic See, but also the creation in various Western orders of branches following the Eastern Rite, such as the Benedictine, the Capuchin, Jesuit, Oblate, Salesian, and others. The Redemptorist Fathers already possessed an Eastern Rite branch.

To this period also belong the organization of the St. Petersburg Synod which took place under the Metropolitan's leadership in 1917, and *Propozytsiya v spravi reformy tserkovnoho prava Skhidnyoyi Tserkvy* (A proposal regarding reform of Eastern Church canon law), 1927. This time also saw the beginning of work on the *General'nyi Ustav Chynu Brativ Studytiv* (General Statute of the Order of Studite Brothers) which was completed in 1936. This work was also referred to as the *Velykyi Typikon* (The Great Typikon).

In 1929 a translation from the Greek original of the ascetical works of St. Basil the Great, begun in 1910-11, was published.

To this second period also belong addresses delivered before the Upper House in Vienna of which the Metropolitan was an *ex officio* member. Pastoral letters were also written. Of these, unfortunately, not many have been preserved.

There are several reasons why this second period was not as productive in terms of volume as the first. The exiling of the Metropolitan to Russia following the occupation of Western Ukraine (Halychyna) by Russian troops in the early months of the First World

War made serious authorship impossible for the three years that the exile lasted. Afterwards, in the immediate post-war years Metropolitan Andrei was occupied not only with reorganizing church life in the metropolia, but also with endeavouring to heal or at least ease the pain of the wounds the war had inflicted on his flock. He was particularly solicitous of its individual victims: invalids, widows, and orphans.

He visited Western Europe in search of justice for his people from the mighty of this world, as well as to solicit funds to assist victims of the war. With the same goal in mind he travelled overseas to Canada and the United States attending conferences dealing with Church union in Toronto and New York (1921). As Apostolic Visitor he was with the Ukrainian faithful in Brazil. Not much time could be devoted to writing, but even while travelling, he wrote epistles to his flock in Ukraine.

The Third Period (1927-1944)

The Metropolitan's most important ascetical works belong to the third period. These are: *Bozha mudrist'* (God's Wisdom), 1932, a work intended to consist of many volumes, but of which only three were written. The third volume in this series was entitled *Khrystyyans'ka pravednist'* (Christian righteousness), 1935. The second volume of *Bozha mudrist'* was not printed.

Dar Pyatdesyatnytsi (The Gift of Pentecost), 1936, is in its way a continuation of the planned series of ascetical works. To this period also belong a historical monograph on Yosyf Veliamyn Rutsky (1574-1637), Metropolitan of Kyiv, and the completion of the *Velykyi Typikon* (Great Typikon), published in 1936. This had been started two decades earlier, together with the Metropolitan's brother, Father Klymentii Sheptytsky. The work was written in French so that it could also be useful in the West.

During this time the Metropolitan wrote a number of letters dealing with Church unity: a collection of documents, *U spravi porozuminnya* (On Understanding), 1943; *Ekzarkhat Bilorusy* (Exarchate of Belarus), 1943; and a longer epistle to the clergy on a sociological and unionistic theme: *Yak buduvaty Ridnu Khatu* (How to build our Native Home), in the sense of state-building, which appeared in December, 1941. Previously, in 1932, he had issued his *Slovo do ukrayinskoyi molodi* (To Ukrainian Youth) a document dealing with sociological issues which became well-known.

16

Many of the decrees issued by Archeparchial Councils held in Lviv in 1940-41 are unmistakably by him, while others clearly reflect his thinking.

To this period also belong pastoral letters, instructions to the clergy, advice to confessors and similar documents. Among his pastoral letters three, *Pro pokayannya* (On Repentance) which appeared in 1937-39, belong to his most profound spiritual writings.

These pastoral works which were published in the *Lvivs'ki Arkhieparkhiyal'ni Vidomosty* (Lviv Archeparchial Bulletin) and, the Metropolitan Andrei's epistles written during his entire archpastorate, still await a separate study, one that would depict him more fully as a pastor and organizer of spiritual life. Such he was first of all, and only secondly, an ideologue and protagonist of union, although the ideal of Church union was central to his life. He was also a liturgist, historian, collector of artifacts reflecting the national culture, a philanthropist, who was active in cultural affairs, and a defender of the rightful demands of the Ukrainian people.

This third period of his creativity was a time in which Metropolitan Andrei was confined to a wheelchair (from 1931) and in ill health for protracted periods. This only enhances the value of what he was able to produce in such unfavourable circumstances.

Style and Language

The writing style employed varied with the nature of the specific work. Major ascetic works, such as *Bozha Mudrist'* (God's Wisdom), *Khrystyians'ka pravednist'* (Christian righteousness) and *Dar Pyatdesyatnytsi* (The Gift of Pentecost) are characterized by a difficult philosophical style.

Style also depended on the addressees or readers, or hearers, for which the letters, epistles, or conference speeches and reports were intended. Consequently the style of materials delivered at unionistic conferences and other writings on Church union, writings and letters on ritual matters, as well as many epistles after 1930, and the style of Archeparchial Synodal Decrees -- less one frequently that of scholarly works, and read much more easily. This includes the monastic statutes which, although dry in presentation, can be read and understood by everyone.

17

On the other hand, the style of many letters is popular, especially to those from the first period (1899 - 1914), of such appeals as *Bozha siyba* (God's sowing), *Kanadiyskym Rusynam* (To Canadian Rusyns [Ruthenians]), *Pamyatka dlya rus'kykh robitnykiv....* (Memento for Rusyn Workers....). on the other hand, the Metropolitan's occasional speeches are characterized by a specific discursive style. Finally, at least those after 1933, had the character of a lecture, and were based on a few words from the Holy Scriptures or from our liturgical books.

It would require a separate publication to discuss the literary devices Metropolitan Andrei employed, his use of contrasts, the structure, etc., of his works, speeches and sermons. A general statement can be made, however, that the Metropolitan possessed exceptional talent in this area.

He wrote in Ukrainian that was current in Halychyna at the time. Here and there we find Polish and Russian forms of expression. These latter probably came by way of the old Slavonic language then in liturgical usage...

The Metropolitan's writings, printed in the *Lviws'ki Arkhieparkhial'ni Vidomosty* (Lviv Archeparchial Bulletin) from the late 1920's to 1944 were edited to conform with the academic orthography. Even here many language peculiarities specific to Halychyna remain, as the editor sought to preserve the flavour of the Metropolitan's original text to the maximum.

Collected Works

...There are two parallel thrusts in the Metropolitan's writings and his speeches and conference reports. One deals with the salvation of the individual and with the raising of the level of priestly and monastic life. The other seeks to correct historical prejudices. It urges mutual forgiveness by both sides, in matters of Church unity and the improvement of social relations within the Ukrainian community.

To achieve these goals, much self-sacrificing work by "saintly and great leaders" would be necessary, and the Metropolitan sought to instil the necessary qualities in those who had been placed in positions of leadership. Already, he demanded from the young that they direct their lives to the doing of great deeds.

This is well-represented by the Metropolitan's works which have begun to be published in recent years.... In them, every reader, whether highly educated or not, whether from the Ukrainian community or from the broader community of the Universal Church, will find something useful and instructive. These works will be of particular interest to those who are active in the cause of Church unity and those involved in sociological research. Translation into other languages will make Metropolitan Andrei's writings even more accessible.

If everything the Metropolitan wrote were to be published, including the materials from the six Church councils held from 1905 to 1944, some twenty or more volumes would be required. Not all of these materials have been collected and some, in view of the beatification process that has begun, are not available even to academic researchers. Many of them, including his extensive correspondence, are in the archives of the Postulature. Others are in the archives of various Holy Congregations. Even without these, what is now available, together with a biography and bibliography, would fill some fifteen volumes of 250 pages each. Pastoral letters alone, ranging from several to dozens of pages in length, would require seven or eight books.

Some of the Metropolitan's writings have already appeared. The *Typikon* was published in Rome in 1964, and some works on union themes have been published in translation in Chicago. Four volumes of epistles have appeared thus far.

I close this brief account of Metropolitan Andrei Sheptytsky as author with the words he so often appended at the end of his writings:

To God, Glory; to Us, Peace!

Anatol Maria Bazylewycz

METROPOLITAN ANDREI SHEPTYTSKY
SOME PERSONAL REMINISCENCES

Whenever I looked at the stately figure of Metropolitan Andrei, I saw a gentle face with its snow-white beard and kind eyes sparkling with great joy. The resemblance of the Metropolitan to the Prophet Moses, as he is depicted in paintings, was so striking as to fascinate me. Seeing the Metropolitan, I had the feeling that I was looking at one of the patriarchs or prophets of God's Chosen People.

Metropolitan Sheptytsky passed from this life on November 1, 1944, but his spirit and influence remain to guide and inspire his people. For his nation he was indeed a Moses leading it out of the darkness of bondage and subjugation into the light of spiritual freedom. For almost half a century he was the living symbol of the Byzantine Rite Catholic Church in Ukraine.

His faithful used to call him the "Great Metropolitan", and indeed, he remains so in the esteem of the entire Ukrainian nation. Not even the Russian Communists dared attack him openly; in fact, during his lifetime, many Russians referred to him as *khoroshy Metropolit* -- a "good Metropolitan".

The stateliness of his person which radiated a remarkable charm, his stature in intellectual and cultural matters, his immense activity in every field of Ukrainian life, and -- above all -- the sanctity of his life, made him the indisputable sovereign of the hearts of the Ukrainian people, whatever their denomination. All Ukrainians, Catholic and Orthodox alike, recognize him as a man especially dear to God.

Metropolitan Andrei Sheptytsky, through the grace of Providence, was father to his people and one of the great Metropolitans in the history of the Ukrainian Church. He was the best of shepherds, ever ready to lay down his life for his sheep; a consoler of the afflicted, defender of the oppressed. He was a life-long patron of Ukrainian culture. As Apostolic Visitor to Canada, the United States, and South America he crossed the seas twice for the sake of neglected souls. He travelled to Jerusalem as a pilgrim. The fact that the faithful in North America received their own Ukrainian Catholic hierarchy was largely due to his unceasing efforts.

He was a true champion of Catholic unity.

His friendship with Pope St. Pius X, himself a zealous apostle, was well known, and he was highly praised in many pontifical utterances. Ever ready to become a martyr bodily, he was truly a martyr in his life and heart. In human terms Andrei Sheptytsky was a genius, in supra-natural terms, a beloved child of God.

Roman Maria Alexander Sheptytsky, Count of Sheptytsi, was born on July 29, 1865 in Prylbychi, Western Ukraine. His father, Count Jan Sheptytski was a descendant of ancient Ukrainian nobility; his mother was Countess Sophia, nee Fredro.

Among the more notable members of the family, Varlaam, Athanasii and Lev had served the Ukrainian Church as metropolitans of Kyiv, and had played an important part in Ukrainian religious and national life. The parents of young Roman, although partly polonized, never denied their Ukrainian ancestry, and spoke Ukrainian in his presence. His mother was his first teacher of religion. Young Roman showed a remarkable interest in the history of the Eastern Church and the Schism. By the time he was ten he knew what he wanted to be when he grew up -- a priest of the Eastern Rite. He completed his high school studies in Cracow at the age of eighteen in 1883. He visited Venice, and shortly after his return enlisted in the Austrian army. After his brief military service he was still a young man before whom bright prospects of a military or political career were open. However, he gave up all aspirations of becoming a great man of this world, and chose instead the humble life of a Basilian monk.

He did not enter the Order of St. Basil immediately. After graduating from university he visited Rome with his mother. At the Vatican he was received in audience by His Holiness Pope Leo XIII. Upon learning of his desire to become a priest, the Holy Father said to him: "Son, you have chosen the better part".

In 1886, Roman graduated from university with the degree of Doctor of Laws and in 1888 began his novitiate taking the monastic name "Andrei" after St. Andrew, Ukraine's patron saint, whom he had chosen as his model and inspiration. In the Collegiate of the Jesuits in Cracow he pursued studies in philosophy, theology, languages, both modern and classical, including Hebrew. Possessing the degrees of L.L.D., Ph.D., and S.T.D. (Doctor of Sacred Theology), he was ordained priest in 1892. After holding several important posts in his Order, he was elevated to the fullness of the priesthood in 1899 as Bishop of

Stanyslaviv. Here he soon proved himself a tireless and energetic bishop. On January 14, 1900 he was appointed to the Metropolitan See of Lviv, holding this office until his death in 1944, even when he was an actual or virtual prisoner of the Russians, Poles, Germans, and Soviets.

His whole life was directed towards the realization of his noblest ideal, the Redeemer's wish: "That they may all be one".

It would be impossible in a sketch as brief as this to give an adequate idea of the Metropolitan's enormous activity, both pastoral and charitable, during the 52 years he was a priest, 45 years of which were spent as Bishop of Stanyslaviv and as Archbishop-Metropolitan of Lviv.

Through his life, his pastoral letters, sermons and visitations of the faithful, the great Metropolitan was an example of a good Christian, not only for his flock, but for every person living in this fallen world. For him, "Be a good Christian, love your neighbours" were not meaningless phrases. In theory and practice his charity knew no distinction between persons. Anyone, regardless who he might be, could see him at his own convenience, seek the Metropolitan's advice or help, or simply talk about personal problems.

Like his divine Master he strove to be a "Good Shepherd". He was a great defender of all in need whether Catholics, non-Catholics or Jews, whom he protected from brutality during Austrian, Polish, German and Russian occupations. In trying times he showed remarkable selflessness without regard for his own health, comfort or safety, putting everyone else before himself.

The great Metropolitan preached constantly a need for cultural as well as religious progress, a need for respect of law and custom, and a need for moral rebirth and strength. By these means he tried to make his people more fully aware of their duty to make Christianity the whole basis of their lives. He taught his flock to love their Orthodox brethren who, knowingly or unknowingly, had found themselves outside the Fold of the Catholic Church.

This good shepherd never faltered in the performance of his pastoral duties. Neither was his zeal limited to his archeparchy and metropolitan province of Halych. It also reached out to the hundreds of thousands of Ukrainian immigrants living abroad in England, Canada, the United States, Brazil, Argentina, and other countries.

It was due to his intervention and petitioning that the Holy See established a Byzantine rite hierarchy for Ukrainians in the United States in 1907, and Canada in 1912.

In 1910, Metropolitan Andrei took part in the Eucharistic Congress in Montreal. As Apostolic Visitor, he visited the United States in 1921-22. He also travelled to Brazil and Argentina to ensure adequate spiritual services for Ukrainian immigrants living there.

At home, his pastoral zeal reinvigorated the Ukrainian Church. An important task was the restoration of monastic life in Western Ukraine, and the founding of numerous Basilian and Studite monasteries. Metropolitan Andrei was always an energetic supporter of the idea that Latin Rite Orders and Congregations for men and women should each form an Oriental branch and contribute thereby to the sacred cause of Union.

However, Andrei's greatest ambition was to accomplish something instrumental for the return of the Orthodox to the Universal Church, especially those who lived in Tsarist Russia. He was the moving spirit behind the Congresses for Reunion held at Velehrad in which he took a most active part. These were held in 1907, 1909, 1911, and 1927. He supported the College of St. Andrew in Munich, established by Cardinal Faulhaber in 1932.

Metropolitan Andrei took part and delivered insightful and wise speeches in many conferences, congresses, and consultations dealing with the theme of Union. He preached an apostolate founded on a Christian charity that accepted no limitations. In his opinion, before all things, it was necessary to pray for the grace of cooperation and the grace to work together with others. This could mean the sacrifice of one's own feelings, but its reward would be to discover "...how good and how pleasant it is when brothers dwell in unity" (Psalms 132:1).

The Metropolitan stressed the need for study and elimination of difficulties of a political nature and of psychological obstacles derived from different mentalities, and to search for means of obtaining a mutual coming together. He maintained, that the separated brethren ought always be treated with affection, because for the most part, they were of good faith. He thought that to reestablish unity among Christians it was necessary before all else to know and love one another. He realized that the hindrances to a general union between East and West were great and that the removal of the walls of separation required much good will and noble effort on both sides.

The great Metropolitan was always on his guard against a false conception of the Union. It must be clearly understood that union with Rome would not latinize the Eastern Rite Catholics. The Metropolitan charged his clergy to keep the purity of the Eastern Rite intact, for he was conscious of the fact that any Latin innovation, however legitimately acquired, might prove a stumbling block to the separated brethren. The Church has had many sad experiences in the area of reunion in prior centuries. The rights, customs and privileges of the Eastern Catholic Church had to be preserved, and the separated brethren had to be convinced that Union means a unity of faith with the Holy See of Rome, and not the latinization or denationalization in favour of their Latin Rite neighbours.

As far as the separated brethren in Imperial Russia were concerned, Metropolitan Andrei saw to it that his writings reached them, and on two occasions visited them in person. In 1902 he was in Belarus, and in 1908 in Russia. Those visits enabled him to make direct contact with leading personalities, both Catholic and non-Catholic.

It was providential that the Metropolitan of Halych had retained the title of the Suffragan See of Kamianets-Podilskyi despite the fact that the city lay within the boundaries of the Russian Empire. Because of this, Pope St. Pius X endowed him with jurisdiction over all Catholics of the Byzantine-Slavonic rite in the vast empire of the Tsars. In 1908 the Metropolitan nominated Alexis Zerchaninov, a Russian priest, as his Vicar General, and fixed his residence in the very capital of the Tsar, St. Petersburg. Thus, the foundations for the restoration of Russian Catholicism of the Oriental Rite were laid. This organization was eventually destroyed by the Russian police in 1913 but the Metropolitan reappeared the following year to find a remedy for the situation. In fact, the Metropolitan arrived in the city as prisoner, having been arrested by Russian forces of occupation in Lviv in September 1914. This happened after a famous sermon in the Church of the Assumption in which he put the faithful on their guard against the schismatic propaganda which had begun with the Russian occupation of Western Ukraine in the early weeks of the First World War. He was to spend three years as prisoner.

He was released with the outbreak of the revolution of 1917 and was able to summon a Council-Synod at St. Petersburg which lasted three days. Among the participants was a group of Russian Catholic priests, one of whom, Father Leonid Feodorov, was nominated Exarch for all Muscovite Russia, while a Vicar General was nominated for Ukraine, with his residence at Kyiv. Metropolitan Andrei knew that this state of affairs would not last. The Tsarist government which had been hostile to Catholics, had been succeeded by a Communist regime hostile to all religion. But it must be said that the work of the Metropolitan certainly bore fruit in this most difficult soil. The Russian Exarch was able to exercise his apostolate, albeit beset with great difficulties, for another five years until 1923, when persecution became general, and the Exarch was condemned to ten years' imprisonment on the notorious Solovets Islands where he died. Nevertheless, the experience of those five years of apostolic work carried out by the Russian Church will be a precious lesson for the future.

It would be difficult to supply statistical data about the fruit reaped from the work of Metropolitan Andrei on behalf of Church unity, but it can be said that he was truly a man of Providence and that he began a new era in that field justly earning for himself the title of the great Apostle of Unity. He was the man who sowed generously the seed which others would reap in abundance in the years to come.

Successive Russian governments, both Tsarist and Soviet, exhibited a real fear of the Ukrainian Catholic Church, as shown by the savage persecution directed against it. The life of the great Metropolitan, his efforts to set up an Exarchate in Russia, and the reaction there to the mere existence of the Eastern Catholic Church, leading to the virtual martyrdom of the entire Ukrainian hierarchy and hundreds of thousands of the faithful, are proof that the Catholic apostolate in the Slavic East was a difficult task, but not impossible.

Such, at any rate, was the lively faith and firm hope of the Metropolitan when the Iron Curtain descended on his people (in June 1944). The wound inflicted upon the Catholic Church by the Soviet atheistic regime of Moscow will one day be transformed into its banner of glory echoing the words of St. Paul: "But it behooves us to glory in the cross of Our Lord Jesus Christ, in whom is our salvation, life, and resurrection".

Before he passed into eternity, the Metropolitan lapsed into a prolonged period of absolute silence preparing his soul for the task of leaving this world, and to beg of God unqualified abandonment to the dictates of His Divine Will. As the great St. Paul had done so many centuries before, he had "fought a good fight and had finished the course and had kept the Faith", and Andrei knew that "as to the rest, there is laid up for me a crown of justice".

It was the general opinion of all Ukrainians, notwithstanding their creed or denomination, that Andrei died a man of God and a saint.

The numbers of people who flocked to his funeral were so extraordinarily large that the Soviet authorities did not dare to interfere as the procession moved slowly through the streets of Lviv. Khrushchev himself led the government delegation and placed a wreath on his tomb. For many years this was to be the last solemn external manifestation of the Catholic Church in Ukraine. After laying that body to rest, it became the Church of Silence driven by persecution into the catacombs.

The Sacred Congregation of Rites has already initiated the movement for the Beatification of Metropolitan Andrei. Let us pray that through its successful conclusion Almighty God may be pleased to manifest the special love He bears to His Servant Metropolitan Andrei Sheptytsky.

Ilarion Holubowycz

ON PRAYER

First Published
in
L'vivs'ki Arkhieparkhial'ni Vidomosty
(The Lviv Archeparchial Bulletin)
October 15, 1932 - February l5, 1933

INTRODUCTION

While staying in Pidliute[1] in September of this year, I wrote a pastoral letter on prayer. The treatment of this subject became so extensive that I decided to publish it as a separate booklet, On Prayer. The last chapters, those on "God's Wisdom", are given here at the beginning with the thought that they are more suitable as the introduction to the complete work.

I dedicate this publication to the Honourable Clergy of the Eparchy, my helpers in pastoral work, with the request that they convey the matter which has occupied my thoughts to our Beloved People in their sermons.

In Pidliute I did not have an adequate library at my disposal. More than one passage from the Holy Scriptures had to be quoted from memory. Patrological texts were not available. After my return to Lviv, I made additions.... Lacking the opportunity to rewrite the whole work, I submit it to you, Honourable Fathers, imperfect as it may be with my wish which is also a prayer that this work may help you and all those into whose hands it comes -- to overcome the unusually grave difficulties of the present moment -- and to deal with them in a Christian manner, armed with Divine Wisdom and the prayer of Christ.

Lviv, October 8th in the year of Our Lord 1932.

---

1   A village of Lviv, the summer residence of the Metropolitan.

GOD'S WISDOM

A PRECIOUS TRAIT OF OUR PEOPLE

Ukrainians hold learning and education in high esteem. Both the children, who approach school with great zeal and eagerness to learn, and also their parents and the elderly among our people consider learning, education, and knowledge as the first and most important of the people's needs.

Perhaps the condition of humiliation and of subjugation in which our clergy and people have found themselves in past centuries; perhaps an intuitively felt need; perhaps the realization that nothing is more important than knowledge to move the people forward -- are the reasons that learning and education are an ideal for all of us towards which our young people strive even at an age when they scarcely understand what constitutes true knowledge. Generations which suffered greatly because they lacked knowledge, who often were illiterate, pined and still pine for knowledge. The desire for knowledge is wide spread among all Ukrainians.

In accordance with that desire for knowledge that is so widely shared by the people, we are not far removed from judging a man by his intellectual worth. Clearly, a man's worth is his worth before God. A man is not what he appears to be to other men, but what he is to God. That real and substantive value of a man is often hidden from our eyes and it is impossible to base a social judgement on God's hidden power in a man's soul.

Among the social values, we cherish the intellectual power of knowledge and learning the most. This judgment would, it seems, be the most equitable one as concerns peoples' worth; obviously, people who are ethically sound. Everyone puts those who are ethical cripples or deviants, those who are without ethical worth, even if they are very intelligent, outside the pale of human society. No one considers bandits, even if they are clever, or traitors, or thieves, as those whose merit could, in general, be worth discussion. But even with these men, reason, knowledge, wisdom, constitute the most important social power -- greater than physical strength, greater than riches.

33

The history of literature, as taught in secondary schools, assesses a man according to a somewhat one-sided skill -- the ability to write verse or works of what is called *belles lettres*. It must be admitted that the history of literature or of creative writing cannot do otherwise because, by its very premise, it is the beauty of what the human intellect produces that it evaluates. It may touch tangentially on philosophy, the exact sciences, and other manifestations of human thought, but by its very nature it is condemned to look at the world from a point of view from which it is the beauty in the expression of human thought that is perceived.

Since there is no subject in the secondary school curriculum in which the creativity of the human intellect in general is presented, an unhealthy, because one-sided, conviction results: that *belles lettres* are the primary and most important product of human thought.

Because our people are still in the first, so to say, epoch of national development, it follows that poets are gladly considered to be leaders of national thought. It is easy for us to forgive this bias when we recall that in European universities philosophy is being taught in a way that makes no mention of the philosophy of India, despite the fact that India represents at least 90% of the intellectual development of mankind outside of Christianity. All the chairs of philosophy and history of philosophy still ignore the highest and most perfect works created by human thought.

Life corrects the bias of our schools by reflex. Only very briefly does a young person entertain the notion that he is most wise who can write a little verse. The first encounter with life smashes this rather naive notion, but that life, at least, does not lead our people into a materialistic assessment of a man, thank God. For us, a man with a golden ring does not take precedence over a wise man.

The superficial, although so necessary, polish that school gives: classical education, though so important; a knowledge of Homer and Horace even though it captivates not only the young, but the old, does not foist on us the view about intellectual life that we should not value wisdom above education or general knowledge above specialized knowledge, knowledge of one subject above a knowledge of life. No matter what value we place on education or knowledge, recognition of wisdom remains, all the same, the highest form of praise.

A man about whom it is said, or even thought, that "he is a fool", will always be disdained, if only covertly, no matter how rich he may be

34

and no matter what position in society he may occupy. Neither wealth, nor high office, nor strength, nor power can offset stupidity and will not replace wisdom. Without wisdom, power or importance will at best create an impression of some rare physical phenomenon. Wisdom alone provides the impress of a spiritual human quality.

It seems that all of this is a general human conviction, much of which remains even with those who have become accustomed in life to judge a man by how many dollars he has. Among us and for us Ukrainians this high regard for wisdom is possibly so general and so decisive that I would not hesitate to consider it our national characteristic and to take pride in it. Even though we are weak and poor and even yet have not produced world-renowned geniuses, that is to say, leading minds recognized as such by the whole world or who have pointed out new paths for mankind to follow, or who would conquer for mankind new worlds of truth or creativity -- this one trait of valuing wisdom properly as it is and what it is, should undoubtedly give our whole national life some great power which other nations cannot have, if they are weaker or lower in this respect. It is possible that I am mistaken. It may be that my love of self or of my own people generates mirages before my eyes. Yet I know that I would not hesitate for a second in my inner conviction, in the depths of my conscience and in my soul, to give priority to a wise beggar over a foolish ruler, regardless of where he may rule. Neither would I hesitate for a second in making a choice between these two conditions, not according to ascetic or monastic standards, but from a human point of view and "according to the flesh", as the Apostle says. I would always choose to be a wise beggar, rather than a foolish ruler. I think such a choice would be the right one and that, with me, most Ukrainians would judge and choose rightly.

A CHARACTERISTIC FEATURE OF OUR RITE

Our Rite and its beautiful components which, so far as I know, are absent from or rare in other rites, correspond to this national, so to say, character. A problem presents itself here, however. In the old church language "wisdom" (*mudrist'*) is called "great wisdom" (*premudrist'*). In popular usage the term "great wisdom" is now given some shading of irony. For this reason in my presentation I will use the word "wisdom" where in the old church language "great wisdom" is given.

The cult of a Divine Wisdom that existed before the ages began

35

is specific to our Church. Divine Wisdom was the hypostatic *Hagia Sophia* to which Justinian's cathedral in Constantinople and the cathedral in our capital, Kyiv, were dedicated. It is possible that this cult has somehow over the centuries even been lost and I do not know whether there is in the Archeparchy of Lviv a church dedicated to Eternal Wisdom, except perhaps the church in the Studite *Lavra* of St. John the Baptist in the Lychakiv district of Lviv dedicated about a year ago.

Nevertheless there have remained in our church Rite many moments which testify to the persistence of this cult and point to it. In these moments, during a service the deacon, more precisely the priest, calls to the people with the word "Wisdom!". To what else does this call refer except to a solemn plea to heaven for this precious gift -- the gift of wisdom for one's self and for the people?

Liturgists usually explain these words in the service -- which in a number of prayers glow in every way with a heavenly splendour -- to the effect that the call "Wisdom!" according to them does not much differ from the call: "Let us be attentive!" And yet what a boundless difference exists between them! I would say that these two words differ from each other simply as heaven does from earth.

This word or exhortation "Wisdom!" is used during services before the reading of the Holy Scriptures, before the Psalm of which there remains only the prokeimenon with its verse before the Epistle, before the Gospel and before the Readings. This word also comes before the ecphoneses (the audible intoning) in the Liturgy of the Faithful, and before the hymn *"Higher in honour than the Cherubim..."* and after the reading of the Epistle before the *"Alleluia"*.

According to the explanation of some liturgists the priest, or the deacon, in the name of the Church through this word, draws the attention of the people to the profundity of God's wisdom, contained in the revealed books, or to God's wisdom with which we should repeat the priest's call in our souls, or respond to it with our affirmation: *"Amen!"*, or with which we should magnify the Most Holy Virgin -- higher in honour than the Cherubim. In passing, I would find it interesting to see how the call for "Wisdom!" is explained by those liturgists who teach that the prokeimenon, the Epistle and even the Gospel should be read so quietly that even the altar boy cannot hear them.

Even though were we to accept this ecphonesis as making us aware of the importance of that what is to follow, it would no less also

36

have the meaning that I ascribe to it. By this word the Church blesses the faithful with God's wisdom, begs for them this gift of wisdom, and reminds them that they should strive to plead for this gift in order to understand the Psalms, the Epistle, the Gospel, etc. This word is a word of blessing, of request, reminder, instruction, the leading word in Christian preaching. For all of Christian preaching has the aim of transmitting to the people the wisdom of God's scriptures - God's Logos.

Here we are dealing with something supernatural, something divine; with something which is either a gift of the Holy Spirit or the Holy Spirit itself, or the wisdom of God's Logos or God's hypostatic wisdom. In every way, the word is replete with mysteries, it reaches the very heaven and in its mysterious depths expresses the mission of two Divine Persons, their action and their teachings.

After the word "Wisdom!" the deacon, or the priest, adds: "Let us be attentive!". With the first word he expressed heaven, with the second phrase, earth; with the first word, Godhead in Its infinite wisdom, then, an abyss of human weakness and helplessness; the first, light, the second, darkness; the first, God's gift, the second, human struggle. These latter are obviously also necessary, but what meaning do the efforts of humans have in God's affairs, and what part in understanding Scriptures inspired by God does the power of human reason have?

But apart from that, (and it seems that this is also found in the Roman Rite), our Rite quite often prescribes that paroemia, in excerpts from the Old Testament Books of Wisdom, be read. As in the Roman Rite, the words from the Book of Wisdom are often applied with reference the Most Holy Virgin Mary. Thus, for example, on the Feast of the Annunciation and other feasts of the Mother of God, the passages from Proverbs 9:1, "Wisdom has built her house, she has set up her seven pillars", and from Proverbs 8:22, "The Lord created me at the beginning of his way", are read.

Along with everything that has been said, one passage from Holy Writ stands out as something priceless, something that is in keeping with our deepest desires and needs, and yet is no less characteristic of our Rite, a passage that is also an excellent school of prayer.

A TEXT FROM ST. JAMES

This is a passage of which, it seems, no Christian can be aware without its leaving in the soul a deep and lasting impression. It belongs to those passages which affect our minds and our hearts with such mighty force that it can become the guiding idea of our whole spiritual life, above all the guiding idea of the whole life of prayer, and a well of immeasurable good and gifts, no less in our experience just as it is in God's revelation.

Saint James the Apostle says this in his Epistle (1:5), "If any of you lacks wisdom, let him ask God, who gives to all men generously and without reproaching, and it will be given him. But let him ask in faith, with no doubting...."

First, our soul must be struck by the words: "If any of you lacks wisdom..." for who, indeed, does not feel this lack? Who can think of himself as being wise as God is wise? It seems that to the extent of our Christianity, of our faith, of God's grace in us, to an equal extent is our conviction that it is wisdom that we lack. There is not the slightest doubt that the presence of these attributes is measured by our humility.

We would have to be very deprived of humility to think that we possess God's wisdom. When we consider, moreover, that this word is found in Holy Scriptures, which are often so hard for us to understand -- and often so impenetrable and full of difficulties as to be insoluble even for the most scholarly and devout of Christendom's theologians -- then even with a generous dose of confidence in our own knowledge and reason and without an excess, even with considerable lack, of humility, we cannot yet consider that passage from James does not apply directly to us.

The eminent French preacher, Bossuet, in a series of sermons delivered in the presence of the then still-young King Louis XIV, strove with all his genius as a preacher by means of indirect examples and even by direct hints to draw the king's attention to the evils resulting from his immoral life. The king could not, or did not want to, understand. Finally, Bossuet cited the example of David, fallen into the sin of adultery, and of the Prophet Nathan. Skilfully the preacher developed his sermon to the point where he could cite from Scriptures directly: "You are the man." James' text, too, points directly at each of us and repeats: "you are the man".

The impression is even more powerful when we realize that James' passage belongs to those exceptional texts in which the divinely-inspired Book calls for a prayer asking for something particular, and adds the commitment that it will be granted. In the divinely-inspired books of the New Testament at least, there is no other such directive. Christ's instruction to pray for labourers for the harvest does not contain the promise that the prayer will be granted. In another case, Christ says: "Pray that your flight may be in winter or on a sabbath." There He does not, however, promise that the request will be granted. Of the three passages in the New Testament which recommend prayer for something specific, the text from James is the only one that asks for such prayer and gives assurance that it will be heard. In this it is exegetically unique.

Rare also is the case where Holy Scripture expresses censure which must be accepted as applying to everyone. The well-known and marvelous letters sent by St. John to the seven churches in Asia contain extraordinary reproaches that simply shake the soul of the pastor. Among them are those which it is hard not to take to ourselves, as well.

To the bishop of Laodicea, for example, his letter says: "I know your works: you are neither cold nor hot. Would that you were cold or hot! So, because you are lukewarm, and neither cold nor hot, I will spew you out of my mouth" (Revelation 3:15). It is hard not to apply this passage to ourselves.

When, however, we remember that in the spirit of prophecy St. John probably saw the times of the Antichrist and, in addition to the church in Laodicea at the end of the first century and the beginning of the second, also had in mind the church in the time of the Antichrist, this prophetic admonition does not impact as directly on the reader's soul as does the text of St. James. That text has this characteristic -- one perhaps typical of all Holy Scripture -- that the more often the mind returns to it, the more strikingly its admonition reaches the reader's soul. It is an intimation of both a reproach and a promise, as if in those words the way God acts is confirmed.

Already in the Book of Samuel we encounter a characteristic and so-interesting song of Samuel's mother, Anne, who had so beautifully poured out her soul in prayer asking God for a son. In this song of gratitude she exclaims: "The Lord kills and brings to life; he brings down to Sheol and raises up. The Lord makes poor and makes rich; he brings low, he also exalts" (1 Samuel 2:6-7).

A thousand years later, the Virgin Mary, thanking the Almighty for her exaltation, repeats the same thoughts: "He has put down the mighty from their thrones, and exalted those of low degree; he has filled the hungry with good things, and the rich he has sent empty away"

(Luke 1:52-53).

James' text in its first half humbles us, in the second half, raises. It is this that creates the impression, indeed this is what faith teaches, that here Jehovah himself is speaking. Does not all this suffice for us to take special note of the text, to study it thoroughly, penetrate its meaning and follow its advice?

It happens when we are reading an ascetical book that we come across a text by some devout author who gives us sound advice that corresponds to the needs of our soul. How deeply at times such a passage engraves itself on our soul and into our memory. How often we return to it, even though the passage or the counsel it gives is of little meaning, for such passages are to be found often in various books of devotion.

But our passage, on the other hand, is so important that the more recent ascetical literature and all the writings of the Church Fathers are worth less than that one sentence of St. James'. It is understood of course that here I am speaking of the writings of the Fathers and of the ascetics to the extent that they are human products and not to the extent to which they quote Holy Scriptures and that text, and also not to the extent that they are the testimonies of the teaching of the Church, the episcopate, or the ecclesiastical schools of their times. Comparing human, although Christian, literature we not only can but must conclude that one word of divinely-inspired Scripture is worth more than everything the human mind as such has created. Thus, confronted by the text of St. James, we are forced on the one hand to confess our helplessness and our deficiencies, our spiritual blindness, the darkness in which our mind by its very nature dwells, and on the other hand long for the light of God's wisdom which divine revelation promises to us, the light we lack, the light of wisdom which is described in such captivating, such beautiful and lofty terms in the books of wisdom in the Old Testament.

And how many beautiful descriptions of it there are in the New Testament! James the Apostle himself, contrasting the "earthly, unspiritual, devilish" wisdom, with wisdom "from above" introduces it, as it were, social features: "pure,... peaceable, gentle, open to reason, full of mercy and good fruits, without uncertainty or insincerity" (James 3:15,17). The description of the results brought about by the lack of this social wisdom or this part of wisdom is such that we must consider the advice contained in the text of the Apostle as advice directed to all peoples, to the whole of mankind.

40

This is especially apt in our times. "What causes wars?" asks James, "and what causes fightings among you? Is it not your passions that are at war in your members? You desire and do not have; so you kill. And you covet and cannot obtain; so you fight and wage war. You do not have because you do not ask. You ask and do not receive, because you ask wrongly, to spend it on your passions" (4:1-3).

If we consider that the word "ask" refers both to the struggles and desires of mankind, and if the words of St. James be applied to these tremendous efforts and struggles of mankind to win peace and order in the world, then this terrible criticism: "because you ask wrongly", becomes clear. You follow the wrong path, your efforts will be futile.

WISDOM IN THE OLD TESTAMENT

The wisdom about which St. James writes is surely all-embracing, and in the mind of that God-inspired writer and in the mind of the Holy Spirit, is certainly the wisdom about which the Old Testament speaks.

Considering the time when it was conceived and written, the Epistle of St. James is probably one of the earliest books of the New Testament. This fact alone would indicate that in this epistle the word "wisdom" is still used in its Old Testament meaning. The very person of St. James, that zealous champion of the law, whose whole spirituality is still so close to the Old Testament type, would also lead to this conclusion. It will thus be proper to look in the Old Testament for the meaning of this word as he used it, and only then to discover that meaning also in the New Testament. Finally we will consult St. Thomas Aquinas, the paragon of all scholasticism, about the meaning of God's wisdom.

In the Old Testament there are four books whose whole subject is God's wisdom. Undoubtedly, a more profound study of these four divinely-inspired books of wisdom would lead to unusually interesting and fruitful contemplation.... Nevertheless, the subject appears to me to be immeasurably interesting and immeasurably important for each of us individually and for all of us collectively. For me it would be a wonderful ideal if, in part at least the Honourable Clergy, and even the faithful could be encouraged to energetic and constant effort in search of, and supplication to heaven for, this mysterious yet mighty gift, the great power of God's wisdom. Thus I cannot refrain from presenting at least a brief account of God's wisdom as it is described in those four books.

These descriptions draw the mind into such depths of enlightenment, and in a distant perspective show what the authors of the Old Testament did not know but that we now know and experience and live by, that their books are a considerably more interesting subject for us than they were for people in Old Testament times. In the passages about God's wisdom they perhaps beheld Messianic glimmerings. Perhaps they surmised that *Sophia* was not just a human trait, or while also a human trait it is a personification, which assumes the form -- hypostasis -- almost of a living person. Could they have identified this hypostasis with the Messiah? Did they guess that *Sophia* would become flesh; that, not in poetic metaphors, but in actuality, in the real order of this world, she will build for herself a house and set up seven pillars, that she will offer her sacrifices, mix her wine and set her table (Proverbs 9:1-2)? [Did they surmise] that in the living flesh, *Sophia* would call to the people: "Come, eat of my bread and drink of the wine I have mixed"? All this could not have had a place even in the dreams of the greatest saints of the Old Testament. Nevertheless, I think that when the prophets of the Old Testament read such passages, and the first three books were read perhaps by Jeremiah, Ezekiel, and the prophets minor and great, and they were read by Daniel, Elias, and Elisha, they must have grasped the Messianic meaning. On these occasions their heart must have throbbed with a longing they themselves could not understand. They must have felt a hunger for this bread of wisdom, a thirst for its wine.

We are fortunate that some of the mysteries that were so completely closed to them have been unveiled to us, fortunate that this treasure is to us at least partially revealed. But, regretfully, how unfortunate we are that we feel so little the hunger and thirst with which they burned. Is this not because, as the same Book of Proverbs writes: "bread eaten in secret is pleasant" (9:17), because that which is a mystery attracts and draws us to itself? If that is the cause of our indifference, then it can and should cease. Although the treasury of wisdom which was closed to the prophets of the Old Testament has been largely opened for us, yet other prospects have been opened for us in the distance, a distance about which the people of the Old Testament probably did not even have an inkling.

The temple veil that denied access to the Holy of Holies has been pulled aside before us. Because of that we can better understand all those further veils, those endless problems, those bottomless depths, which God's wisdom still keeps hidden from us, even though she is so approachable that we touch her, eat her bread, drink her wine, sit at her feast. Yet this wisdom is so little understood that every minute we become convinced anew that she dwells in unapproachable light. In every way, both reading and pondering the Old Testament books on wisdom bring us immeasurable benefits. Sometimes it is by the crumbs that we better recognize the weight and value of bread.

The Book of the Proverbs of Solomon

The first book [of the four Old Testament books] of Wisdom is called *Mishle* in Hebrew, and the Hebrew names of the first two books [of Wisdom] are used quite freely to distinguish them from the others. In the book *Mishle* are found first, encouragement to acquire wisdom (Chapters 1-9); then two collections of proverbs, one older (10-24), the other newer (25-31). Both collections contain the proverbs of Solomon and other Hebrew sages, collected during the reign of King Hezekiah of Judah.

The proverbs...express practical everyday wisdom of Old Testament times, little is said about wisdom as a distinct subject. The whole of the first part, an introduction as it were to the parables, speaks simply and specifically about wisdom, about the fruits and benefits which possessing wisdom brings, about her excellence, about how to search for her, how to avoid her opposite. Finally, in the last two chapters, 8 and 9, there is a very eloquent and convincing call to her.

Naturally, it is impossible, as it seems to me, to provide a brief presentation of a doctrine contained in a whole series of sayings often ambiguous and difficult to understand, which do not have any connection with each other or whose connection is very difficult to grasp. This much is certain: almost all that is great, beautiful, good, pleasant, comes from possessing wisdom, particularly a whole gamut of virtues, knowledge, mental gifts, which it is difficult to differentiate from wisdom herself. Wisdom gives correct understanding, knowledge, fear of the Lord, justice, judgment; wisdom sets one onto the right path. With her are associated simplicity and uprightness (Chapter 2). She grants a long life and peace, teaches truth, mercy does not abandon the man who searches for wisdom, for he shall find favour with God and men and a well-ordered life (3:1-7). Happy is the man who finds wisdom (3:13). Having wisdom is more valuable than trading in silver and fine gold. Wisdom is more precious than all possessions; one cannot compare with her anything that men desire (15). The length of days is in her right hand and in her left hand are found riches and honour (16); her ways are ways of pleasantness and all her paths are peace (17). Those who lay hold of her possess the tree of life (18); have a sweet and peaceful sleep (24). Finally, she gives true glory (35). Thus, she must be loved. She safeguards men (4:6); and will place a garland of grace on your head.

Wisdom is a good counselor, teaches justice, gives fortitude, she is a quality of kings, a teacher of lawgivers, a leader of leaders (8:15-16); she loves those who love her, and she is easily found by those who search early for her. With her are riches and honours and enduring wealth and prosperity (8:17-18). Wisdom was brought forth before the ages when there were no springs abounding with water, before mountains were shaped, she was there when God established the heavens, when He assigned the sea its limits...but her true delight was with the sons of men. Happy are those who keep her ways.

Ecclesiastes, or "Koheleth"

The main idea expressed in the Book of Ecclesiastes is: "vanity of vanities.... All is vanity." The [first six chapters of this] book are a broadly-developed treatment of this idea. Beginning with Chapter 7, the book gives various sorts of advice, directions, principles of righteousness, of order. It speaks about those in authority, about the king, about the rich, about the poor, and finally expounds certain principles on how wisdom should be valued. An interesting example is given of how the wisdom of a poor man saved a city when it was besieged by a mighty king. From this it follows that wisdom is better than weapons of war (9:18).

The "Song of Songs"

The book of Proverbs (*Mishle*) is intended for beginners, while Ecclesiastes (*Koheleth*) is for those more advanced in God's ways. The *Song of Songs* is for those who are perfected. This book describes the spiritual tie of love between Christ and the Church; or, rather, between Christ and human souls. It is filled with endless mysteries and is the source from which all mystics draw...

The last two books of Wisdom date from the second or third century before Christ. They repeat much of the teachings of Solomon, but belong to the canon of inspired books and possess many and varied divine qualities.

In the first part, which is in effect a philosophical treatise on wisdom, the author speaks about conditions for acquiring wisdom (1,2); about the benefits of acquiring her (3-6), and about the nature of wisdom.

The second part is, so to say, a presentation of the history of the chosen Jewish people. It shows how wisdom was the guide of the Patriarchs (10:1-14), how she ruled the Jewish people (10:15 - 19:19), and led them out of captivity (10:15 - 11:4), how their enemies were punished (11:5 - 12:27). Wisdom preserved the chosen people from idolatry (13:1 - 15:19), and also protected them from punishment when they did stray.

To be gained, wisdom must be sought with sincerity of heart (1:1), with faith (1:2). She must be sought in righteousness (1:4) because she will not enter into a wicked soul and will not dwell in a body burdened with sin because the Holy Spirit flees before deceitfulness (1:5). The spirit of wisdom is gracious, friendly to mankind.... God does not rejoice in man's destruction, for "God created man for incorruption". He made the nations of the earth capable of being healed.

A multitude of wise men is the health for the world, and a wise king is the strength of his people. Thus, "I prayed and understanding was given me...and the spirit of wisdom came to me" (7:7). "I preferred her to sceptres and thrones, and I accounted wealth as nothing in comparison with her" (7:8). "Neither did I liken her to any priceless gem, because all gold is just a little sand in her sight, and silver will be accounted as clay before her" (7:9). I loved wisdom more than wealth and beauty and I chose her to be my light (10); all good things came to me with her and in her hands uncounted wealth (11). I rejoiced in all who had wisdom, not realizing that she was their mother (12). What I learned diligently I shall pass on without grudging; I do not hide her wealth (13). For humans she is an inexhaustible treasure: and those who acquire wisdom share in God's friendship, "commended by the gifts that come from instruction" (14-15).

Wisdom, the fashioner of all things, taught me (7:21). Within her is a spirit of intelligence, holy, unique, manifold, subtle, mobile, incisive, unsullied, lucid, invulnerable, loving the good, keen, irresistible, beneficent, humane, steadfast, dependable, free from anxiety, almighty, all-seeing, embracing all virtues, pure, and most subtle. Wisdom is quicker to move than any motion: she pervades and permeates all things by her purity. She is as if a counterpart of God's power, and like an immaculate reflection of the light of almighty God and no shadow falls on her (25). For she is a reflection of eternal light, untarnished mirror of God's majesty, the image of His goodness. Although she is one, she can do everything. Remaining in herself, she renews the world, and through generations passes into holy souls, making them into friends of God, and prophets. God loves only those who dwell with wisdom (28). She is indeed more splendid than the sun, she outshines all constellations...is brighter than light (29). Light must yield to night but against wisdom evil cannot prevail. She extends from one end of the world to the other, governing all well (8:1).

It follows then that if wealth is desirable, what can be richer than wisdom which gives everything (8:5)? Nothing in life is more profitable (8:7). In addition, "Because of her, I shall have immortality, and leave an everlasting remembrance to those who come after me" (8:13).

All of heaven's gifts come through wisdom, even the gift of understanding those gifts, because it is a mark of insight "to know whose gift she was" (8:21).

"God of my fathers and Lord of mercy...give me the wisdom that sits by thy throne (9:1,4).... Send her...from the holy heavens... that she may be with me and toil, and that I may learn what is pleasing to thee" (9:10). Who among men can know God's judgment and understand His intentions? "Who has learned thy counsel, unless thou hast given wisdom and sent thy holy Spirit from on high?" (9:17).

Ecclesiasticus, or The Wisdom of Jesus the Son of Sirach

The longest among the books of wisdom is that of Jesus, son of Sirach, written in Hellenistic times and translated into Greek during the reign of Ptolomy Euergetes by the author's grandson, himself a righteous sage.

In order not to overburden my text with too many quotations, I will only present the Son of Sirach as an example of a man who throughout his entire life sought and prayed for God's wisdom. Towards the end of his book (51) in a prayer of thanksgiving, he says about himself:

"When I was still young...I sought wisdom openly in my prayer. Before the temple I asked for her, and I will search for her to the last. From blossom to ripening grape my heart delighted in her; my foot entered upon the straight path; from my youth I followed her steps. I inclined my ear a little and received her, and found for myself much instruction. I made progress therein...to him who gives me wisdom I will give glory" (51:13-17).

The Old Testament texts concerning the wisdom of God were in part also Messianic texts. They represented both the birth of the hypostatic wisdom of the Word of God as well as the granting of this wisdom to the people. This wisdom, obviously, is Jesus Christ -- the Word of God that has become Flesh. According to this fundamental truth of Christianity, wisdom -- as a human quality, as the people's virtue or strength -- will be at one with Christ's Spirit and with Christ's wisdom in them. But because Christ's Spirit in everything meets the needs of individuals and of nations and epochs, and particularly all facets of human nature, the word wisdom acquires a more definite, a narrower, meaning and begins to have application to only one aspect of Christ's Spirit. In Isaiah's Messianic passage (11:2), of this Spirit the Prophet writes: "And the Spirit of the Lord shall rest upon him, the spirit of wisdom and understanding, the spirit of counsel and might, the spirit of knowledge and the fear of the Lord."

In ascribing to God's wisdom all the virtues, we apparently do not stray from the consensus of the Old Testament. This not only because from heaven all benefits are given together with wisdom. As the Book of Wisdom (7:11) says: "All good things came to me along with her, and in her hands uncounted wealth". In many passages in all books of the Old Testament that speak of wisdom as if ex cathedra, wisdom is shown as being associated with all intellectual qualities, no less with qualities and gifts that are related to reason and the will.

Moreover, the very word *wisdom* is often replaced by another, a related, concept, understanding *(prudentes)*, for example. Thus in the Book of Proverbs 8:1 "Does not wisdom call, does not understanding raise her voice?" These two words, *wisdom* and *understanding* have the same meaning, in keeping with the rule of parallelism in Hebrew poetry. The second part of the verse, using different words, repeats the sense of the first. Substitution by the word *understanding* of the word *wisdom* occurs quite often. One example is Proverbs 7:4: "Say to wisdom you are my sister! Call understanding your relation". I am not citing other passages, because from many such instances it is clear that the God-inspired author more than once referred to *wisdom* as *understanding* and united these concepts in a way that ascribed to *wisdom* a meaning broader than that given in formal philosophy. The same should be said about the equating of other intellectual qualities with the quality that these holy books call *wisdom*.

47

WISDOM IN THE NEW TESTAMENT

The New Testament writers, obviously accept both the word *wisdom* and its corresponding meaning from the Old Testament, although one should consider that since, in the majority of cases, they use the Greek language and a Hellenistic translation of Scriptures, they also take into consideration the Greek meaning of this word. In translations into Church Slavonic and Ukrainian quite often the words *wisdom* or *wise* are also expressed by such concepts as "understanding", "intelligent,intelligence", "prudent, prudence".

In Christ's parable recorded by Matthew (25:1-13) we read about the wise and the foolish virgins. It was *wisdom* which led the wise ones to make ready for the Bridegroom and keep their lamps filled with oil. In Matthew 10:16 Jesus calls on the disciples to "be as wise as the serpents and innocent as doves". The Greek text renders *wise* as *fronumoi* (*prudentes*).

The man who built his house on a rock (Matthew 7:24) is called in our translation wise, and in the Greek intelligent. This, however, does not prevent us from seeing here Divine Wisdom, which we can easily obtain through prayerful entreaty, a quality possessed by the wise virgins and the serpents -- a quality which is directly commended to us, pastors -- and also the quality of the sensible man who builds on a rock. In these passages in the Greek original *fronima* is used to which translation again gives a somewhat different meaning, when it says that "to set the mind on the flesh is death, but to set the mind on the Spirit is life and peace" (Romans 8:6).

The meaning of the word *wisdom* should also be sought in those passages in which Holy Scripture speak about light. This word is at times applied to moral life, to moral qualities, in the sense of purity, lucidity whether of soul or relationships. However, there should be no doubt that when Holy Scripture speaks of the light which illuminates understanding, by this word it very often means Divine Wisdom, for it cannot be doubted that Divine Wisdom is anything but light, illumination, or a valuable and great gift from heaven. It is this which allows the human intellect to understand truth by some more lofty and fuller means than the intellect alone can do.

We must, however, limit ourselves to those passages in Holy

Scripture, that speak directly of *Sophia*. Thus in Luke (21:12-15) Jesus Christ tells his followers that they will be persecuted for their faith. "They will lay hands on you and persecute you, delivering you up into...prisons.... I will give you a mouth and wisdom, which none of your adversaries will be able to withstand or contradict."

It is characteristic that this promise of wisdom made by Christ was recorded only by St. Luke, a physician with a Hellenistic education. In St. Matthew and in St. Mark Christ's promise reads differently. In Mark 13:12 Christ says, "...It is not you who speak, but the Holy Spirit". From this it would follow that wisdom is the quality through which, in man or through man, the Holy Spirit speaks. As St. Luke puts it: "The Holy Spirit will teach you in that very hour what you ought to say" (Luke 12:12).

The man who, when prosecuted before the courts, through his speaking can put judges and adversaries to shame, deserves in the eyes of all to be called wise.

St. Stephen was obviously such a man, "full of grace and power", whose adversaries in dispute "could not withstand the wisdom and the Spirit with which he spoke" (Acts 6:10). Indeed, his defense, as recorded by St. Luke, possibly from St. Paul's dictation, even with slight errors of memory, is so striking a fulfilment of Christ's promise, that it sounds like a battlefield signal of victory and a routing of the enemy, even though it led to the stoning of St. Stephen. Such, in any case, are all Christian victories, and such was the victory of Christ.

No matter how ideal was the apologia delivered by Socrates, which inspired another sage, Plato, to record Socrates' defense, every knowledgeable literary critic must grant primacy to St. Stephen. In St. Stephen's apologia Divine Wisdom and some inner invincible power manifest themselves, not only strength of spirit but also of mind.

I cite Greek sages not without good reason, because the Greek word *sophia* had, through a long and old tradition in Greek culture, its own defined and developed meaning. When a Greek said about someone that he was wise, *sophos*, it was as if he was comparing that man with one of the seven mighty, great, leading geniuses who held an exceptional position in the development of Greek thought. The New Testament is written in Greek and we must look to Greek culture for the meaning of the words used there. The meaning of a word in a language also influences the development of thought. The God-inspired writers of the New Testament used the Greek language and the Greek words with the meaning which the Septuagint translation of the Bible had given them.

In his first Epistle to the Corinthians (3:10) St. Paul speaks of himself as being "as a wise master builder" who "laid the foundation", referring to the building of the structure and doctrine of the Church. It would seem that here the Holy Apostle gives the word "wise" a meaning that we express through "good organizer". Although Jesus Christ is the foundation laid by the Apostle, laying the foundation is not only preaching Jesus Christ but also organizing the Christian Church.

The Apostle speaks of Divine Wisdom, but in a different sense, in the first two chapters of this same epistle. Here God's wisdom is contrasted to the wisdom which the Greeks seek (1:22-23). God's wisdom, or, to judge according to the flesh, "the foolishness of God is wiser than men, and the weakness of God is stronger than men" (25-26). For the Apostle this is God working through people.

Yet again but with a slightly different meaning, St. Paul speaks in the second chapter: "among the mature we do impart wisdom" (2:6). Here he contrasts the most lofty and the most profound mysteries of his teaching with those more simple and more approachable truths, which he calls milk for babes, because, as he writes to the Corinthians "you were not ready for it; and even yet you are not ready, for you are still of the flesh" (3:2).

From this we can see that as in the Old Testament, so in the New, God's wisdom is in itself, or grants, or is united with, all the qualities of a mind illuminated by the light of heaven. Holy Scripture mentions only infrequently that Christ is Himself God's Wisdom in the flesh, God's Word which became flesh (John 1) "in whom are hid all the treasures of wisdom and knowledge" (Colossians 2:3). Everything that Christ gives, all His teachings, all His grace, all that He has established, is the work and gift of this Word of God, which itself is also a gift to us.

From this arises the necessity to ascertain what among the many gifts is the so-special gift that Holy Scripture calls wisdom. Is it that which Apostle Paul calls Christ's mind, when he says "But we have the mind of Christ" (1 Corinthians 2:16)? Is it Christ's spirit which, too, is a gift given us? Or, finally, all or any one of the qualities of the soul, the created but supernatural powers of the soul, through which we become participants in Christ and the Holy Spirit?

The above gives rise to the need to differentiate all the qualities and also for a psychological analysis of them, from which the doctrine of

50

St. Thomas about the gifts of the Holy Spirit emerged, and in a more particular way about the gift of God's wisdom. This doctrine is exceptionally important for all teaching about prayer and leads the human spirit to such heights or into such understanding of God's profundity, that we must yet return to it after having presented all of the teaching of the Holy Scriptures about prayer.

A PRAYER FOR WISDOM

It follows from all that has been presented thus far that God's wisdom, no matter how we define it, is like a teacher, or a treasury of all virtues and of all spiritual gifts. Therefore, as guided by St. Thomas Aquinas, the great teacher in the school of theology now approved by the Roman Pontiffs, let us review the virtues of Christian life, for which we should ask every day, gathering them into the form we are here discussing, namely the form of God's wisdom. Through this we remember that God's wisdom either contains these virtues, or leads us to them, teaches them to us and is a guide on the way to them.

O Great and Almighty God!
Bestow on me from Your high and holy heaven and from the throne of Your glory, Your holy wisdom, which is the first by Your throne.

Grant me the wisdom to know Your will, so that in life I might do what pleases You -- to desire fervently, to search wisely, to seek with truth, flawlessly to fulfil every task for the glory and honour of Your holy Name "to the praise of his glorious grace" (Ephesians 1:6).

Give me, O God, the wisdom of my calling, that I may fulfill everything that You demand. Grant that I understand my duties, give me the wisdom of my duties and grant that I discharge them as is fitting for Your glory and for the benefit of my soul.

Give me the wisdom of Your ways and the wisdom of walking in the paths of Your holy will. Grant me wisdom of success and failure so that I might learn not to exalt myself in the former, nor fall in the latter. Give me the wisdom of joy and of sadness, so that I might rejoice only in what leads me to You and find sadness only in what leads away from You.

Give me the wisdom of all that is transient and all that is lasting; may the first diminish in my sight, and the latter grow. Give me the wisdom of labour and of rest; may labour on Your behalf be my delight and my rest without You be my fatigue. Give me the wisdom of honest and simple intention, the wisdom of directness, the wisdom of candour; may my heart turn to You and search for You in all things, all my life.

Grant me the wisdom of obedience, obedience to Your law, and to Your Church. Give me the wisdom of poverty: may I never value possessions other than according to their real worth. Give me the wisdom of chastity according to my calling or vocation.

Give me the wisdom of patience, the wisdom of humility, the wisdom of cheerfulness and of solemnity, the wisdom of the fear of the Lord, the wisdom of speaking truth, and of good deeds. May I be patient without the least complaint, humble without the least affectation, cheerful without excessive laughter; solemn without severity, fearing You without despair; truthful without a shadow of equivocation. May my good deeds be free from self-satisfaction.

Give me the wisdom of admonishing, if need be, my fellow-men without self-aggrandizement; give me the wisdom to build by word and deed without hypocrisy; give me, O God, the wisdom of sensitivity, attention and caution; may no empty thought lead me astray.

Give me the wisdom of integrity, may no attachment that is unclean or unworthy bring me down. Grant me the wisdom of uprightness, may no selfish intention lead me from the path of duty. Give me the wisdom of courage and strength, may no tempest bring me down. Give me the wisdom of liberty, may no compulsive passion enslave me.

Give me the wisdom of the theological and the moral virtues: faith, hope, charity, prudence, justice, temperance, fortitude. Give me, O God, the wisdom of the Apostles, the wisdom of the martyrs. Give me the wisdom of a priest and of a pastor; give me the wisdom of preachers and of teachers. Give me the wisdom of servants at the Holy Sacrament; give me Eucharistic and mystic wisdom -- the wisdom of prayer and of contemplation.

Most of all, O Lord, give me the wisdom of heartfelt contrition, of imperfect and of perfect regret. Give me the wisdom to know myself in my weakness and my malice; give me the wisdom of mortification and fasting; give me the wisdom of self-denial and self-sacrifice. Give me the wisdom of sacrifice, the wisdom of the Cross, the wisdom of Blood.

O God, give me finally the wisdom that leads, according to Your holy intent, to the unification of the churches under one supreme shepherd -- the Bishop of Rome. Give me the wisdom to cherish, to love this cause of holy union, and to dedicate my whole life to it.

Give me the wisdom of our Eastern Rite, its preservation, renewal and progress. Give me the wisdom of the Fathers of the Holy Eastern Church and of all the great Teachers of the Church. Give me the wisdom of Your great Apostle, St. Paul, so that I can at least understand his epistles well, remember them and explain them to your people.

Give me the wisdom of Your first Vicar, so that I can understand the intentions of Your Divine Providence which rules the Church through the Bishops of Rome. Give me the wisdom of obedience to them and to the Universal Catholic Church. Give me the wisdom of Church history and of theology.

Give me that wisdom which I and my people lack most: give me the wisdom of true contentment, true happiness. Amen.

The Wisdom of Prayer

Among all the graces and gifts from heaven which we can obtain through the prayer commended to us by St. James, the most important grace, the most valuable gift that is most closely tied to God's wisdom is, without a doubt, the gift of prayer. Prayer is not only our obligation, not only our right and our privilege, not only our primary need, but also the most valuable gift which we can and must by supplication obtain from heaven. When God's wisdom illuminates our souls with heavenly light perhaps in response to our prayers, she may show us the importance, the necessity and the benefit of prayer.

Thus, having presented these thoughts about God's Wisdom as an introduction to the subject which, in the measure of my meagre powers, I am to place before you, my dear Brothers in Christ and my Helpers, with God's good grace, I now pass on to my main subject.

ON PRAYER

THE NEEDS OF OUR TIMES

Christian feeling induces everyone to turn to God more ardently in difficult and trying times, to seek consolation, aid, and strength in Him. This feeling arises almost unconsciously in the soul of every Christian. It leads me too, in these unusually difficult times to appeal to you with a fervent and vehement call: the more life becomes increasingly difficult and trying with every day, the more to turn to Almighty God with more urgent, more humble, and more frequent prayer.

I have no doubt that priests have long been doing that. They would not be priests, they would not be Christians, if they faced life's difficulties differently and if they thought differently. I have no doubt that among the faithful the majority understands and feels the need for prayer throughout the whole lifetime, and the even greater need for it in difficult times. Apart from this, I think that we all, not only by the wishes of each individual heart, but as a Church, as an eparchy in the Church, as God's family made one and united by bonds of Christian charity and God's grace -- that we should reverently gather around Jesus Christ and all of us together before Him determine to increase our efforts more fervently and more completely as regards everything that is called our life of prayer. Therefore through today's epistle I wish to recall and to repeat those vehement and fervent summons of the Holy Spirit in the Scriptures that counsel, encourage, and remind us of the necessity, importance, holiness, and benefit of prayer. I also want to emphasize that today we are in greater need, and to unite all of you, for whom I answer before God; and, by repeating this truth again, and by putting it into practice, to gather you around the Cross of Christ.

I think that I could not find a more suitable subject for our times, nor help you more in your difficulties. If God were but to grant me this great, albeit undeserved, grace: that through the preaching of God's word I might convince you of all the infinite benefits which you can find in prayer and to arouse your hearts to all the infinite gifts and heavenly graces which, without the least doubt, await you on that path! If I could raise by my unworthy words the level of your life of prayer; improve the quality of your prayer, teach to pray those who do not pray enough or

55

who pray without sufficient love, I would thank God for the greatest gift given me and to you. I could not even wish to do more for you, or to give you more.

And yet, I am quite aware of the fact, however, that human words mean little and can accomplish but little in such a lofty and truly heavenly cause. It is characteristic of saints to speak in a way that human speech, reaching human hearts, brings them something from heaven and elevates them to heaven. Therefore I approach the subject about which I wish to write rather timidly. I am powerless in this subject in relation to you, worse than the paralytic in the Gospel.

The Most High can, however, add His power from the heavens to the plain words of an unworthy preacher. This power can accomplish miracles of grace in the souls of men. And since Jesus Christ in the Holy Gospel promised many times to grant everything for which we beseech Him, I do beseech Him in the introduction to this letter, that through the intercession of the Blessed Virgin Mary and of St. Joseph her Betrothed, St. John the Baptist and the Holy Apostles, to give my words the strength of heavenly thunder to proclaim the holy truths of faith concerning prayer and to soften all your hearts and to change your lives by the holiness of His grace. I ask this not for myself: "not for us, Lord, not for us -- but give glory to your name". I ask on behalf of a cause, I ask for the gift of grace most necessary in the lives of Christian laity and priests, I ask for the graces without which a priest cannot be a priest and a Christian a good Christian -- I ask for the grace of prayer for them all.

O Saviour Christ!

I beseech you for graces and gifts which are most needed for Your cause -- the salvation of human souls. I ask for grace for Your Church, O Christ, for the souls redeemed by Your blood. I ask in Your Name, for Your cause -- for You.

I ask the Heavenly Father through You in Your Blood which You shed for our salvation; I ask through the sacrifice of the most Holy Eucharist.

I believe in Your love, in Your goodness, in Your promises, and I know with certainty that what I ask for I will obtain. Amen.

RELIGION

Prayer is one of the most important religious obligations. In order to explain what prayer is and what it ought to be, it is necessary to recall, at least briefly, what religion is.

To begin, we should distinguish religion in itself: religion considered objectively on the one hand, and religion considered subjectively -- that is, in human souls -- on the other.

Objectively, religion is all those laws and norms taken together which relate to the obligations of people towards God. Subjectively, religion is that bond with divinity into which people want to enter according to their convictions and their will.

Had there been no divine revelation, human nature and its laws would govern our obligations towards God. Among several religions which would have to be considered as natural, the one which best corresponded to the laws of man's moral nature would be the best. Among individual men, whoever adhered most completely and consistently to the religion based on natural law would be the most religious. That would be one who not only possesses the theory of those natural laws and of natural obligations regarding the Creator and Lawgiver of nature through which human reason recognizes God, but one who also lives his whole life in conformity with those concepts and laws.

In reality, natural religion can be adequate only for people who know nothing about revealed religion and only as long as they know nothing about it. The moment a person conceives the idea that God has spoken to men and revealed to them His will, given them His law, they have an obligation to verify the fact of God's revelation, to know it, and to look in it for laws that are binding on them. They are obligated to do so on the basis of natural religion, as well. Their reason and their conscience present them with this obligation towards divinity, the Creator of nature and its Lawgiver, whom they have come to know through natural reason.

It is self-evident that the obligation of the created towards the Creator cannot depend on men's will alone. By the nature of things, obligations towards God are what God wishes them to be.

Faced by the fact of God's revelation, of religion which proclaims itself as revealed by God, one is obligated to come to the truth of this revelation, and to weigh its arguments. Even before accepting religion on the strength of natural obligations recognized by reason, one must be so disposed that, if indeed it is true that God has revealed religion, to accept it and be ready to fulfil the obligations imposed by it.

The fact of revealed religion is as old as God's revelation, as old as mankind. There cannot be two and there are not two different and mutually-opposed revealed religions. The whole of God's revelation always relates to one and the same religion. To the extent that this revelation was granted gradually, and with the passage of time more explicitly, this religion developed according to the development of revelation, still remaining one and the same. The religion of the Patriarchs before the flood and Noah in essence was the same as the religion of Adam. It differed only by the degree of its development. The religion of Abraham, then of Moses, David, and the Prophets, was that same religion. The essence of religion through all the degrees of its development is always the same: to know God, worship, and serve Him.

Our religion -- Catholic, universal -- is in essence the same revealed religion to which Adam, Noah, Abraham, Moses and all the Prophets adhered. People always had the same obligations towards God. With the development of revelation came the development of the understanding of these obligations. As revelation becomes clearer, mankind learns to know God better, and learns more and more from God's revelation about the worship which God demands of people. The essence of the knowledge and worship of God does not change.

The same is true of the obligation to obey God. As the revelation of God's law develops, people learn to obey the law. Obedience in essence remains the same even though the law changes or undergoes development. Changes occur in what God demanded of people in various epochs. The Apostle Paul speaks thus about the development of revelation: "In many and various ways God spoke of old to our fathers by the prophets; but in these last days he has spoken to us by a Son" (Hebrews 1:1-2).

Christ came not to abolish the law but to fulfil it. He did not change the original revealed religion, but only developed and completed it. He changed the law of dread into the law of love. Obedience to God remains the same, only the actions which God demands of people change. God demanded different things in the times of the Patriarchs, different things from the Jews in the time of Moses, and demands different things from Christians.

Subjectively, for a religious person who sincerely wishes to fulfil his religious obligations, the first and most important question is: what are these obligations? What is God's law? What is God's will?

The more sincerely and more often a person ponders these questions and searches for answers to them, the more religious he or she is. The less a person ponders them, the less he or she thinks about them, the more that person distances himself or herself from religion and from God in general. Then the more he or she approaches the type whom St. Paul so succinctly and unreservedly characterized by these words "Their god is the belly" (Philippians 3:19).

People can in their notions and in the practice of their lives so belittle the highest and the most perfect Divine Being and reverence of and service to Him, that in their stead they put gross and brutal selfishness. This by its nature is above all materialistic and carnal.

People make a god out of their own interests, preferences, gratification of passion, or as the Apostle puts it, make of their belly a god whom they worship, whom they serve, and who occupies the position that belongs to the Almighty.

In practice there are no true atheists, people who are indeed godless. Those who bear that name are people for whom their god, or law, or morality, or the highest good, or object of worship is they themselves. Alongside that selfishness they might in theory admit the existence of an infinite and eternal God, or as they say, some highest power, architect of the universe. This theory can sometimes mitigate the brutality of their selfishness, but this selfishness can reach a degree of ruthlessness that, through being practised, itself becomes a theory.

It is quite possible that there is no theory in any philosophical or religious system according to which every person is his or her own god. And yet, there are philosophical and religious systems that stand out quite vividly in which the deity is mankind or human nature, or the fatherland, or the state. To include that kind of heathen humanism, according to the theory of which it is mankind that has created God, in a discussion about religion would give religion a very inappropriate and broad meaning.

But even in the revealed Christian-Catholic religion, to the extent that selfishness, the passions, or what Holy Scripture calls "the old self",

59

exist in us, they can be said to be in us an anti-religious element. This element is always opposed to the proper worship of God, it always represents a tendency to self-adoration, to make of one's self a god. "You will be like God"-- this was the catch-phrase associated with the fall of our first parents.

Thus, the religion in our hearts is, so to say, a plant that requires constant and intensive cultivation. For those who do not make efforts for it to flourish, do not water it, the abyss between practice and theory grows ever greater. Theory soars higher and farther into the heavenly spheres, where the eye does not reach, but practice descends more and more to the earth. All of life is more and more reduced to the life of the body, a person becomes less and less religious; in the heart of such a person religious life withers and disappears.

Only by fulfilling their religious obligations, and primarily the obligation of prayer (frequent prayer, we say, would not be enough, for the Holy Scriptures call for prayer that is unceasing) can people sustain their religious life, strengthen and make more permanent the bond which joins all of us with Almighty God, One in the Trinity.

THE NATURAL BASES OF RELIGION

If we are created by God, like a pot made by the hand of a potter, and if our Most High Creator has endowed our immortal soul with reason and free will, thereby making us like Him, then our nature itself demands that this reason and free will be directed towards our Creator so that we might know Him as He can be known through His creation, and to love Him. That directing of reason and free will to God our Creator is, as it were, the natural basis, the natural condition for prayer. Because God "so loved the world that he gave his only Son" (John 3:16) for our salvation, that Son of God -- Jesus Christ -- has, by His teachings, revealed to us God's being, God's nature, and God's works. Through supernatural grace He has given us light from heaven, the light of faith to know God. He has made our souls holy by His grace and through the virtue of God's love.

Embellished thus by heaven's gifts, the soul in turning to God by the most natural and most simple acts of knowing and cherishing Him, discharges its first and most important obligation to God: the obligation of prayer. This is because prayer is knowing God as He is: as the highest good, our Father, the supreme aim of our life, the essence of love, because "God is love" (1 John 4:8, 16).

Having come to know Him as such, we cherish Him as such, our supreme good, and we love Him above all, and hope to obtain from Him the gifts that are needed in the supra-natural life for our salvation.

Thus prayer rests on the most basic, most simple, most natural acts of our reason and will. Thus has God made us, in our very creation, beings who are in need of prayer and inclined to prayer. In the supra-natural order of salvation God gives us, as it were, a higher heavenly nature, which again, from the depth of its power, from an inner necessity, from its natural inclination, of itself turns to God through prayer. For us, to be is to pray.

The essence of our reason and our will, their nature, the stuff of which they are made, all those both push and pull towards prayer. The existence of our reason and of our will is prayer; that is, they need and demand prayer. Without prayer, reason and will lack what for them is primary, most important, most basic. What is reason, created to know truth, if it does not turn to the Highest Truth and does not know It? What is will, created for the good, for which the good is everything, if it does not recognize, cherish, love, the Highest Good? And in his spiritual life, what kind of believer is he who does not turn to God in prayer? What faith does he have, if faith does not give him an actual, living knowledge of God? What kind of Christian is he who can cherish everything that is good, but cannot cherish God, the highest Good, turning to Him with love?

It would be easy for a person to pray to God, call on His holy Name, and consider Him the best Father, were human nature not spoilt by the original fall, by original sin.

Prayer After the Original Sin

Even though such is our nature, such is God's revelation, such the grace of faith, hope, charity; it is not easy for us fallen sinners to turn to God through prayers of faith, hope, and charity. We need long and assiduous effort in order to understand the need for, and to cherish, the most beautiful flower of Christian life, and at the same time the greatest need of that life: namely, prayer.

From this comes the need for the struggle of prayer and for prayer itself. From this comes the need ceaselessly to convince and remind ourselves what prayer is. There is a need to struggle for prayer, for without this struggle we would forget about prayer, we would cease to pray. We need to know what prayer means in the general battle of life, because only thus can we evaluate prayer for what it is: the most important weapon in this war and the only means of gaining victory.

What is life's struggle about? Is it about conquest of sin?

He will not conquer sin who does not cherish prayer, does not love it, and does not pray enough.

What is this struggle about? Is it about repentance for past sins?

He will not repent who does not pray for that grace.

What is life's struggle about? Is it about victory over temptation and evil?
He will not vanquish temptation or avoid evil who has not received that grace through prayer.

What is life's struggle with one's self about? Is it for eternal salvation?

He will not achieve eternal salvation who has not received that grace through prayer.

THE GRACE OF ETERNAL SALVATION

At times people entertain the illusion that eternal salvation is in their hands, that a baptized person who has Christian faith through God's gift of grace freely given, already possesses sanctifying grace and with it the gift of hope and charity, and thus everything necessary for salvation. To be sure, one who has received Baptism is placed in a state of supra-natural sanctifying grace, and will certainly be accepted into Christ's heavenly kingdom if he dies in that state, for he belonged, through sanctifying grace, to Christ's kingdom on earth.

Our situation, however, is incomparably more difficult than that of the fortunate person who dies immediately after Baptism. Perhaps we have committed sins in our life after Baptism, mortal sins perhaps, or sins about which we have reason to be in doubt: whether they are not or were not mortal or were indeed forgiven? Perhaps our repentance has not been sufficient? Who knows whether he put enough ashes on his head in contrition, whether he lay and slept enough on the bare ground, whether he wore a hairshirt long enough and mortified his passions sufficiently with sackcloth? Who knows whether he has merited the Almighty's complete forgiveness, that the Almighty has expunged and cancelled His judgment against him, as He did with Nineveh, the great city to which Jonah preached repentance? This is the kind of repentance Christ demanded in His sermons when, because Bethsaida and Capernaum remained unrepentant, He said that the heathen cities of Tyre and Sidon, possessing the grace given Capernaum, would have repented in sackcloth and ashes (Matthew 11:21).

What still awaits us in life? Will we withstand in times of temptation? Will we betray in time of persecution? Will we not lose the grace given to us? Will we persevere in goodness to the very end?

True, all this depends to some extent on us. But immeasurably more does it depend on God's grace, which we can in no way earn, which is always in God's gift without our deserving it, which we can only obtain through good, long, humble, and persistent prayer.

Often we are confused by the misunderstood, and in practice perverted theological thesis about predestination *post praevisa merita*. Eternal salvation is the gift of God's grace. There is no doubt that through eternal salvation God rewards good deeds "through grace given" more, this should be said, than "out of grace committed". Good deeds done in a state of sanctifying grace are rewarded in heaven. But we do not attain this reward except through God's grace freely given us.

This is taught by all the Fathers and theologians. This, too, is thought by those who favour the idea of predestination *post praevisa merita*. Remaining in the favour of God until death is grace freely given. The circumstance that at the moment of death one possesses sanctifying grace is a gift granted out of God's goodness. Remaining true to this grace is again thanks to God's grace, as is victory over temptation.

In a word, we cannot be saved without God's grace. This grace is necessary to us not only in the first moment of justification but in every minute following justification until death. It is not in our power to make use of God's grace so as to be saved, because the very good will by which we desire to make use of grace, again is grace freely given. Our will alone cannot protect us from sin. Only God's grace can and will.

We repeat in sermons and in catechism quite properly that God's grace is necessary for everything and that we cannot do anything good without God's grace. Above all, also, that God's grace is necessary for salvation. Did not Christ say "Every branch of mine that bears no fruit, he [my Father] takes away, and every branch that does bear fruit he prunes, that it may bear more fruit... As a branch cannot bear fruit by itself, unless it abides in the vine, neither can you, unless you abide in me. I am the vine, you are the branches. He who abides in me, and I in him, he it is that bears much fruit, for apart from me you can do nothing. If a man does not abide in me, he is cast forth as a branch and withers... (John 15:1-6). All that can be good in us comes from our unity with Christ. Outside of this unity there is no good will in us, nor can there be. But it is impossible to remain in this union without diligent prayer.

To maintain that unity means not to offend God by a mortal sin -- this feat is also a gift of God's grace. The vessel in which we carry our supernatural life is so weak, so clayish, that no one who depends on his own powers, can be assured that he will not fall into mortal sin (2 Corinthians 4:7). This is why the Apostle Paul says: "Therefore let any one that thinks that he stands take heed lest he fall" (1 Corinthians 10:12). The Apostle does not say "who stands", but "who thinks that he stands", to show that many who think that they stand, have already fallen long ago. That means no man should be self-sure but should humbly ask God's grace for himself. That was indeed Christ's admonition to Peter, James, and John in the Garden of Gethsemane "Watch and pray that you may not enter into temptation" (Matthew 26:41).

Jesus Christ tells us to make the same request in the Lord's Prayer: "and lead us not into temptation".

In this way, prayer is a means to obtain God's grace which Jesus Christ often mentions, introducing in many places in the Holy Gospel entreaties that we be shown how to obtain it.

The Holy Sacraments are truly pre-eminent sources of God's grace. They are visible symbols or signs of the invisible grace which they impart. Besides the sacraments, good deeds performed in the state of sanctifying grace are also the means for multiplying that grace. Yet prayer is the most comprehensive and the most successful way to God's grace, because during the receiving of the Holy Sacraments prayer is necessary and without it the Holy Sacraments do not grant God's grace. Exceptions are: Extreme Unction of the ill, and Baptism, Confirmation, or the Eucharist given to children. These in themselves suffice for God's grace to be received without the prayers of those receiving it. To receive

64

other Sacraments worthily, however, preparation, disposition, and active participation through prayer on the part of the recipient are required.

Apart from the Sacraments and good deeds, there is no other way to enter into God's grace except prayer. Thus as is said about God's grace that it is necessary for everything and without it nothing that is good can be done, so also it can and must be said about prayer. Prayer is necessary for everything, without it we cannot lead a Christian life or be saved. This shows clearly the almost infinite importance and value of prayer and how much a Christian life depends on praying well and praying sufficiently.

Most important of all is -- to know how to pray.

If the teachings of the Gospel in general constitute a school of Christian life, a school in which we are all learners until our death, then certainly the most important part in this school is the teaching of prayer. Indeed, there is nothing more important for the Christian life than the school of prayer.

WHAT PRAYER IS

Usually prayer is defined with St. John Chrysostom[2] as conversation with God. We shall see that prayer does indeed merit this description because in praying not only do we talk to God, but God talks to our soul. In prayer ties are established between the human soul and our Heavenly Father, the most Holy Trinity, Jesus Christ, the Blessed Virgin, the Holy Angels and Saints in heaven -- relations that exist in a mutual granting of whatever can be granted to another according to reason and will.

For now let us reflect about prayer, inasmuch as on our part it is only the raising of our mind and heart to God. We will speak about prayers to the Saints in another place, but for now let us define prayer

---

2   Second homily, on prayer, beginning, and XXXth homily on the Book of Genesis towards the middle: "Consider, what great good fortune is given you, how great your glory, that you can in prayers speak with God, with Christ, as with a friend, in your conversation share, desire what you want, ask for what you desire."
Dionysius, *On the Names of God*, Chapter III, Lesson I, at the beginning: "First of all, to begin with prayer is a very profitable thing; in this way, it is as we give ourselves to God and unite with Him."
Augustine, in his book, *On the Word of God*, 5th discourse: "Prayer is a kind of request."
John Damascene, *On the Orthodox Faith*, Book III, Section 24, the beginning: "Prayer is asking for things that are needed from God." Prayer is "the raising of thought of God."

as the raising of our mind and our heart to the Lord God and let us consider how great the benefits for the human soul from the mere fact of prayer are; that is, even without taking into account what, through prayer, we might ask and receive from God.

The Reverence of Worship

Our first and most important obligation in prayer is to give glory and honour, the reverence of worship due to God our Lord Almighty and which in Latin is called adoration (*adoratio*) and in Greek *proskinidis*. Holy Scriptures use various terms when they speak of the act of rendering the highest honour to God. The whole of the Scriptures is replete with wonderful prayers that express this act of rendering only to God the respect that is rightfully His. To bless God, praise Him, glorify Him, magnify Him, call to Him, seek Him, sing His praises, appear before His face, confess Him.... In all these forms of prayer is found the reverence of worship.

Every approach made to God is that that reverence of worship which almost equals the act of love. To worship God as the Highest Good is the same as to love Him. When we worship God, as God, in all the acts of prayer whether we are pleading with God, or begging His forgiveness, or proclaiming His glory or His works, in all these acts we are rendering Him the same honour, the same reverence.

Why is it then that the Scriptures or the God-inspired men who wrote them, or gathered them, use so many terms to designate the one and same act of worship? Perhaps because when the Christian soul stands in faith as if before God's throne, to unite with all the angelic and archangelic heavenly choirs, and compete, as it were, with the angels and Saints in heaven, the soul feels its inadequacy and looks for ways to express what human words can only say so incompletely, unclear, weakly.

Resolving to magnify and glorify God, the human soul cannot be satisfied with the first word that comes to mind, it looks for another, a better one, because it sees through faith the light which is God, for God is light (1 John I:5). At the same time it is aware that this light is unapproachable, because God dwells in unapproachable light (1 Timothy 6:16). Even though this light is unapproachable it discloses itself to the soul, unveils itself. God reveals Himself as love, because "God is love" (1 John 4:8). Thus God's revelation may appear to the soul like a father's arms reaching out, calling the soul into the embrace of His infinite goodness, His love.

The soul can understand that just as the sick woman in the Gospel who only touched the hem of Christ's garment and was healed from her many years' illness, even so would the soul's ills, troubles, suffering, dimness of reason, passion, and weakness of will would also disappear, as wax melts before fire, if the soul could but touch God's infinite goodness and love. It is as if the soul asks itself:

Where shall we find strength to praise Him? For He is greater than all His works.

Terrible is the Lord and very great and marvelous is His power.

When you praise the Lord, exalt Him as much as you can; for He will surpass even that.

When you exalt Him, put forth all your strength, and do not grow weary, for you cannot praise Him enough (Sirach 43:28-30).

Faced with God's greatness, our weakness forces us to look for ever-new forms, ever new words, in order to express what the soul would wish to express but which it feels so powerless to do. When it finds in Holy Scriptures words which express the prayers of the holy angels, in those prayers (which without any doubt are rays of heavenly light) it searches and discovers something of the angelic prayers that corresponds more both to God's glory and the soul's need to praise the Lord.

St. John in Revelation 4:8 sees the heavenly Seraphim and hears their song: "Holy, holy, holy is the Lord God Almighty, who was and is and is to come!"; or again in 4:11, "Worthy art thou, our Lord and God, to receive glory and honour and power, for thou didst create all things, and by thy will they existed and were created"; or in 7:12: "Blessing and glory and wisdom and thanksgiving and honour and power and might be to our God for ever and ever! Amen."

There are other similar passages in Holy Scriptures. The soul gladly uses this angelic language, the more gladly for it sees that the Seraphim, too, have the same difficulty as we do. Of the angelic prayers in heaven, Holy Church makes prayers to be used in her services of worship, through this striving to raise human souls to heaven.

It is from here that those pearls of almost boundless value in our church services, to mention only, for example, the ecphonies in the

67

Liturgy, come. Their greatness, their power, the light that shines from them, the aroma of paradise with which they are replete, the reflection of heaven in every word, lead the soul to unimaginable heights. All this is so extraordinary, so mysterious, so great, that it appears strange that these words, printed as they are on paper do not burn, do not shine, with some supernatural light, which is hidden perhaps under the black printer's ink.

Among the prayers that are included in church services or prescribed by church law come the prayers by which the Prophet David praised the unspoken Name of the Most High, almost infinite in number and wonderful in their variety. A Christian recalls that the Psalter belongs to the canon of God-inspired books of the Old Testament, and that Jesus Christ himself used those heavenly words in His prayers. In reciting on the Cross Psalm 21 that begins with the words: "My God, my God, why hast Thou forsaken me?" He commended this book to us as the best prayer book. When a Christian recalls that all the Saints, beginning with the Virgin Mary, repeated these prayers and were sanctified by them, how can he but think that through saying these prayers with and after them he in spirit truly, as it were, touches God's goodness and God's love and, like the woman with the flow of blood, will be cured of all sin-related illnesses?

Through Prayer We Touch God

Indeed, "touch".

I have used this expression not by accident and not without purpose, because this expression is in essence strictly theological. Speaking about divine or theological virtues: faith, hope, charity, theologians ask "Why do we call them divine?" They reply: Because they touch God (*attingunt Deum*), they reach up to God. God is their material and formal object; He is the object of the actions of these virtues. This is because to the question, "In what do we believe?" -- we reply, "God". "What do we hope for?" -- we reply, "God". "Whom do we love?" -- we reply "God". He is the formal object, because to questions about the motive-stimulus of the acts of the virtues, why we believe, hope and love, again we reply: we do this for God.

Thus acts based on these virtues relate directly to the nature of God, they touch it directly. Through them God is in our intellect as the object of supra-natural knowledge by faith and is in our will as the object of the will's desires and love. In us He is like what is comprehended in

68

the mind that comprehends, or what is loved in the heart that loves. All three virtues contribute to the act of worship of God.

The act of worship is based on faith in God, because we worship Him such as we know Him through faith.

Worship of God is also based on hope because through faith we know Him as the highest goal that we hope to reach. We know Him as the giver of all gifts, as the source of all the good which we can hope to receive from Him.

Worship of God, finally, is based on love. Through faith we know Him, but through love we cherish Him as the supreme Good and revere Him as the highest, infinite, and eternal Goodness.

These three divine virtues are the foundation and to a large extent the content of the act of worship. They are also the reason why in Holy Scriptures and in our prayers the worship of God takes on the various forms and appearances that it does.

This is also why every prayer and every word of every prayer are in fact acts of worship. Every prayer is the interlacing of endless acts of reverence, faith, hope, and charity. Prayer raises us to heaven and unites our souls with the Lord God. Prayer lets our souls touch God. For this reason, prayer has the power to work miracles in sundry ways. Every prayer and every word in every prayer can and should be an act directly similar to the touching of the hem of Christ's garment by the woman in the Gospel who was thereby healed.

In order to explain this truth of faith we must reply to the following objection: we explained the way in which our intellect touches God by the fact that God is the object that we know as well as the stimulus for our consent to recognize revealed truths as being the truth. We believe in God, believe because of God, believe because He has revealed [Himself]. Through this belief, this faith, we know God. In this knowing Him, God is for us as He is known by the mind that knows Him. To this someone could make the following comment: for the mind doing the comprehending, what is comprehended is not the object itself, but only some kind of image of that object. What is comprehended, the object of our comprehension, is accessible to our intellect only in an intentional way, as a kind of reflection, it is reflected in the mind as in a mirror. It appears then, that it would be most incorrect to say about the relationship of the intellect to the comprehended object that it is a touching of the object, that it has a bond with the object.

I may know about a Chinese emperor from a book, but from this reading and from this knowledge there is no understanding, there arises no bond with that "Son of Heaven". To this we reply as follows: neither our intellect nor our will have in their natural powers the possibility, the power, to rise to a knowledge of God and His love!   Our soul can be raised to have this power only by supra-natural means, means higher than mere nature, only by infusing the soul with the supra-natural virtues of faith and love.

In order to be able to love God, the soul must be raised to the supra-natural state by the sanctifying grace of God. For the act of faith the soul needs the supra-natural gift of the virtue of faith, which can remain in the soul even without sanctifying grace. In this way the light by which we know God in the soul is a supra-natural gift of God, and each gift from God is a participation in God, a certain participation in His nature; I would say some kind of physical touching of God. Therefore all the analogies that might be used to illustrate this matter, because they are derived from natural knowledge, can reveal only in part what happens in the soul when it knows God and loves Him. When "appearing before God's face to pray" with the desire to give God the reverence due Him, the soul is immediately illuminated with the "quiet light" about which we sing at Vespers, which illuminates the soul with supra-natural heavenly knowledge and places it in heaven -- above all nature.

In our Church, at the end of Matins during Lent, we chant: "Standing in the temple of Your Glory, we envision ourselves as standing in heaven" and St. Paul, speaking about the life of prayer or generally about the supra-natural life, Christian life, says: "Our commonwealth is in heaven" (Philippians 3:20). St. John Chrysostom speaking about prayer, "You have not even begun to pray, you are just preparing to pray, and already God has heard you", has in mind it seems, this infinite thirst that God's love has -- to give Himself to His creatures and to hear our prayers. We will speak later about this thirst, but Chrysostom could have said the same about the supra-natural light which immediately bathes the soul in the moment it turns to pray. This first moment of prayer is already the healing touch of Christ's robe, and even something more, because it is the healing touch of God's light, that is: God's nature, God's love.

It is clear that this touch must bring to the soul that is humble and prepared something that is extraordinary, something that is not found in all of nature and cannot be. This very first touch must already bring the soul something from paradise, something from heaven, something not of this world, something that heals, elevates, sanctifies, strengthens. In a word, it must bring something of what we hope for when we begin this labour with the Psalmist, who says: "O God, thou art my God, I seek thee...."

The Sign of the Cross

It seems unnecessary to say that all this comes about when the soul approaches prayer with a truly sincere intention and good will, for example, when the holy Sign of the Cross is made.

This is an act of worship of God, an act of faith, an act of hope, an act of love, an act of public confession of one's allegiance to Jesus Christ, an act of searching for salvation in Christ, an act expressing faith in the Holy Trinity, in redemption through the death of Jesus Christ, in the three Persons of God and the two natures of Christ. All this is contained, quite naturally, in the Sign of the Cross.

When, therefore, this most wonderful Sign of the Cross -- that is composed of such a multitude of angelic thoughts and truths -- is made without thinking by someone; then, obviously, that person's "prayer" is no prayer at all. It will not bring any benefits but probably will bring great harm for how can one make a caricature of the truths of faith and the outward signs of faith without risk? Can one, without risking punishment, provide others with an example of indifference, lack of seriousness, and carelessness concerning the things of God, the affairs of God? Is this not simply inviting God's wrath from heaven, and God's punishment? How is it possible to treat sacred matters with such a lack of reverence and with such an absolute lack of piety? After such a beginning the prayer that follows is not worthy to be called a prayer. Rather it is flippancy that deserves punishment relating as it does to the most important, most sacred obligations of a Christian's life. It is a thoughtlessness that could lead to the most horrid crimes and blasphemies.

VENERATION OF JEHOVAH

The act of veneration of God can relate to God as our Creator and Supreme Benefactor, irrespective of the revealed truth of faith about the three Persons of God. Such an act of veneration can, or rather should, be, or by the nature of things is, an act of faith, love, and hope.

71

Through this act we venerate God as best we can; we give Him the highest possible honor, or as we often say it, honor above everything; we recognize Him as the Being that is above all things, the Being that is higher than any other possible being, or better still, the only Being in comparison with which all created beings are not really beings, do not actually exist.

God's Being is eternal, infinite, almighty. It is so much higher than any created being, that there is no comparison which could explain that difference clearly enough.

Were we to compare, for example, the extent of God's Being with the extent of the whole universe (with those millions and millions of stars, among which our solar system is a minute disappearing atom) together with all that God has created, we would have to admit that such a comparison is infinitely removed from reality. Taken together, all created things, material and spiritual, including all the angelic choirs of the Cherubim and Seraphim, are in their sum infinitesimally small in the face of the greatness of God's glory. It is like an atom compared with the whole universe, it is simply nothing in the strictest sense of the word.

It was appropriate that God, when revealing His fearsome Name to Moses, said: "I am who I am". Thus whenever we say "is" or "to be" in relation to creatures, we are using the expression in a completely different sense than when we say about God that He "is". It would be the same were we to say about a squirrel that it is "wise" and about a great sage that he is "wise". The word is the same, but the sense is completely different, for there is no comparison between these two "wisdoms". When we speak about a live expression of a face in a portrait or about how live the colours of that portrait are, we are using the same word but in a different sense! Philosophers say that only through some analogy, some relative comparison, can one word be used in such different senses.

Geometry provides examples which might clarify these relationships. Compared to a line, a point has no existence. A line, therefore, no matter how short, can contain billions of points, each different from every other. The same relationship holds between the existence of a line and the existence of a plane, and the existence of a plane and the existence of a three-dimensional solid. Mathematics presents this fact by stating that each unit of a higher kind contains an infinite number of units of a lower kind. In these examples we have at least a shadow of how some existence can be simply nothing in comparison with a higher existence.

From this essential and fundamental difference between God's existence and created existence follows the fundamental difference between the worship of God and the worship of what He has created. The worship of God, and it alone is of this kind, is called "divine worship", *latreia, latria*, while worship of even the highest of God's creations is worship of a completely different kind. In Greek it is called *doulia, dulia*, or "service". Thus we render service to angels and the Saints. Because the Virgin Mary surpasses in dignity all the highest angels and the highest Saints, for the dignity of a mother surpasses that of the highest servant, we call the worship of the Virgin Mary by the Greek word *iperdoulia, hyperdulia*, that is, "higher service".

These two kinds of worship, of God and of the Saints, are in essence so different that it is impossible to mistake one for the other. To give a created being the honour of worship due to God alone is the sin of idolatry, it is paganism. This difference between the worship of God and veneration of the Saints must be kept in mind by every Christian during prayer, because in prayer human thought passes from the Saints to the angels, stands before the dreaded throne of Jehovah and then descends to the veneration of the Virgin Mary. That is to say, it passes from the *latria* type of worship to the *dulia* type, returning to *latria* then again to *dulia* or *hyperdulia*.

All this was said in order to emphasize in our praying those prayers, or words, or acts which constitute the veneration of God. It is as if in prayer books we were to underline or print in gold those sections which relate to the worship of God. From them we should draw or pour into them the pure gold of God's love.

REVERENCE OF PERSONS

Even though worship belongs to Most High God himself, for it is written "You shall worship the Lord your God and Him only shall you serve" (Matthew 4:10), as the Scriptures show, a type of worship also applies to persons. This, however, appears to be only in the sense that reverence to God is shown through reverence of His creatures, or to what is Godlike in the created. It was in this way that Abraham in Genesis showed reverence to the three men who visited him. Abraham "bowed himself to the earth" in rendering honour to those three men or angels, venerating them as messengers from God, or perhaps giving reverence to God directly, venerating the Holy Trinity in the persons of those three angels.

73

It is significant that in our iconography the Holy Trinity is depicted in the persons of three angels. That this was indeed Abraham's intention would appear from his words: "My lord, if I have found favour in your sight..." (Genesis 18:3). This mysterious occurrence in Abraham's life shows that just as God spoke to people and appeared to them through angels, so also people adored God through angels and spoke to them, addressing God directly. Similarly, Jacob after his mysterious struggle with the angel says to himself: "For I have seen God face to face" (Genesis 32:30). So did Joshua the son of Nun worship an angel, falling on his face to the earth, in spite of the fact that the latter said, "...as commander of the army of the Lord I have...come" (Joshua 5:14). In the same way, the Prophet Nathan bowed to the ground before King David (1 Kings 1:23). Mordecai (Esther 3:2), however, did not bow to Haman because he feared to transfer to man the honour due to God, and to bow to anyone but God, even though he would willingly have kissed his footprints for the sake of Israel (as the deuterocanonical addition found in the Vulgate and certain Greek codices as Esther 13:14 tells us).

Even the angel who appeared to St. John (Revelation 22:9) did not allow him to worship him, saying: "You must not do that! I am a fellow servant with you."

By this worship of God or what is Godly in people we can explain in a word those prayers in which we give honour together both to God and the Saints. Such, for example, is the prayer translated from Latin and included in our prayer books in the introduction to the church Rule, and also in the prayer which should be read after the church Rule. In this prayer we say "Praise and honour to the Holy Trinity...to the Virgin Mary and to the Saints."

People who do not pay particular attention to the meaning of words in all European languages instead of using the expression "I value very highly and love very much", use such words as "worship", "idolize", "deify" (*vergoettern* --- German; *adorer* -- French). This kind of talk is so pagan and so glaringly scandalous, that such words when used in this sense should be stricken from the dictionary.

Although in worship the difference between what is due to God and what is due to the Saints may become slightly blurred, there is one act of divine worship which all people of the world agree cannot be rendered to a created being -- and that is sacrifice.

From Acts (14:7-17) we know how people of Lystra thought

mistakenly that Paul and Barnabas were gods and how the pagan priest of Zeus wanted to offer sacrifice to them. We also know with what indignation the apostles reacted to this proffered act of divine worship.

WORSHIP OF THE HOLY TRINITY

Acts of divine worship acquire a higher meaning and can in a special way be saturated with God's love when our *latria* relates to the most Holy Trinity or to one of its Divine Persons.

The saints of the Old Testament also worshipped God, and this worship was also based on their faith, their hope, and their love, according to the way these virtues could be practised in the Old Testament. Through the revelation of the New Testament heaven was opened up to us, and with faith, hope, and love we enter as it were to be among the divine Persons themselves. With the revelation of Jesus Christ, the heavenly Father makes us a gift of the second divine Person -- the Word of God -- and the Father and Son make us a gift from heaven of the third Person, the Holy Spirit.

The act of reverencing God in the Old Testament was the highest form of worship relating to God, because through it people acknowledged the highest Being. It was at the same time the highest form of worship of which people were capable because it conformed to Sirach's prescripts, mentioned above, that men should praise, magnify, glorify, and bless God, as best as they can and to the greatest extent possible. But even so, this highest form of worship was still helpless to render to God even a tiny sliver of real glory. Perhaps hope in the future Messiah could alone have given this Old Testament worship of God something of the power needed to carry it to heaven.

In this wretched atom which is the entire human race, in this grain of sand which is the whole of the universe, there could not even have been talk that it would be possible for human thought to rise all the way to the throne of Jehovah, into those infinite heavenly spheres in which on the throne of God's majesty sits Jehovah the Father, Jehovah the Son, and Jehovah the Holy Spirit. There before that throne the seven highest Spirits worship, rendering *latria*, which the Seraphim and Cherubim take up in chorus so that the echo of that glory might resound through the heavens from end to end. These mysteries were so closed to all that is material or tied with matter, that, once again I repeat, in this atom of mud there could not have been even the least talk that there ever could have arisen in the hopes or dreamy visions of these tiny insignificant dwarfs, even the minutest thought about what was happening in heaven.

Today, washed by Christ's Blood, holding in our hands the chalice of His sacrifice, carrying in our hearts the Holy Spirit, bearing Christ and bearing the Holy Spirit, we stand before the throne of the All-Highest there high in heaven together with those seven we render to Jehovah the worship that is worthy of Him.

Such approximately is the difference between the Old Testament act of worship which we, too, can repeat, and the worship of the Holy Trinity.

When we worship the Trinity we must be like those who "have washed their robes and made them white in the blood of the Lamb" (Revelation 7:14). We carry in our souls traces of Christ's blood and the robes of our souls are redeemed and washed white in the blood of the Lamb. For our worship to be accepted by the Most High, our soul must be sanctified by God's grace. We cannot do otherwise because only through Jesus Christ can we glorify God. "...that in everything God may be glorified through Jesus Christ. To him belong glory and dominion for ever and ever. Amen" (1 Peter 4:11).

It seems to me that our worship must have a eucharistic character. Its words, the actions of our soul, must be bathed with Christ's blood shed on Golgotha for our salvation, the price with which we were bought (1 Corinthians 7:23), the blood of the Eucharist which we drink from the chalice. If the prayer book from which we pray were to be compressed with tremendous force, from it would flow Christ's most Holy Blood. The prayers in the book are marked with blood. That is why it has such immeasurable value, that is why we can draw angelic holiness from it.

How sad, how dreadful it is that, being Christians redeemed by the blood of Christ, we priests sometimes say prayers carelessly, that we approach the altar of God without reverence. Without concentration, without deliberation, without any thought and reflection, we repeat the holy words of prayer. And sometimes we can be so forgetful and reach such a level of mindlessness and impiety that even at the very instant we stand before God's altar in order to worship the Almighty in heaven, to bring the sacrifice of the Holy Liturgy, we are capable of doing this with impure lips, a sinful soul, and a defiled body. We can be so forgetful, that the state of our soul in this most solemn moment of sacrifice, when we as God's angels should be praying for the whole people, is simply despicable and foul.

What terrible abasement, what extreme senselessness, and what misfortune! Not only for himself the miserable priest, who has lowered himself to sacrilege, but also for the people whose spiritual shepherd he is, and for the church in which he is celebrating the Liturgy, and for those who receive Communion from his hands! To take the Most Holy Body from a loathsome cesspool!

What misfortune for the children he baptizes! What bottomless abyss of evil and misfortune for the destruction of his own children he is! Wretched are the children who have such a teacher. Unfortunate are the children who have such a father.

The worship offered to the Holy Trinity is such an immeasurable and such an infinitely important part of our prayers, that even with insignificant effort and attention we can easily attain a state in which these words, at least these words, would be said in a pure love of God. When we pray for our needs or the needs of those close to us, or of the whole people, we are certainly doing a good deed, but which of us can know how much selfishness there might be in these prayers? Even in the love of those closest to one, in the love for one's people, there can be much love of self. We do well to wonder if in such prayers we do not merit Christ's admonition: "...even the tax collectors do the same" (Matthew 5:46) and "...even sinners love those who love them" (Luke 6:32). They, too, love their children; they, too, care about their health and worldly goods.

But when, during prayer, we can at least for a moment forget about ourselves and about those who are close to us, and worship God in the Trinity for His own sake, such a moment in prayer can have an immeasurably greater and higher significance. Such a moment can be one of those in which the Spirit of God prays in our souls and hearts with that inexpressible sighing about which the Apostle says: " the Spirit himself intercedes for us with sighs too deep for words" (Romans 8:26). Such prayer without the slightest doubt will give us infinitely more than all of the prayers in which we are still thinking of ourselves.

Of course, we must pray for ourselves and pray much, as well as for those close to us. We must ask heaven for many spiritual and temporal gifts for ourselves and for them. But let us, from time to time, with a contrite heart and humble spirit remember God, and bring a pure sacrifice of worship and love of God.

The special place in worship, or cult, of the Holy Trinity is a characteristic feature of the Rite of our Church. The passages in which the Holy Trinity is remembered are possibly the oldest passages in our whole Liturgy. It is as if they bear the imprint of the fourth century, when after the decisions of the First Council of Nicaea in 325 AD on the divinity of Christ and the First Council of Constantinople in 381 AD on the divinity of the Holy Spirit, the cult of the Holy Trinity was bound to flourish in the Church. Before this Christians, according to the words of St. Basil, believed and glorified the Trinity as when they were baptized; that is to say they remembered the Holy Trinity in their prayers in the same way as during baptism, only without the certainty and conviction that the dogmas enunciated by the ecumenical councils gave them.

The divinity of Christ was asserted in the formula: "of one substance with the Father". The divinity of the Holy Spirit was affirmed through the words: "who together with the Father and the Son is adored and glorified". With these words the Ecumenical Council stated the confession of faith in the Holy Trinity through the equal worship of all three Persons. This fact found expression in the prayers of the Church in which the three Persons are glorified together.

THANKSGIVING

The second essential aspect of our prayer should be the giving of thanks for all the benefits received. It is so essential to prayer that St. Paul, speaking about supplication, adds to this "with thanksgiving". In Philippians 4:6 he writes: "...In everything by prayer and supplication with thanksgiving let your requests be made known to God".

The very nature of the matter demands it. To approach someone from whom we have just received some exquisite gift with a new request and to forget to thank him for the previous gift would be a mark of gross and boorish insensitivity. Such ingratitude would justify our never receiving another similar gift.

When of the ten lepers who were healed by Christ only one came to thank Him, Christ felt the ingratitude of the others painfully. "Were not ten cleansed?.... Was no one found to return and give praise to God except this foreigner?" (Luke 17:18).

Such thanklessness harms the soul more. It does harm not only because it hinders further benefits, but because it pushes people into sins worse and more grievous than ingratitude. Who does not give thanks behaves like one who considers a gift to be something that is owed him, and himself to be someone who has a right to receive what was given. In his eyes the benefactor is a debtor who was obligated to do what he had done. The ungrateful person not only behaves this way when he to thinks this way, and in time he does. This is shown particularly when one boasts of a gift as something that is his. Such a person deserves the Apostle's censure: "What have you that you did not receive? If then you received it, why do you boast as if it were not a gift?" (1 Corinthians 4:7).

Ascribing to one's self God's gifts clearly leads to pride. In itself it is already almost pride in the gift. Anyone who knows the Holy Scriptures even superficially understands what danger lurks in such behaviour. Is it not written that "God opposes the proud, but gives grace to the humble" (James 4:6)? St. Peter says literally the same (1 Peter 5:5). Jesus Christ teaches the same in the parable of the tax collector and the Pharisee. "Everyone who exalts himself will be humbled, but he who humbles himself will be exalted" (Luke 18:14).

Does not the Virgin herself in her most wonderful song of thanksgiving which St. Luke committed to writing for us, point out as the greatest glory of God the fact that He "has scattered the proud in the imagination of their hearts, He has put down the mighty from their seat...and the rich he has sent empty away" (Luke 1:51-53)? Among God's deeds, to the Most Holy Virgin this is what appears as the most notable and noteworthy of His actions, as His banner, as His character.

St. Paul wrote in his epistle to the Hebrews: "It is a fearful thing to fall into the hands of the living God" (10:31). If we were to apply this text to ingratitude, then it is a fearful thing for one to show a lack of gratitude to Jehovah because He is jealous of His praise. "I am the Lord...my glory I give to no other" (Isaiah 42:8). Lack of gratitude offends Him. In this we all offend Him in many insidious ways, for if each of us were to reflect, even only a little, we could find hundreds of great and valuable gifts we have received from God for which it has never occurred to us to thank Him. Yet we consider this state of gross and vivid ungratefulness to be so natural that this becomes a sin we scarcely ever confess.

Just as lack of gratitude leads to pride, is itself perhaps concealed pride, so gratitude is the school of humility and to a high degree prepares roadways to heaven for prayer. It teaches to observe God's actions in the soul and to recognize the workings of God's Providence even in the smallest things. It continually places our own insignificance before us, in contrast to God's greatness. It reminds us of our weaknesses and sins and teaches us when and how to pray and what to ask for. It leads to love, for it teaches us to look to our greatest Benefactor, to our true Father, and teaches us what the "best gifts" and "perfect gifts" that proceed from the Father of Light that we should ask for (James 1:17).

Gratitude towards God takes away that kind of self-confidence that even among men is considered rash. "Instead you ought to say, 'If the Lord wills , we shall live and we shall do this or that'. As it is, you boast in your arrogance. All such boasting is evil" (James 4:15-16). Finally, gratitude easily and quickly leads to love, because it teaches to discern God's love and goodness everywhere, it teaches to believe in God's goodness and in God's love, and from day to day, as it were, to touch that love.

In the Holy Liturgy and in the Eucharist, following which it is obligatory that we not leave the church for at least half an hour, we priests have the opportunity to pray for and receive what I would call the wisdom of gratitude. I say to pray for and receive, and I call gratitude wisdom, because gratitude has this in common with wisdom: from it flow streams of grace (James 1:5).

Even without this wisdom it is easy to sense the criminal brutality of the materialist, to whom Jesus with infinite love, out of the desire to do him good, brings a chalice of His Blood shed out of that love on the Cross. But he drinks out of this chalice with no more piety than he would have when emptying a glass of any drink and then immediately turns to his daily, often base, preoccupations.

And yet an act of gratitude done well following the Liturgy is so precious! It gives so much strength during the whole day and, first of all, pours so much heavenly light on our prayers.

When, in the guise of the Eucharistic bread, Jesus Christ enters our hearts, He teaches us to put directly into practice His precept, one that is perhaps even difficult to carry out, but which in His teachings is the basic condition of every prayer. "But when you shall pray, go into your room and shut the door and pray to your Father who is in secret; and your Father who sees in secret will reward you" (Matthew 6:6). Jesus Christ has in mind the room of our heart, because He is talking to people who are poor and simple folk. There could hardly have been among His listeners those who had separate rooms in their homes in which they could shut themselves. It is certainly unthinkable that Christ spoke these words only to those who had homes so large that they contained some room in which they could be alone.

Therefore He is obviously talking about a room that is accessible to everyone: the chamber or chapel of our heart.

For us priests particularly, for about half an hour after Communion it would be the chapel in which the Holy Sacrament is deposited. It would be a chapel because we are also the temple of the Holy Spirit. "Do you not know that your body is a temple of the Holy Spirit within you, which you have from God?" (1 Corinthians 6:19).

Through these words and through the Holy Eucharist, and through being with us in the chapel of our heart, Jesus Christ teaches us to shut ourselves in this chapel during prayer. This is a necessary condition if we are to concentrate on our praying, for without concentration good prayer is not possible. When we are about to pray we should accustom ourselves to enter this chapel of our heart and to remain there for the whole duration of the prayer.

In practice this should be done as follows: in our imagination to visualize a chapel complete with an altar, icons, and other appropriate things. In this chapel on the altar is Jesus Christ with whom we have just been united through Holy Communion. We should visualize ourselves as being in this chapel throughout the whole time we are at prayer.

Another aspect of thanksgiving, particularly expressing gratitude to God, necessary to the Christian soul and bringing benefits, is that it keeps the soul on the heights, the mountain tops, of spiritual life. It does not permit the soul to lose the Christian outlook on life and thus contributes greatly to the growth of Christian life in the soul. It is no less beneficial or necessary for the life of prayer, because it does not let a man forget who he is and who God is, or that by himself he has nothing and continuously needs help and God's grace. It reminds him of how much he can ask for through prayer every day. It brings him to the realization of what a priceless treasure to the soul prayer is, what strength and joy it gives, what a sure way to heaven it provides. In a word, there is no better teacher of prayer and the Christian life than gratitude. There is no better counsellor in the difficult and hard circumstances of life.

The giving of thanks, just as in every valid and good prayer, is a ceaseless exercising of supra-natural virtues. It supports them, makes them easier to practise, multiplies them. Through gratitude to God for all the benefits He provides, the soul's faith develops and grows. That

81

faith blooms and bears fruit. Hope is strengthened, leading to a state where a man almost already possesses what he merely hopes to have forever. In him the fire of love slowly begins to glow, gradually growing into a fire of love of God and fellow man.

PETITIONING -- ASKING

To encourage people to pray, Holy Scriptures almost incessantly repeat one great, immeasurable, important truth: that God willingly and always listens to our prayers. It says this about all prayers or about prayer in general, but since hearing depends on beseeching, these scriptural passages refer primarily to asking through prayer for some grace and gifts from heaven. Perhaps in this way of describing prayer there is contained a teaching. According to it prayer, though not necessarily a petition for something but perhaps an expression of praise and gratitude, is nevertheless always heard in the sense that God receives it with kindness, that it is pleasing to God, that it deserves not only a reward but also a response from God: the pouring down on the petitioner of various kinds of grace.

In the Lord's Prayer, about which we shall speak later, everything is presented in the form of a petition even though this prayer also contains praise of God and expressions of gratitude.

In the same way, in the well-known parable in Luke 18 which appears like a gate to heaven and to which we shall also return later, Jesus Christ, in order to teach how we should pray persistently and without ceasing, shows us a widow who by constant petitioning finally moved an unjust judge to action. From this it would follow that incessant prayer is the same as petitioning.

It is possible that the whole question should be considered as follows: that there is a prayer, apparently an obligatory one, which Holy Scriptures refer to as unceasing prayer. This is what we find in the passage in Luke 18, a passage for which we will never be able to show enough gratitude to that great Saint. Had he given us nothing but those eight verses he would still have earned the immeasurable gratitude of all mankind. From this parable it follows that we must pray incessantly, and St. Paul in his first epistle to the Thessalonians repeats this literally: "Pray constantly" (1 Thessalonians 5:17).

St. Luke's parable encourages us to continual prayer by that brilliant demonstration of the immeasurable benefit of prayer, and that every prayer achieves its purpose.

That teaching is necessary for us, weak ones, for whom it is a difficulty to recite the Lord's Prayer three times a day. (I say this because, according to the *Didache*, which recorded the teachings of the Apostles, this was the practice of the first Christians who considered this the obligatory minimum of daily prayer). Because it is so difficult for us due to our weakness to pray and because God wished through His revelation to lead people to unremitting prayer, He presented the whole matter of prayer in Holy Scriptures in such a graphic way, so that the reader, no matter how dull-witted, would be forced at least to reflect on the matter. Prayer is presented simply as: pray, ask for what you want, and you will receive everything.

Herod, when he promised Herodias' daughter: "Whatever you ask me, I will give you, even half of my kingdom" (Mark 6:23), allowed himself against his own will to commit the basest crime against St. John only to keep his word. "Will not God be as faithful in keeping His word as was Herod?" is a question everyone who gives some thought to the comparison will ask.

Herod placed a reservation on his commitment. God's revelation is given without any reservations whatsoever. For Herod half of his kingdom was the extreme limit of his royal magnanimity; the poor wretch failed to see that Herodias was asking for 100 times more than not half, but the whole kingdom, because she was asking that he destroy his soul.

God's revelation, however, does not place any limitations.

Ask what you will, I shall give everything. Here, in your hands I put the key to all My treasures. I leave you, a Christian, as the steward of My house, My treasure, My possessions, My kingdom. I repeat what a Pharaoh once told Joseph: "...You shall be over my house, and all my people shall order themselves as you command; only as regards the throne will I be greater than you" (Genesis 41:40).

The solemn promise of Holy Scriptures on the part of God's Supreme Majesty as regards each of us individually is with mathematical precision equal to what the Pharaoh promised Joseph. "Then Pharaoh took his signet ring from his hand and put in on Joseph's hand, and arrayed him in garments of fine linen, and put a gold chain about his neck; and he made him to ride in the second chariot; and they cried before him 'Bow the knee!'. Thus he set him over all the land of Egypt" (Genesis 41:42-3).

Is it therefore conceivable that a Christian, having received that gold chain of prayer, been dressed in royal purple -- no, even in better and more costly robes about which Joseph, already dressed in Pharaoh's robe, had not even dreamt -- and having been placed in a chariot more like the chariot of Elias than that chariot of Joseph, can understand nothing and appreciate nothing? Even stones would understand and crumble into dust at that message.

Who among us can doubt that such an unconditional and comprehensive promise by God which is truly equivalent to the key to all God's treasures, has actually been given?

Only listen. In John 14:13 Jesus Christ says: "Whatever you ask in my name, I will do it, that the Father may be glorified in the Son." And again in John 16:23-24: "Truly, truly, I say to you, if you ask anything of the Father, he will give it to you in my name. Hitherto you have asked nothing in my name; ask, and you will receive, that your joy may be full".

Do you want to have an explanation from one of the Apostles, perhaps from the one who rested his head on Jesus' bosom and who lived for a number of years in the same house with the Virgin Mary? He will tell you: "And this is the confidence which we have in him, that if we ask according to his will, he hears us. And we know that he hears us in whatever we ask, we know that we have the requests made of him" (1 John 5:14-15). St. John maintains that we, one and all, possess the same power to produce miracles through prayer as had the ascetic monks in the desert during the early centuries of Christianity.

Do you want other witnesses? In Matthew 7:7-8, "Ask, and it will be given you; seek and you will find; knock and it will be opened to you. For everyone who asks, receives, and he who seeks, finds, and to him that knocks it will be opened."

The other Evangelists bring the same message from Christ. Mark (11:23-25) carries His words: "Have faith in God. Truly, I say to you, whoever says to this mountain 'Be taken up and cast into the sea', and does not doubt in his heart, but believes that what he say will come to pass, it will be done for him. Therefore I tell you, whatever you ask in prayer, believe that you have received it, and it will be yours".

In Luke 11:9-13 we find: "And I tell you, Ask, and it will be given you; seek and you will find; knock and it will be opened to you. For every one who asks, receives, and he who seeks finds, and to him who knocks it will be opened. What father among you, if his son asks for a fish, will instead of a fish give him a serpent; or if he asks for an egg , will give him a scorpion? If you then, who are evil, know how to give good gifts to your children, how much more will the heavenly Father give the Holy Spirit to those who ask him!".

In Matthew 21:22 Jesus Christ says: "And whatever you ask in prayer, you will receive, if you have faith". In 18:19 He tells us: "Again I say to you, if two of you agree on earth about anything they ask, it will be done for them by my Father in heaven". To this yet should be added these arresting words of Our Lord from John 15:7: "If you abide in me, and my words abide in you, ask whatever you will, and it shall be done for you". And again in 15:16: "...so that whatever you ask the Father in my name, he may give it to you".

In three chapters of the Gospel according to St. John (14, 15, 16) Jesus returns to this same thought four times, and repeats with emphasis the same promise. Obviously, the Gospel gives us only some of Jesus Christ's teachings, for He probably repeated the same lessons several times. The emphasis which He places on prayer and with which He repeats His solemn promise, causes us to think that this thought must have recurred more often in his teachings than might have been recorded in the Gospels. We are justified in thinking so because just as that promise is the key to all the treasures of heaven, so is that teaching the key to the knowledge of the Gospels. It is what reinforces and gives strength to the edifice of Christian life.

In all the texts quoted above only one condition is made: ask in Christ's name, and it will be granted according to God's will. A prayer not in Christ's name and not according to the will of God will not be heard. This limitation is more than justified and natural. And yet in all the passages of Holy Scriptures on prayer God's pre-eternal will is presented so clearly: that it is precisely through prayer that men may come to various accomplishments. It might appear that God bends His will to accommodate men's prayers, that He hears not only when He already wishes to give and only waits to be asked in prayer, but also even when at first He did not wish to grant the petition. It might appear as if the human will, within some limits permitted by the will of God, contends with God and, as it were, forces Him to do what He is asked to do in prayer.[3]

85

It is difficult to say what precisely the meaning is of the mysterious event in which Jacob wrestled with the Angel who represented, or deputized for, God, as told by Moses in Genesis 32:24-30. In memory of that struggle God changed Jacob's name to *Israel*. This victory of Jacob over God, this strength of his against God about which God's angel said: "...You have striven with God and with men, and have prevailed" is in its spiritual meaning a very suitable picture of the power of prayer. Obviously, according to God's pre-eternal will, human prayer is as if power against God.

The fact that God sometimes wishes that we, as it were, apparently force Him to grant us some great gifts of grace, is demonstrated in the wonderful parable replete with deep mysteries in Luke's Gospel. Here a godless and unjust judge was forced by a widow's persistence to do what he, in the first place, did not wish to do. How much more then will God hear urgent and persistent prayer! All the more so when He so gladly wants to give that He only waits for prayer to give.

Even when the petitioner is unworthy and what is asked for is immeasurably great and precious, His infinite love and goodness keep Him bound to the promise He has made, whose purpose was to evoke lasting, urgent, fervent prayer. It was His wish both by His promise and His gifts to bring at least some to unceasing prayer. It was His wish through a wondrous vision of the joys of paradise and of heavenly treasures to cultivate among Christians, or at least among priests, an ideal towards which one strives, albeit indolently and with difficulty, but which one does not reject. This ideal is: "that it is needful to pray always and not to cease".

---

3   It is necessary for us to explain the usefulness of prayer in a way that would not appear to predetermine what the outcome of human affairs under the guidance of God's Providence would be, or to impute changefulness to God's Plan. In this explanation it is necessary to accept that God's Providence not only directs that something happen, but that it happen as the outcome of a series of causes. Among these causes are also the actions of humans. Thus it is necessary for humans to act not with the goal of changing God's plan through their actions, but through their actions to achieve effects that are in accord with God's decrees. This is the situation with regard to natural causes, and also should be with regard to prayer. We do not pray to change God's directives, but to achieve what God has from beginning of the ages ordained to be achieved through prayer. St. George Dialogos puts it thus: "People achieve through prayer what Almighty God has determined before the ages to grant them" (Dialogue, I,8).

We do not pray in order to acquaint God with our needs, for "...Your heavenly Father knows that you need them all" (Matthew 6:32), but for us ourselves to understand and remember that it is necessary to ask for God's help.

In the whole doctrine about prayer there is some hidden thought which, it seems to me, has great power.

In the New Testament God promises to hear all prayers made in Christ's name, but the same promise is found in the Old. It is a common thread that runs from the beginning of Holy Scriptures, through the Prophets to the Gospel and the Revelation of St. John, throughout all of Holy Writ.

What does the Old Testament promise mean? There is, after all, no mention of Christ's name there. In none of the texts that touch on prayer is there mention of the Messiah. Obviously, all Old Testament hope subsumed hope for the Messiah and was sanctified by it. All its power lay in this hope.

On one hand, the very breadth of this hope, which included all the righteous petitions of believing Jews, explains how broadly the words "in Christ's name" should be understood. On the other, the Old Testament silence regarding this precondition for God's attending to a prayer is, I think, a convincing argument that these words should indeed be understood in the broadest sense. God in the Old Testament did hear and grant prayer, as witness prayers of the mother of Samson, and the mother of Solomon; and of Moses, and Joshua, and Gideon, Elijah, Tobias, and others.

Despite the fact that their souls and their prayers reflected only dimly the light of the yet-far-off Messiah, God heard when they petitioned. He heard when they asked not bearing in mind, or perhaps not remembering at the time, the promise regarding the Messiah. Through all the Prophets He repeated this promise to the Jews, even those who were weak in their faith, a promise which he was in time to reinforce so immeasurably through the Word of His own Son.

Then how much more (but reflect: a million-fold!) will He hear the prayer of one who wears the vestment that is red with Christ's Blood, whose words preach Christ and breathe the sacrifice of Christ's death! How much more will He listen to his prayers when he asks with foreknowledge and explicitly in Christ's name. When He asks for the benefit of His cause which is the salvation of men's souls, for the Church which is Christ's Betrothed, for her children who are called to God's service to be the great future Saints, Martyrs, and Apostles of the latter days.

If God gave the Jews the promise in the Old Testament and

always faithfully kept His word, how much more would He do so now that in the New Testament He has repeated the promise so many times and has kept it for almost two thousand years! From time immemorial it has been unheard-of for God not to keep His promise. How much more then in the future will He hear all our prayers and always keep the promise given us!

"Elijah was a man of like nature with ourselves and he prayed fervently that it might not rain, and for three years and six months it did not rain on the earth. Then he prayed again and the heaven gave rain, and the earth brought forth its fruit" (James 5:17-18).

TEACHINGS ABOUT PRAYER IN THE OLD TESTAMENT

What are God's promises in the Old Testament to hear prayer?

I do not intend to present the whole doctrine of the Old Testament concerning prayer, it would be necessary to cite thousands of passages that deal with prayer. Even a superficial knowledge of the writings of mystics would suffice to realize how often they use Old Testament texts to explain the highest and the profoundest laws or manifestations of the mystic life. I would almost be inclined to say that they quote the Old Testament more often than the New. In every word the Song of Songs contains an infinite depth of mystery and books like the Psalms of King David, and the Prophets are replete with teachings about prayer. Indeed, I do not know if there exists another as interesting and profound a treatise about prayer as the one revealed in the Old Testament.

For our purposes it would suffice to assert and show through passages from Holy Scriptures that in Old Testament times God clearly promised to hear every good prayer and that devout Jews in general were convinced of that this was so.

A few passages will do.

Jeremiah 33:3 reports God's words: "Call to me and I will answer you, and will tell you great and hidden things which you have not known". And Isaiah 30:19: "...You shall weep no more. He will surely be gracious to you at the sound of your cry; when he hears it, he will answer you". In 65:24: "Before they call I will answer, while they are yet speaking I will hear".

"For what great nation is there", asks Deuteronomy 4:7, "that has a god so near it as the Lord our God is to us, whenever we call upon him"? In Sirach (Ecclesiasticus) 35:17 we read that "The prayer of the humble pierces the clouds", and in 2:10 "...Who ever trusted in the Lord and was put to shame? Or who ever persevered in the fear of the Lord and was forsaken? Or who ever called upon him and was overlooked?". The Psalmist tells us (34:15,17): "The eyes of the Lord are toward the righteous, and his ears toward their cry," and "When the righteous cry for help the Lord hears, and delivers them out of all their troubles."

In Job 22:27 it is written: "You will make your prayer to him, and he will hear you". Judith 9:16 affirms: "...Thou art God of the lowly, helper of the oppressed". In Tobit 12:8-9 we find: "Prayer is good when accompanied by fasting, almsgiving, and righteousness".

True, in all these texts, with the exception of those from Jeremiah and Isaiah, these is no explicit promise from God, but there is given the doctrine of God's revelation and that is equivalent to God's promise.

A SCHOOL OF PRAYER

Whoever reflects, if only a little, on the words of Jesus Christ about prayer, some of which words have been quoted here, that person cannot doubt that in prayer we in fact possess the key to all the treasures of heaven and an infallible way of obtaining them. We can also say a key to all treasures of this world; obviously, treasures understood in the Christian sense. This would be all that in this world is the most beautiful and the most precious.

How can it be then, that so few attain these treasures, and so infrequently? That they fail to reach them is readily seen from the fact that so many are impoverished, so many complain, suffer because of misfortune, lose their mental balance, and even commit suicide. Instead of a life which could have been filled with all sorts of good things, they choose the worst kind of death, one without a Christian preparation in the moment of a terrible crime. They prefer that the stain of their crime remain on their memory and on the honour of their family forever, rather than to continue to live. This was obviously because life had become unbearably difficult for them. Yet it could have been replete with joy through prayer and through God's wisdom, and through the stilling of the passions that flows from them.

All this is a sure sign that people, though they have the key to riches, do not know how to use that key to open the door to the heavenly treasurehouse. I say they do not know because of a lack of light on their reasoning, for I cannot say they do not wish to. Who would not wish, if he only knew how? They do not know. Therefore for them, for all of them, for all mankind, the primary and the most important thing is to know how to pray.

If there were a school in which one could learn how to pray, then every Christian would surely devote some time and some effort to this learning. Among us in the church of Christ, among Christians, there is such a school.

I invite all of you to this school today. Come all, young and old, even the very old, lay people and priests! I call you, men and women, to this school. I call you, Christian mothers; I call you, children and girls. I call you, Christian families, Christian communities, Christian institutions. All of you come, and enrol in this school.

I would like to shout this invitation so loudly, that my voice would carry to every city, to every village, to every home, to every Christian soul, where I cannot be in person. Let this booklet reach you wherever you might be, let it encourage everyone to begin learning in this school of God.

I am asking you, good and pious Christians, you who care for God's glory, you zealous leaders in all parish brotherhoods and sisterhoods, and you of the youth who are returning home from school for vacations. I ask you, cantors, who are called by God to assist priests, to assist me, to assist Christ in His holy work of saving souls. I urgently ask all of you: carry this word of God which I proclaim to you in this booklet to the souls of the illiterate, to those who attend church infrequently, to the ignorant who do not know the faith. Enlighten them with God's word, read this booklet yourselves, share it with others, and remember this great and holy word of the Holy Spirit spoken through St. James: " ...Whoever brings back a sinner from the error of his way will save his soul from death and will cover a multitude of sins" (James 5:19).

In Christ's church there is such a school: the preaching of the Gospel and the teaching of the truths of the faith. This school may assume many forms. It may be as God's truth revealed and preached during a mission, or a pastoral letter from a bishop, or a pious book approved by episcopal authority, or the teaching of catechism in schools when it is taught under the authority of the bishop of the eparchy, or by teachers of catechism, religious and lay, or the teaching of catechism as given by a mother to her child. All this is part of that school of the Gospel which we have in God's church.

We must all attend this school, priests and bishops no less than lay people. We all remain pupils in this school until death. I am not dealing with the whole of this school here, rather with but one part of it.

A separate part of this school is where people learn how to pray. Fortunate and blessed is the one who in the school of the church has attained that learning. Happy is the pastor to whom the faithful can say: "You have taught us how to pray".

When you find a book from which you garner this teaching, keep it as a precious treasure and pass it on to your children as a possession greater than all other possessions. Here I am going to mention at least two books in which you will find such a school of prayer and which I advise you to read very carefully, not once but several times.

One such book is the precious work on the power of prayer by St. Alphonsus Ligouri. The other is *The Imitation of Christ* by Thomas a Kempis. *The Imitation of Christ* is a book which should not simply be read, it should lead to reflection and meditation. The words that are read should be interwoven with the words of prayer.

Whoever searches will surely find a school of prayer, whether in a good book or in the sermons of one's pastor, for every pastor knows well that it is his duty to convey the school of prayer to his flock. Or perhaps, brother and sister, you will find this precious treasure which I call the school of prayer during a Lenten retreat, or a mission, or recollections.

It is not about this school, however, that I intend to speak today. You, my fellow-Christian, can have the school of prayer about which I write, in your home, and in your heart. As there is a God in heaven, you will find hidden heavenly treasures in this school. Hidden they might be, but how great, how rich, how plentiful!

It is likely that all the Saints who worked for the salvation of others, and perhaps even more so those who prayed for the salvation of humankind, had each of them his or her own school of prayer. Whoever searches will find in the lives of the Saints, that many of those great heroes of the Holy Faith, mighty before God and before men, had their own school of prayer and that they passed this school on to their disciples.

What a wonderful variety of schools of prayer, what a rich flower-bed of prayer! There we find millions and millions of different flowers, each more beautiful than the next. There is the lily, white as snow on its stalk as if reaching to heaven; the wonderfully-fragrant violet which hides in the grass; a proud full rose, blood-red, and so many others. Such are the schools of prayer that the Saints have given to humankind in books that are filled with God's wisdom....

I will not describe at length here, not even to cite as examples these various schools of prayer of the Saints that we have in God's church, although I would wish to talk about them, because each of them seems to resemble the paradise our first parents lost through disobedience to God's will.

Today, however, I do not wish to talk about these particular schools of prayer.

The greatest among men born of a women, an angel in human body, that prophet of Old and New Testament, that hermit and man of fasting, teacher of the Apostles, the Great Precursor and Baptist, had his school of prayer and taught his disciples to pray. Unfortunately, his school has not survived and the Holy Scriptures mention only that he taught people to pray. How and what he taught, we do not know (see Luke 11:1). His must have been a large and excellent school, considering the possibility that several of the Apostles emerged from it. We only know with certainty about St. Andrew (John 1:40), and we guess that St. John was another. There certainly must have been more, although the Holy Scriptures are silent about that. Of the seventy-two holy Disciples of Christ, on August 21 we honour the memory of the Apostle Thaddaeus, about whom is written that he was also a disciple of John the Baptist.

What the Baptist's school of prayer was we can only guess. Its motto, however, must surely have been John's great pronouncement (John 3:30): "He must increase, but I must decrease". We find a trace of that teaching in a passage in the Greek patrology reporting on St. Andrew's martyrdom. There we find Andrew's beautiful words, who, when he saw from afar the cross on which he was about to be crucified, fell to the earth, reached his arms out to the cross and cried: "I greet you, o honourable cross. Long have I desired you, long have I searched for you, long I have prayed God for you".

Neither is this the school of prayer about which I wish to talk today.

THE POWER OF CHRIST'S EVERY WORD

By the grace of God, I now want to talk about a school of prayer which Jesus Christ, our Saviour, Himself instituted when He gave us the miracle-working prayer, the "Our Father", the Lord's Prayer.

The Lord's Prayer is not only a prayer, words, a prayer formula. It is a holy creation, an institution, a school, equal in significance with other acts of Jesus Christ. Before we explain what the Lord's Prayer is for a Christian, we must recall that each word of Jesus Christ, though expressed in human speech, the language of human nature, was the word of the Creator. As such, it had, or through God's will could have had, the power to create millions of suns out of nothing in a fraction of a second. Thus, when we hear Christ's words in the Holy Gospels, let us remember that in them, in each of them, is a bottomless well of power, light, and holiness. Each of them works and conveys miracles. Before each, millions of angels bow, worshipping with their whole being the word of the Word, striving to understand it, to penetrate its meaning, and yet every word even for them remains an unapproachable depth of depths.

Of those words of Christ in the Holy Gospel, one led thousands into the desert; another called hundreds of apostles to convert pagan peoples to Christ; the echoes of another toppled Roman emperors from the throne; another gave direction to the whole history of the Church for many centuries; yet another became the salvation of nations peopled by millions.

Some day, in heaven perhaps, we will understand something of the power and importance that the words spoken by Christ had. But even here in this world we already have an excellent example of what each word of Christ was or might have been. Consider: throughout His whole life Christ wishes to die for humankind, for his brothers, wishes to die because "Greater love has no man than this, that a man lay down his life for his friends" (John 15:13).

"I have earnestly desired to eat this passover with you", said Christ (Luke 22:15) for it was during that Passover that He was to make the sacrifice of his life. Through the last Old Testament sacrifice was the

93

first of the New Testament to be made, His death on the Cross. The real would replace what had been prefigured. The prototype of the Lamb would be replaced by Christ Himself. His desire to die for humankind was so immeasurable, so infinite, that, as it were, one death would not suffice for Him. To satisfy the infinite love in His heart an endless array of deaths was needed. To quench the fire of this love in His soul oceans of blood needed to be spilt.

Having consumed the Passover lamb and by this Passover having fulfilled the Old Testament, He sets out to bring His sacrifice. To draw all people to the road He will follow, He provides an image, a symbol, of what He will in a moment do. Through the washing of their feet He gives them an example of service to others extending even to humiliation of self and further...even to the limit. The disciples hardly understand these first steps along the road, even St. Peter does not comprehend, and resists. In time, however, they will remember His words: "...You also ought to wash each other's feet. For I have given you an example, that you also should do as I have done to you" (John 13:14-15). That example will carry them to the limits and in time they will understand that Christ wished to wash their feet not with water, but also with His heart's blood.

Now having shown His disciples the New Testament road and the New Testament service of brotherly love, He prepares to bring His sacrifice, Himself.

And because His sacrifice on the Cross would become sustenance for humankind, because humanity would derive eternal life from that sacrifice, as humans derive earthly life from the bread they eat, He takes into His hands the symbols of that blood sacrifice. He takes what is food for people -- bread. But as the sacrifice is to be made through the spilling of blood, He takes into his hands a chalice of wine. Wine is the blood of the noblest of fruits created by God, wine which warms and stirs the human blood. Now wine is the symbol or image of the Blood that is to be shed on the Cross, and He says these words: "This is my body", "This is my blood", and gives them bread to eat, and wine to drink.

Now behold the depth of power contained in each word of the Creator. Through the power of these words for centuries and centuries to come, in all countries of the world, His blood will flow and generation after generation will wash away its sins. All the peoples of the world will eat this bread and be fed through His sacrifice on the Cross.

With the saying of those words the sun could have just as easily have ceased to shine, or millions of new suns could have come into being. The earth could have been consumed by fire, all of heaven could have come down to earth. None of these resounding and to-the-eye great things happened, however. But something is happening that is millions of times more important, grander, and holier. A new world that is millions of times worthier and better than that existing until now has been created. This world, almost invisible to people because hidden under a piece of bread, is the Most Holy Eucharist.

The Eucharist is the world, many worlds. In it and through it all of humankind lives this hidden life, which alone is the true life. It is a world which encompasses earth and heaven. It is a world because it brings to life millions of saints in a triumphant march, though one incessantly marked by blood, which conquers both the earth and heaven. It is a world, even though the veil before our eyes is lifted but for a moment. It is a world because it brings with it God's kingdom, because it is that kingdom of the Father that begins amid the bloody sweat on the way to the Cross taken by Christ and all who follow Him along that way. It ends in this world with the words "It is finished" (John 19:30) which resound from generation to generation and after which begins the triumph of the resurrection of all humankind, renewed and sanctified by Christ.

Such is the power of Christ's words!

Do not be surprised that I have called the words through which Christ gave His disciples the Lord's Prayer an "institution". They have given us a perfect school, a school that works miracles, which takes people "...Out of darkness into his marvelous light. Once you were no people but now you are God's people; once you had not received mercy but now you have received mercy" (1 Peter 2:9-10).

St. Peter uses these words to describe the entirety of Christ's works. They, however, can also apply quite well to Christ's action which He accomplished more particularly through the institution of the Lord's Prayer. This passage from St. Peter describes well what happens to the human soul in that school, how it changes a person, how much it gives that person, and how it sanctifies it.

Certainly only some day in heaven will we realize what God's gift of Christ was and is. But even here we can with our limited powers at least see from afar and see at least something as in a mirror or a picture of what the Lord's Prayer is a school, how we can benefit by it and what can be learned in it.

Most Holy Mother of God help me, give my speech clarity in presentation, power in expression, and success in persuasion!

PREPARATION FOR PRAYER

We have already mentioned that concentration is one of the pre-conditions for prayer that Christ demands ("...Go into your room and shut the door...." Matthew 6:6). This is one of the preparatory steps which Jesus Christ demands of those disciples who want to learn from Him how to pray.

We can only add that concentration consists in two things.

One is to enter our "room" or "chapel", or, as St. Paul would put it, into the temple of our soul. That is to say, in thought or imagination to enter into the temple of rational reflection and spirituality, which is our heart, our soul. This is an absolute condition for every prayer and it is absolutely necessary to train one's self to achieve it. This is an image which, in a beautiful way, expresses love of others, because I cannot express that love better than through this symbol of embracing the object of my love with my heart; that it exists spiritually in my heart. This practice as regards people whom one loves or should love, such as enemies or opponents, those who have done me harm, is in itself a most beautiful act of virtue, and a necessary one, at least from time to time.

The second is that, in order to concentrate, we must shut the door. It is abundantly clear that by "door" Jesus means the senses which are in fact the doors of the soul, for everything that enters the soul comes through the senses. In this way Christ asks that in order to learn how to pray we must learn and become proficient in stilling the senses, to be blind, deaf, mute, without even the tactile sense, at least for that short time of prayer. This will leave the soul the freedom to speak with God. The very nature of prayer demands this. Who ever, while at prayer, continues to look around, pays attention to every sound, keeps shifting hands and feet, cannot but be distracted and preoccupied with something else and be therefore incapable of praying.

Such a person behaves in the same way as one who would stand at the door of the church with his back to the altar, looking outside the church, talking to someone outside the church. What kind of prayer would that be? Those who while praying search with their senses for things of this world, that is to say, do things like looking at something in

96

The Sheptytsky family: Leon, Zofia (mother), Stanislaw (standing), Roman, Jan (father), Kazimierz (standing), and Alexander, in 1887. Source: P.R. Magocsi, Editor, Morality and Reality, p. 86.

**Metropolitan Andrei Sheptytsky
as Bishop of the Eparchy of Stanislaviv, 1899.**

Metropolitan Andrei Sheptytsky,
Archbishop of Lviv and Metropolitan
of Halych, Bishop
of Kamianets Podilskyj, c. 1906.

**Metropolitan Andrei Sheptytsky,
Archbishop of Lviv, c. 1921.**

**Metropolitan Andrei Sheptytsky
during the Velehrad Congress, 1927.**

**Metropolitan Andrei Sheptycky
in a Studite religious cassock.**

**Metropolitan Sheptytsky and his brother,
Archimandrite Klymentii, in Pidliute, c. 1928.**

Metropolitan Andrei Sheptytsky in his residence, Lviv, 1939.

their surroundings, listening to stray sounds, fiddling with their hands, turn their back on the sanctuary that is their soul. By doing these things they turn their back on God's altar which is in this sanctuary, in which God appears to the soul through His grace, listens to prayer, and speaks to those who pray.

"...The Lord was not in the wind", it was said to Elijah (3 Kings 19:11), nor is He in the turbulence of the external world, not in the waves of air or light, not in material nature, not in the world which eyes see, ears hear, hands feel. God is the inward anointing which we have from Him "the Holy One" (John 2:20). God is in the eternal life, "...which was with the Father and was made manifest to us" (1 John 1:2) which gives us "...fellowship with the Father and with his Son Jesus Christ" (1 John 1:3). These ties that bind us to God are not in the body but in the depth of the soul, in the hidden depths of our heart. That is where we should seek God. There we will find him.

This thought can be expressed in the following, albeit strange, analogy.

When we seek God, and that can be said about every prayer, we are doing something that is similar to a search for hidden treasure. Indeed what we are searching for, that anointing, that fellowship and bond with God, His grace, the benefits that prayer gives us, all these are a hidden treasure. In order to find it we must dig as if a well. At the bottom of the deep well we will find this living water which has in it all the goodness which has just been mentioned.

Where should we dig this well? In the depths of our soul.

Let us try this strange exercise: let us enter this well with our head down. The well will be the deeper the greater our humility, the greater our effort, the greater our separation from all that which was until now around us and over our head. Now it is at our feet because our head is at the bottom of the well, searching in its depths for living water.

The world is upside down, you say? Yes, exactly. Everything is contrary to the way the world thinks. What for the worldly is good: luxury, sensuality, gluttony, drunkenness, for us is bad. What is bad for the worldly: the Cross of Jesus Christ, suffering, the wounds of Jesus Christ which St. Paul the Apostle carried on his body, the crown of thorns, scourging, the crimson raiment, the Cross, Golgotha, all those who are worldly scorn them. But they are all that is dear and precious to us. And because we want all this and search for it, we plunge head-first into the well from which we can get this living water.

It is possible that we will have to undergo privation, struggle, labour, search a long time and go through much suffering for the sake of Christ's name. But what will be the end result? The water will spring forth, we will have dug through to reach another world. Again we will have above us a bright sun and wonderful flowers of paradise, and the joy of the angels and the blessed. And, while we live in this miserable world, we will have the blessedness of the humble and those who weep, of those who are persecuted, of peacemakers and the merciful. After labour and tears there will be blessedness to which there is no other way than the way we have described: by digging that well head-down.

And where is this well to be dug? In the depths of our heart!

There we will find God. Do not look for Him elsewhere. There through prayer we will gain all of heaven; there we will find the door to heaven's treasury. The key to that door, my brother priests, is in our hands -- but we do not know how to use it. By that well-digging analogy, which might appear strange perhaps, can be represented nothing other than that state of readiness, that concentration which Christ demands, and in which we must begin every prayer.

FURTHER PREPARATION

Apart from concentration, Jesus Christ very decisively demands one more thing. He says: "...In praying do not heap up empty phrases as the Gentiles do; for they think they will be heard for their many words. Do not be like them, for your Father knows what you need before you ask him" (Matthew 6:7-8).

Christ does not ask much of us when He says: do not babble like the heathens. But He demands that resolutely. Can He ask less?

What is the prayer of the heathens like? It's a lot of words, little thought, little heart. "This people", says Christ, "honours me with their lips, but their heart is far from me" (Matthew 15:8). Jesus Christ does not in general censure words as such. A prayer spoken by the lips and in words is good. But it is not enough when the mouth alone speaks and the spirit is far from the words. When the mouth speaks ten words and the spirit only one, there are exactly nine words too many in the prayer

98

that the lips have spoken. This means, it was the lips that spoke, not the heart. This is the prayer of heathens: to babble and rattle on, not to think about what is being said. But then, it is very difficult for the soul to express everything that is contained in prayer. Certainly, it is difficult. That is why we need to be taught by Christ in that school of prayer that the Lord's Prayer is.

IS ATTENTIVENESS NEEDED DURING PRAYER?

We should differentiate between those means which make it easier to achieve an objective, and those means without which achieving that objective is impossible.

Oral, spoken, prayer has three objectives.

The first objective is one that is common to all good acts of a soul that is sanctified by grace -- to earn merit. To reach this objective it is not necessary to be attentive throughout the whole prayer. The power of the initial good intention with which one approaches prayer acts to make that person and that prayer worthy of reward, just as would other actions that merit heavenly recompense.

The second objective of prayer is to petition, to ask, for a benefit. For this an intention to achieve the first objective is sufficient, because God, first of all, pays attention to the objective towards which the will is directed. If that first good intention is absent, then such prayer neither has merit nor can it successfully petition for anything. As St. Gregory says: "God does not hear a prayer which the one that is praying does not truly want granted".

The third objective of prayer is to provide nourishment for the soul. To attain it, attentiveness, concentration, during prayer are necessary. St. Paul says: "For if I pray in a tongue, my spirit prays but my mind is unfruitful. What am I to do? I will pray with the spirit and I will pray with the mind also; I will sing with the spirit and I will sing with the mind also" (1 Corinthians 14:14-15).

It should be noted, however, that there are also three kinds of attentiveness that are needed, as well. In oral prayer we pay attention to the sounding of every word so that there is no mistake. The second type of attentiveness relates to the meaning of the words used in the prayer. The third attentiveness concerns the objective of the prayer; that is, God, and the purpose of the petition, what is being requested of God.

This third kind of attentiveness is the most necessary. Even those who may not understand the exact meaning of the words can still be capable of this kind of attentiveness. The words of Jesus Christ to St. John also point to this. "God is spirit and those who worship him must worship in spirit and truth" (John 4:24).

This is how one prays who approaches prayer, led by the good will that is granted by the Holy Spirit. This is why no obstacle is created even should thoughts, because of human frailty, stray from the objective of the prayer. This happened even to the Saints. The Prophet David expresses it in these words: "...My heart has abandoned me" (Psalm 39:13).

THE *OUR FATHER...* -- THE LORD'S PRAYER

The Gospel according to St. Luke (11:1) recounts the time that Christ gave His prayer (for we rightly call the "Our Father..." the Lord's, Christ's, Prayer) to His Apostles. Christ had been praying "in a certain place" and one of His disciples, was encouraged by Christ's example and because of it realized that prayer is far from being what people have at times called "prayer" (that is, not "many words" or heaping up of "empty phrases"), but something infinitely more lofty. Desiring to learn Christ's way of praying, he said: "Lord, teach us to pray, as John taught his disciples".

Christ answered: "When you pray, say; 'Our Father....'".

Matthew (6), however, tells us that Christ taught his disciples the Lord's Prayer during a longer discourse in which He warned against giving alms as hypocrites do, in a way that would earn praise from people. He further cautioned against the hypocrites' way of praying "in the synagogues and at the street corners" so that they "may be seen by men".

Then He taught them: first to prepare to pray, "go into your room"; and, second, not to think that they "will be heard for their many words". Only then did Christ give the words of His Prayer.

It is difficult to say whether Luke simply did not cite the whole conversation, whereas Matthew kept the disciple's request in his account, or whether, as appears more likely, Christ taught His prayer on several separate occasions.

What does appear undoubted is that, just as all of His teachings, just as this, which is not only a teaching but a veritable school, Christ gave to those who had at least some desire for it, who, like the disciple, said or thought: "Lord, teach us to pray...". It is natural that this request, this desire to learn, is necessary if teaching is to be absorbed; and that teaching is imparted and assimilated to the extent that it is desired.

In response to the request, "...teach us to pray...", Jesus Christ gives more than simply a formula for prayer, more than the words alone,

He teaches the best way to pray. More important, He teaches the best way to learn to pray, gives us His school of prayer.

When accepting this teaching of Jesus Christ, we should not only use those words in reciting the Lord's Prayer. To recite that prayer is good, praiseworthy, necessary, essential, but not sufficient. Apart from saying it, we should seek in the Lord's Prayer the teaching about prayer and the school of prayer which Christ gave to the Apostles and which He has given us. In other words, those who want to learn how to pray, to receive from Heaven the gift of prayer; who aspire to have the words of the Prophet: "...I will pour out on the house of David and the inhabitants of Jerusalem a spirit of compassion and supplication" (Zechariah 12:10) apply to them, must seek that learning and that compassion in the Lord's Prayer.

The words given us by Christ are like a gate to heaven, that heaven which already in this world is the "spirit of compassion and supplication" and to which prayer leads along the direct way. Let those who desire to learn to pray enter this school, remain in this school, and be convinced that in this school they will find what they desire. They will learn to pray, will receive prayer, their souls will be filled with prayer, will ascend to the state of prayer. Together with that spirit of prayer their souls will be filled with the many, wonderful, heavenly graces which, taken together, can be expressed in one word, transcendental, full of power: *Sophia* -- Wisdom.

Let us try together to enter into that Lord's Prayer, and to remain in it at least for a while. Let us try to enter that shrine, for the Lord's Prayer is the shrine of God. Let us try to scent the fragrance of the incense that rises before God's Throne. Together let us breathe that pure, clear, life-giving and healing air with which the shrine is filled. Let us strive, if only for a moment, to raise our eyes to that far, distant, wondrous panorama, turn our eyes to that scene, those visions which are unveiled before our souls in that shrine. Let us aspire to see and taste how good God is. Nowhere else will we experience this in such measure as in that shrine. Let us try to accept that Holy Communion of prayer, to enter into that community of prayer, to feel how well and welcome we feel in that shrine of God, which is also our home. How fulfilling it is to live in this boundless, wonderful, divine world that this shrine of God is!

The Lord's Prayer would not be a school of prayer if it did not lead souls into that state of acceptance which is essential for all prayer and without which prayer would not be prayer.

It must not only lead the soul into that state of acceptance, but must infuse the soul with that acceptance, strengthen it there, make it permanent. I say: that state of acceptance -- although it is many-sided and can be expressed only partially by human speech. What is it like? It reflects every word, every petition, of the Lord's Prayer.

FATHER

The first[4] word, "Father", leads our souls to the acceptance of our state of being sons, children, of God: acceptance of something that was so novel to the Jews at the time when Jesus taught.

In the Old Testament -- the Testament of the fear of God -- God's name seemed so terrible that when that *tetragrammaton* was written in sacred texts, those reading them did not dare to speak the name and say "*Jehovah*" or "*Yahweh*", but replaced that fearful name with another word, "*Adonai*", which means "Lord".

It was the New Testament that revealed to men the Fatherhood of God, and permitted us humans to call the Most High: Father. That we are sons, children, of God is a fundamental truth of Christianity, it is the gift to us from Jesus Christ. In itself it is the New Testament in its entirety, the testament of grace and love. That is why that word "Father" is a word of grace and love, possible only in Christ and in the Holy Spirit. To be able to say it, we must truly be sons, "And because you are sons, God has sent the Spirit of his Son into our hearts, crying, 'Abba! Father!' So you are no longer a slave but a son, and if a son then an heir" (Galatians 4:6-7).

Who can measure the profundity of this word, of this favour, this dignity, this sonship? Who can evaluate the importance and worth of this relationship to God, this inheritance, this tie that joins us to God? Is not the very word, "Father", in itself a wonderful communion which introduces us into a mystery -- a new bond with the Deity? I say a new bond, because we may call God "Father" not because we are His creation. Sonship to God belongs to the supra-natural life. To speak of it worthily would require the language of angels, and even that would be unequal to the task.

---

4   In Ukrainian, as in a number of other languages (e.g., Latin, Greek, German) *Father* is the first word of the prayer, "our" the second. Here the order of the Ukrainian text is preserved.

Because of that supra-natural sonship we have become, in the words of Peter, "partakers of the ·divine nature" (2 Peter 1:4). To be conscious of this sonship, to acknowledge Jehovah as father and to feel ourselves his son (through a different sonship, not like the actual sonship of our Brother through His human nature, Christ Jesus) is the first element of the state of acceptance needed for prayer.

The Lord's Prayer leads us into that acceptance with its very first word. The saying of that prayer, which is Christian practice, fixes that acceptance in the soul. Who recites the Lord's Prayer at least once a day with even the slightest attention will find that imperceptibly the thought of "God the Father" will become a part of his life. This thought will become a guiding light and a prayer. It can become ceaseless prayer, even though it might not be repeated often. It can remain forever in the depths of the soul. It can itself pray in our soul. That thought can itself become a ceaseless filial prayer to the good Father in heaven.

Thus Christ's school of prayer immediately, from the first moment, pours into our soul streams of light and strength from heaven. If we understood this completely then it would be easy for us to have happen, or at least have possibly happen, to us as happened to St. Arsenius the Hermit. One evening Arsenius began to pray facing the East (our churches, as did early Christianity, pray to the East), and the opening words of his prayer were: "O God!". In these two words he found such plentiful nourishment for his soul that he did not continue in words. It was only the rising sun which interrupted his prayerful reverie which led the saint to exclaim with naive directness: "Why, sun, are you interrupting me? I have just.begun to pray. Indeed, I have not even begun".

With its very first words the Lord's Prayer leads us into the prayerful mood of preternatural Christian spiritual life, one turned to heaven, to God as to a father. These words not only induce this mood, but maintain and strengthen it. These same words are an excellent heavenly school of prayer which the entire Christian life, from beginning to end, can be: unceasing prayer, day and night. Fortunate is already he, who imitating Christ and with Christ, repeats those words by how he lives his life. Fortunate is he who learns but those words from Christ, even though he were to go no further in that school.

Fortunate is that Christian home in which that word sounds from time to time. Fortunate is the soul of the child who first meets that word on the road of life at the time when the concept of love of parents and that love itself first waken in the soul.

OUR

The second word of the Lord's Prayer leads the soul into a new world. It awakens a readiness in the soul that is equivalent to a new and better life. Taught by Christ to pray as sons to their father, we pray not only for ourselves, but embrace in Christian love our brothers in Christ, or in God. We render worship to the Heavenly Father for ourselves as individuals and on behalf of ourselves as a community, remembering that God is not only *my* Father, He is *our* Father, Father of all of us.

We ask: Who is "all of us"? Is it those who are close to us, in the narrower, somewhat egotistical sense, those with whom I identify? Is it all of us who belong to one people, or is it all of us who have been redeemed by Christ's Blood, who have received Baptism, and who have the grace that comes with being sons of God in our souls?

Or is it, perhaps, all who have been baptized, even the sinners; or even all those who have persecuted and wronged us, our enemies? Or does it even include the unbaptized Jews, Mahometans, pagans? Does it relate to those who live, or also those who have not yet been born, or even those who died long ago? Or, perhaps, does it even include the angels of heaven?

"Our" is such a small word, but how many problems it contains! What boundless prospects it presents, how it expands the heart and soul to yet unknown limits -- is this not a new world? Community with them, with Christ's Apostles (I John 1:3) and with all those who are, or who may yet become, sons of God, is that not a new life?

The feeling of human solidarity knows no bounds, nor does it know the limitation of a heart which, satisfied with what it possesses, is unwilling to share with others. Brotherly love, love for others, love which embraces all, is reluctant to see anyone for whom it would not wish the good which it itself has received at no cost. The human intellect cannot envision how far that brotherly love for others might go. That love led Christ Himself to Golgotha. Christ's Apostle, St. Peter -- who himself was to glorify God through his crucifixion (John 21:19) -- addressing all the Christians of Pontus, Galatia, Cappadocia, Asia, and Bithynia, taught them as follows: "Since therefore Christ suffered in the flesh, arm yourselves with the same thought" (I Peter 4:1). He also said, even more forcefully and clearly: "...Christ also suffered for you, leaving you an

105

example, that you should follow in his steps.... By his wounds you have been healed" (1 Peter 2:21-24).

It is Christ who leads us into those distant vistas of love. When, before His Passion, He washed the feet of his disciples He set an example of humility and love, a symbol of what He was to do on the Cross, saying to those disciples -- and obviously not to them alone: "If I then, your Lord and Teacher, have washed your feet, you also ought to wash one another's feet" (John 13:14). With the washing of feet, the death on the Cross, the Eucharistic sacrifice, as their example, Christ's disciples wash the feet of their fellows with their yearning to serve, their tears, and their lifelong labour. They seek for means how to wash those feet not with water, but with their heart's blood: an example set by Christ. They seek their Eucharist, they ask heaven for that Eucharist, they seek for ways to shed their blood out of love for God and men, not only to shed their blood, but to shed it as had Christ, every day, for each a hundred times a day, throughout their life. They do so that no one might be separated from the Lord's Prayer, from that state of being sons of God, from that fellowship with God and His Son Jesus Christ (1 John 1:3). They do so in order that the word *our* might include everyone without exception.

Thus the first word of Christ's school leads the soul into an acceptance of love for others, to zeal for the salvation of souls, even to self-sacrifice out of a sense of goodness, solidarity, and union with all the chosen of the whole of Christ's Church. That acceptance inculcates and strengthens in the soul that love to which it leads, love which can itself also be unceasing prayer. Again, that word is in itself a school, lofty and beneficial, of prayer not only for one's self, but for all.

WHO ART IN HEAVEN

"Our Father who art in heaven" -- it is there that we need to direct our desires, our whole life. We know from the catechism that God in His infinite, changeless, and eternal nature is present everywhere, in heaven, on earth, in every place. Why then does Jesus Christ in His prayer tell us to turn to our Father who is in heaven?

That is where God reveals Himself before His wise creatures, the angels and Saints. That is where God is seen face-to-face by those who "have come out of a great tribulation; they have washed their robes and made them white in the blood of the Lamb" (Revelation 7:14). Heaven is the place where God's glory is revealed, where the righteous receive

106

their eternal reward; the place given to be the goal of all the effort and aspiration of Christian life. Heaven is the place of eternal life, "eternal peace, eternal gladness, eternal rest, and eternal bliss". To want that life, to live that life, is to be a Christian.

Prayer is the road to that life. This is why the school of the Lord's Prayer must initiate the soul into a predisposition for an eternal supra-natural life, instil into the soul the desire for it. Thus it leads the soul to prayer and teaches it to pray -- and how successfully! Our heart is where our treasure is. To remind us about this so-often-forgotten treasure which moths do not consume and which thieves cannot steal, is to lead the soul directly to the road of longing for heaven -- prayer. Thus this third element of the Lord's Prayer -- "who art in heaven" -- raises us to that life in heaven. It might be said that it leads us into heaven, leads us through hope, for "in this hope we were saved" (Romans 8:24). We already "were saved", not "will be saved".

This third element of the Lord's Prayer again gives us a world, or rather worlds that are brighter and more glorious than all the astral spaces, worlds in whose distant vistas is the true divinity of the soul. "You shall be holy, for I am holy", says God (1 Peter 1:16, after Leviticus 19:2).

This element of the Lord's Prayer puts into our soul the readiness to desire holiness, to work and sacrifice for the sanctification of our soul. There cannot be a finer and higher impulse to prayer than these lofty ideals which were the guiding light for the life, labour, and sacrifice of all the Saints. To go together with them towards the same ideals they held, praising our common Father in heaven -- that is what the introductory words of the Lord's Prayer teach us.

There should be no need to speak of how at every step constantly new, broader, higher ideals are to be unveiled before the soul. This is a task truly worthy of God's School. There should be no need to say that it would suffice to be caught up by these ideals, become accustomed to them, in order to become perfect beings, true Christians, and through the experience of our own life to be convinced and be able to affirm what prayer is in the life of a Christian, and what for the life of prayer the Lord's Prayer is -- a school of prayer.

THE FIRST THREE PETITIONS

Christ's words which express the first three petitions: "Hallowed be thy name; Thy kingdom come; Thy will be done" represent such an unfathomable depth of thought that some commentators believe that in their essence all three of these petitions have one and the same meaning. This is not to be wondered at. Almost every word of Holy Scriptures is a bottomless well of great wisdom. Rather, not almost every word, but *every* word.

When an inspired book interprets Holy Scriptures such unexpected meanings of even an unexceptional word are unveiled (I recall St. Paul's words: "the Rock was Christ" in 1 Corinthians 10:4) that we cannot but ponder about any word in Scriptures if it does not hold in itself some concealed treasure. If every word of Holy Writ contains hidden riches, then how much more ought this to be said about the words of Jesus Christ that have the meaning found in the words of the Lord's Prayer?

These first three petitions have -- we must guess -- hundreds of meanings, or rather one meaning, but so lofty and profound that we are unable to express it even with hundreds of our words. Each one of them is like a sun which not only illuminates and warms the whole solar system and the whole of our earth, giving life to all humankind, and at the same time surrounding with its warmth the tiniest insect and the smallest blade of grass, adapting to their life, their needs, their development. In the same way that word of God applies equally to heaven and to the earth, to all of humanity and to each individual soul, adapting itself to every, even to the most trivial, needs of the most insignificant spiritual being.

It must be so many-faceted so that in every application, and there are billions and billions of them, it might be so complete as if it had no other function. And in every application it will still have all of the endless qualities of God's Word. This being the case, it is only natural that human interpretations vary, as would, indeed, even those of the holy angels...

...It appears that the first three petitions of the Lord's Prayer in themselves, like the first three commandments, contain the whole Godly aspect of the life of humanity and of individual persons. It is not easy to say how one petition differs from another because each encompasses everything. Thus in asking for these three gifts, we ask for what is for each of us something undoubtedly and infinitely good.

First and most important is that we are asking for God in the way that we are capable of reaching for and possessing Him. We are asking for God's Son, the Eternal *Sophia* (Wisdom), and for the Life-Giving Spirit. This is why some theologians simply assert that in each of these petitions we are asking for the same thing. The difference possibly lies in our concepts and in our way of expressing them, the human way of expression to which Christ condescends. Still, I think that this explanation is not sufficient because all of those different concepts must have their own corresponding gifts or benefits. The grace for which we ask can be embodied in a variety of ways. Or when we ask for benefits, whose greatness we receive simply of our own insignificance, those benefits are not only different depending on our concept of them, they are also different, one from the other.

To express my thought briefly, I would make the following differentiation between the petitions: The first petition relates to all that should be called worship or adoration of God, or calling on the Name of God. The second relates to everything that concerns human organization -- the Church, the life of humanity, society, to all the ways in which these touch on the life of the individual. The third petition relates to what flows from the first two -- the sanctification and perfecting of humanity and the individual; and, through this, their penitence or reform and salvation.

In each of these three groups can be found God's Work and our participation in it. God's Work becomes a benefit for us. We take part in serving God or praising Him, and generally in God's Creation. That Creation is God's kingdom in heaven, on earth and in human souls. It lies in God's will in which are our salvation and sanctification. To become participants in God's Work in these three aspects is for us the highest and boundless good. It is nothing other than entering into communion with God, the highest good, also our Good.

To desire that Good is prayer at its loftiest and most perfect. It brings and instils into the soul the loftiest and most perfect virtue: God's love. In this, too, is a school of prayer. A miracle-working school, I can say without any doubt. What else can we call a school that at once gives its pupils what they want to learn in direct proportion to their desire to learn?

One who, in the desire to learn to pray, appears before the face of God to say the Lord's Prayer, is heard directly even before he speaks. His desire is fulfilled according to the power and depth of that desire. He might not have yet begun to present his petition, has but appeared before the face of our Father who is in heaven, but already in those pre-introductory words, in proportion to his desire, God's Name has begun to be hallowed. Into his soul, in proportion to his desire, enters the Kingdom of God, and God's will is done in that soul, in proportion to the human will, as in heaven.

That, obviously, is but the first flicker beyond which open vistas as boundless as God is boundless. But even in that first glimmering is that light, the beginning of the concerns the individual desires to address. The lesson has already been given, already the will is attuned to prayer as much as it wants to be.

Of course, if that will is weak, cold, lazy, that heavenly light, that hallowing of God's name, is but a weak distant reflection. And yet, when in that soul even the most distant reflection of God's love flashes like lightning through the intellect and heart, even for a second, it is sufficient to snatch the soul of the greatest sinner from Hell and save it eternally.

And what is strange about that? That happens when that flicker is the reflection of God's name, and when in that soul, despite all faithlessness, passions, transgressions, through God's gift and grace on the lips -- even though but distantly in the intellect and heart -- God's name is hallowed. Do the words, "hallowed be Thy name", not work miracles?

Exactly the same should be said about the second and third petition. Each of them brings with it the power to work miracles. This is the power of God's grace. This is the kingdom of God which is within you; the kingdom which is the first glimmering of that kingdom of God into which those who do the will of the heavenly Father shall enter (Matthew 7:21). To seek the kingdom which is within and that which is in heaven is to pray. To learn to pray is to learn to seek the Kingdom, or to seek God, or to love Him -- it is all the same.

In this same way and to the same extent, the third petition is also capable of working miracles. To the same extent it teaches prayer, in the same way fills the human will, depending on what kind of will it is -- great or little, profound or shallow. God's will is our sanctity; sanctity lies in grace. Through sanctity we move towards God. In sanctity through love of God and through prayer we possess God and acquire the

110

desire for sanctity. It is impossible to teach one more about prayer that when he is taught to seek the will of God, or to desire God's will, or to say: "Thy will be done".

THE FIRST PETITION: *HALLOWED BE THY NAME*

The word, to be "hallowed" *(sanctificetur)* is used in the Scriptures in a sense completely the opposite of to be "blasphemed" (as used, for example, by St. Paul in Romans 2:24, and found in Isaiah and Ezekiel). Undoubtedly, the effect of "hallowed" is that when used in calling on God's Name it makes that Name holy, represents its holiness in the eyes and soul of the petitioner. It is, however, difficult to say what meaning the word "hallowed" has when used as an attribute of God. When theologians discuss the attributes of God, being "hallowed" is one that is generally not mentioned.

In St. Thomas Aquinas we will find a discussion of God's infinite nature, His omnipresence, and other attributes, but will find nothing about hallowedness. In created beings, whether angels or persons, that word means everything that is noblest, loftiest, best in the soul; everything that must bring us nearer to God, that makes us most like God.

St. Paul says: "...whatever is true, whatever is honourable, whatever is just, whatever is pure, whatever is lovely, whatever is gracious, if there is any excellence, if there is anything worthy of praise.... What you have learned and received and heard and seen in me" (Philippians 4:8). This is perhaps a description of what hallowedness is.

In the Gospels Jesus calls His heavenly Father "Holy" once (John 17:11) and once "righteous" (John 17:25). Generally He refers to God only as His Father.

The angels, however, use no other but precisely the word, "Holy", to praise God, as might be seen in Revelation (4:8). How do they understand this word? -- All of God's attributes taken together: that which in the eyes of the created represents the glory, greatness, love, goodness, infiniteness, wisdom, and other attributes of the Deity. But then it is difficult to understand why when we ask about the nature of God and its essence *(essentia metaphysica)* the theologians, as I recall, seek that essence in the existence of God; existence in itself, absolute existence, being that is in itself, being that is. Theologians do not speak,

111

I believe, about the hallowedness of God as His essence.

It is possible that the angels through that word "Holy", gather together all of the attributes of the Deity, not as they are one with God and one in God, but all of the attributes through which people come nearer to God in sanctity, or become like God. But here again we find difficulties. Created beings seek to approach God as He is in Himself, but all that differentiation of God's attributes is not God's. It comes out of a limited, small, created mind -- whether angelic or human.

Let us put aside this discussion, but it should serve to confirm the mystery that lies in that word. In it there is a depth that is beyond understanding, unapproachable even to the highest intellect, for in it is the greatness of all those uncircumscribable concepts taken together. That word expresses the impossibility of achieving a complete understanding of it. That is possible only to the Divine Logos and the Spirit. And yet, it is so close and approachable that all of our bliss lies in seeing Him face-to-face.

Everything that the word "hallowed" means attracts, entices, inspires, captivates us, and is worthy of emulation. In it are purity, brightness, light, higher than all intellect and filled with measureless mysteries; brightness without blot or darkness. But were there darkness, even it would be higher than any intellect and overflowing with endless mysteries.

Such should the Name of God be or· become when humans call on it. That it be so when called on in worship, in liturgical services, we ask in this first petition of the Lord's Prayer. Only in the very slightest degree can we understand the good for us that this represents.

We were created to know God. Our intellect in relation to God is that of the eye to light. The intellect that does not recognize God is in the full sense of the word blind, unseeing. The intellect is the natural reflection of Deity, through it we are created in God's image. Who does not know his Creator does not know whence he came, of what stock. He is like an orphan or foundling who does not know who, what and from where he is, and what is his name.

The intellect through its capacity to know truth can look not only down to the earth and examine through a microscope what is apparently infinitesimally minute. It can through a telescope also look up into the sky and measure the expanse of the heavens. The intellect that does not know this, or does not see this capacity within itself, in which that power

112

to look upward has vanished through disuse or ill will or passion, is like one who cannot stand on his own two legs, but crawls on all four on the ground like an animal. And yet in an infinitely higher sense our good -- actually, our life, and our salvation -- is, in piety, to call on God's Name. It is an excellent and great good for us on the road of life, from the first sign of the Cross that a mother teaches her small child to that ultimate worship of All-Highest God in which people and angels join in heaven.

People take pride in the swiftness of intellect, but they do not value that acuity which makes it possible to see the highest and the furthest. They value knowledge, but are unconcerned about the highest and most valuable knowledge. They value and boast of the acquaintance and friendship of great and famous, or highly-placed, persons. And yet they do not appreciate what for them are and could be their relationship, conversation, friendship, mutual gifts, proof of mutual love with the Most High. People are happy when they can sometimes take part in some endeavour, or in some event, if only as spectators from afar, particularly when that undertaking or event has a historic significance. Those same people have the opportunity every day to play a part, as great as they themselves choose, not only in the most important, but in the only truly important event that impinges on all of humanity: the work of salvation. Compared with this the greatest events in history have no meaning. Those same people, however, value this work but little and shun it.

They are truly poor, truly blind. They could cross the Alps with Hannibal or Bonaparte a hundred times with less effort that those had. With Alexander they could conquer the East to the Ganges and beyond. They could be full members of international congresses with historic significance. A mess of pottage, however, is dearer to them than that glory, those garland and awards, that prominence. If they were to say the Lord's Prayer with full concentration but three times a day -- such a practice would not take more than three minutes daily -- that practice would slowly make them into Christians, for in them the Name of God would be hallowed. Do they not see how important this is in their family life? Do they not understand what it means to them that God's Name be hallowed already over the cradle of the little ones and also over the efforts, the labours, and suffering of their elders?

Stop! Look around you! Do you not see that glorious angel from heaven who has spread his wings over the humble cottage? God's Name is being hallowed there! Look and see the quiet but bright light that shines in the life and efforts of the righteous man. Do not envy him. You can have the same, for God's Name is hallowed in his life and labour. The righteous Christian hallows Sunday, the Lord's Day. Who does not hallow a holy day does not want God's Name to be hallowed. Even though he says the words with his lips, his heart is far from God. To say "Hallowed be Thy name" worthily he must through his life show that he desires it -- and he dare not utter God's Name with scorn.

Who at every opportunity unthinkingly calls on God as his witness, sometimes even to support a lie, dishonours God's Name. Who labours physically on a feast day and does not attend the Liturgy in church, even though he could do so without difficulty, dishonours the holy day, and by doing so, also God's Name.

That first petition of the Lord's Prayer relates first of all to the whole life of prayer and is completely analogous to that request by Christ's disciple: "Teach us to pray". Through this request we ask for the spirit of prayer, for in prayer primarily is God's Name hallowed. Because of prayer, who glorifies God by his life, prays unceasingly, his very life prays.

Clearly, one's life glorifies God only when one prays sincerely, well, constantly, and in humility. Without this kind of prayer one cannot defend one's self against sin, cannot love God as one should, or love the neighbour as one's self. Although Christ's yoke is light, life's burdens become light only with prayer; without it they are often heavy indeed. Thus our petition also represents a need of the human heart. If one would be a righteous, honourable, and good individual, if duties are to be fulfilled conscientiously, if it is needful to shun egoism, then prayer is needed and also the prayer that God's Name be hallowed in us and through us.

That prayer, that first petition in the Lord's Prayer, is our priestly prayer. It is our function, our duty, to call on God's Name. Through us is God's Name hallowed in the souls of those who have been entrusted to us, and this is achieved more through our example than through our preaching. So that our example and our preaching may be what they ought to be, much prayer is needed -- much prayer: prayer about prayer, and prayer for prayer. The priest who does not ask that his priestly actions receive God's blessing, that in them God's Name be truly glorified, can hardly live up to the difficult duty to pray for all in the name of all and to be that Jeremiah who prays for his people (2 Maccabees 15:14).

May God grant us that all the clergy of our Archeparchy, and my unworthy self, that we might worthily fulfil that first and most important

114

of our obligations and that in all the churches of the Eparchy worship, church services, general and common prayers, be truly an unceasing glorification of the Most High. May He grant that the entire rite of the Church, and all rites, be maintained and practised devoutly so that by them, by all of them, we might glorify God.

Not only in the Holy Liturgy alone should we glorify God. Every Baptism, every Holy Confession, every blessing of a mother after childbirth, and particularly the Office celebrated publicly in church or privately at home, should also glorify Him worthily. In everything should God be glorified. The success of our efforts as pastors of souls will depend on whether we consider this to be the first and most important obligation. It will depend on how it is fulfilled, if worthily, with conviction, with love -- but first of all whether with a pure heart and a soul without even the slightest stain. This will determine the entire success, every bit of it, of our efforts. On it will depend our people's welfare, both temporal and eternal, as well as the worth and happiness of the future generation.

As God's Name is glorified in our Church, so will It be glorified in every Christian home, in every Christian family.

THE SECOND PETITION: *THY KINGDOM COME*

The word "kingdom" is used by Holy Scriptures with a variety of meanings, but all of them combine into one.

The first meaning, and that closest to us, is that in which Christ says: "The kingdom of God is in the midst of you" (Luke 17:17). In this word He sees either God's grace that sanctifies souls, or our belonging -- through that grace -- to the Kingdom of God.

This second petition in the Lord's Prayer can be understood in that first sense. In asking that God's kingdom come, we are asking for the grace that is in our souls, that it grow and multiply. It must be stated here that this request is heard absolutely and completely, even before it is uttered. The very thought to ask that God's kingdom come to us, the desire for that kingdom, is in itself a good deed, one which increases God's grace. Of course, this is only when this request is made by a pure heart, by a soul sanctified by God's grace.

Christ's words, however, have other, more lofty meanings. These higher meanings are more direct, and are more actually the primary meaning, the first thoughts of Christ.

That which by God's grace begins in the soul stretches like an unbroken thread to that kingdom of which Matthew wrote: "Not every one who says to me, 'Lord, Lord' shall enter the kingdom of heaven" (7:21). It stretches to that kingdom of which the Psalms state: "The Lord has established his throne in the heavens, and his kingdom rules over all" (103:19).

When Scriptures say that someone will enter the kingdom of heaven, they can say this with a double meaning. This can mean that the blessed will reign in heaven, or that God will reign over them. There are passages that have one or the other meaning.

John writes in Revelation about the kingdom in the first sense: "He who conquers, I will grant him to sit with me on my throne, as I myself conquered and sat down with my Father on his throne" (3:21). St. Paul says: "If we endure, we shall also reign with him" (2 Timothy 2:11).

The second meaning might be found in David's words: "Thy kingdom is an everlasting kingdom, and thy dominion endures throughout all generations" (Psalms 144:13). Or Matthew: "Then the righteous shall shine like the sun in the kingdom of their Father" (Matthew 13:43).

Between these two pillars of God's kingdom in the soul and that God's kingdom in which the righteous shall shine like the sun, there are many intermediate pillars. These relate to the whole of humanity, its so-to-say social life, to Christ's Church.

When Christ calls that God's grace which is in us a kingdom it is only because it makes of us members of Christ's Body -- Christ's Church. Through that interior grace we enter into that bond with the Apostles and the Church, of which St. John speaks so beautifully in the first chapter of his first epistle. That is why both Christ's petition in His Prayer, and our prayer, must embrace Christ's entire Kingdom of God, all of those pillars which join us with God's kingdom, the kingdom of all the ages. It is only through its ties with Christ's kingdom on earth -- the Church -- that the soul can attain the kingdom in heaven.

This petition in the Lord's Prayer rejects that excessive individualism which the Protestants observe in their religious life. They believe that each soul can as an individual entity unite directly with God and heaven; and accept no mediators. I think that the mention itself of the kingdom in our midst points very convincingly at community, at that holy family made one in Christ. Only such a community, or membership in it, can be referred to as a kingdom.

In Christ's teaching, after all, the expression "God's kingdom" is used primarily with reference to the Church. If the parables comparing the kingdom of heaven to a treasure hidden in a field (Matthew 12:45), or to a trader seeking valuable pearls might be understood in terms of God's grace, then the comparison to the householder who went out early to hire labourers (Matthew 20:1), or the net thrown into the sea (Matthew 13:47), or the man who sowed good seed in his field (Matthew 13:24), or to a mustard seed (Matthew 13:31), or to the leaven which a woman hid in three measures of flour (Matthew 13:33) very clearly represent an understanding of this word in a social or collective sense. It is only in this sense that the parable about the king who gave a marriage feast for his son (Matthew 22:2) can be comprehended.

When Christ uses the word "kingdom" in these many senses, incidentally quite in keeping with the whole of Scriptures, and includes it in His Prayer, the many ways of understanding it might appear to create a difficulty, a problem. The question might be asked: in what exact sense is the word being used? Yet this apparent lack of clarity, completely natural when discussing matters that are so inexpressible, so ineffably lofty and profound, could very well have been deliberate on Christ's part. There can be no doubt that in many of His teachings Christ, speaking in parables, used a mode of expression that was not immediately clear. "...I speak to them in parables, because seeing they do not see, and hearing they do not hear" (Matthew 13:13) so that, as the Prophet Isaiah so forcefully put it, the heart of the people may be made fat so that it might never see with its eyes or hear with its ears (Isaiah 6:9). Both Christ and the Apostles refer to this passage from Isaiah and Christ says the same, but directly: "He who has ears, let him hear".

It would appear that all of the Apostles, too, often spoke in obscure terms deliberately. The aim of this unclarity, when it is dictated by the will of the holy writer, and not by the loftiness of the subject, is to heighten the will of the listeners, to force them to make the effort to search for the meaning, to pray in order to overcome the difficulty. That light which at first is hidden and to which the soul comes through effort, struggle, and prayer is extremely valuable in the whole of spiritual life and encourages further victorious striving.

Obviously, we who preach the good news of the Gospel are obligated to follow a diametrically-opposite course, to present matters with the utmost clarity so that our preaching might to the greatest extent possible illumine human minds with the truth. But even when we try, as we ought, for the greatest clarity of exposition for which complete, even so-to-say extreme, simplicity is necessary, we would be following a very erroneous course in our sermons if we strove to solve every problem, clarify every mystery, as if they were clear to the intellect.

This is not the way it is, or can be.

God's truth, just as God's being, will always have an infinite profundity that is unapproachable for the created intellect. Even the blessed in heaven, who gaze face-to-face at the divine Being of the Holy Trinity, that is, see the three Persons of God, see them directly as they are, still cannot encompass the Deity, do not know Him in that perfection in which He can be apprehended. Only God and God alone can apprehend so completely. That apprehension, that complete perception, is an internal act of the Holy Trinity, through which God the Father bears God the Son, in which God within Himself utters His pre-temporal Word. Only that Word is perfect knowledge of the Deity. Only by the Word of God and by the Holy Spirit is God known completely; that is, as completely as He can be known.

For all creatures, even the highest and most perfect, God is always a bottomless well of unapproachable light. For this reason of all the ways in which He revealed His nature to humans, the thick darkness, the cloud, that filled Solomon's temple, the bright cloud that appeared at Christ's transfiguration, are perhaps the most proper and perfect. They reflect that holy unknowing which is the most perfect knowledge of God. The more one knows God, the more one is aware of that boundless well of unapproachable light which the Deity is, even for those who see Him face-to-face. And particularly from them, for they, immeasurably better than all who are on the earth, understand how infinitely God's essence surpasses every created intellect.

That same rich darkness of God lies on those words: "Thy kingdom come".

We understand this: when we ask for God's kingdom for those who with us call on the Name of our Father who is in Heaven, we ask not only for ourselves and not only for them, but on behalf of that whole Body which joins heaven and earth, unites people with angels and the Saints, that we call the Body of Christ. Do we also ask for that kingdom

118

for those who are in heaven?

A new problem. But it would without a doubt appear that in that petition is also included a petition for the resurrection of the body as they, together with us, "look for the resurrection of the dead". For them this will be a moment of great change in God's kingdom. It will be a moment in which Christ will begin to reign "and His kingdom shall have no end". Even in the Creed we say first that Christ will come "to judge the living and the dead", and only after that "His kingdom shall have no end".

But if in some sense we can hope and ask for God's kingdom for the Saints in heaven, then even more we can and should ask on behalf of Christ's kingdom on earth which is the Church of God. We should ask that day by day the kingdom of God come to it and for it. For the Church which is on earth, although it is Christ's kingdom, is enduring great suffering and terrible struggle even yet. Now, in and of that struggle, amid that suffering and the persecution with its streams of blood, is being developed that pure Church which is Christ's kingdom in the fuller sense.

"...Christ loved the church and gave Himself up for her, that He might sanctify her, having cleansed her by the washing of water with the word, that He might present the church to Himself in splendour, without spot or wrinkle or any such thing, that she might be holy and without blemish" (Ephesians 5:25-7). In that struggle, amid suffering and persecution, the Church bears children for heaven. The Apostles, like Paul, in pain bore their children and bear them "again in travail until Christ be formed in you" (Galatians 4:19).

The Church Militant needs help from heaven every day, unceasingly. It is our obligation to ask for that help unceasingly. We ask for that help through that one phrase that is so immeasurable in it profundity. Through that prayer we answer, according to our powers, Christ's call to pray for labourers for the harvest (Luke 10:2). Through that prayer we ask for the grace needed by all labourers of the Gospel: a pure life, devotion to the saving of souls, the spirit of prayer, boldness in preaching. Paul often asked the faithful for this kind of prayer (2 Corinthians 1:11; Ephesians 6:19).

By this prayer we ask for the sanctity of the Christian family; for good leaders in the Church; for good leaders of the people; for good bishops and priests; for good institutions, and other such matters. How many prayers are needed to be granted all of these graces and so many,

many others!

I draw your attention, Reverend Fathers, to some petitions which we often forget, and to speak about which we almost never have the opportunity.

We must petition on behalf of children who, in their mother's womb, are still awaiting Holy Baptism through which they are yet to become members of Christ's Body. For them we must above all ask for the grace that they not die without Baptism. For the young in general we seek to obtain all the graces that are so necessary throughout life. For children to the age of seven, or six, the pastor can do nothing other than pray -- let him not neglect this duty!

There is yet another sense in which we ask that God's kingdom come. In truth, it is veiled in mystery, but it appears that the first meaning of this phrase is "let God's kingdom come" as it includes a petition for God's grace in human souls, for the Church Militant, and for the resurrection of the body.

In this first sense something is asked for that is not yet here. We do not know whether in this petition Christ did not have in mind, apart from all other meanings, also the subject of John's prophetic vision of: " ...the holy city, new Jerusalem, coming down out of heaven from God, prepared as a bride adorned for her husband" (Revelation 21:2). John heard a loud voice from the throne saying: "Behold, the dwelling of God is with men. He will dwell with them and they shall be His people, and God Himself will be with them; He will wipe away every tear from their eyes, and death shall be no more, neither shall there be mourning nor crying nor pain any more, for the former things have passed away." And He who sat on the throne said, 'Behold, I make all things new'".

This renewal of all, this "rebirth", the reign of God among people is perhaps not identical with that kingdom of God that is of all ages and exists from all ages and needs no renewal. It is possible that in the Lord's Prayer we also ask for that renewed kingdom, for that renewal which John saw in his prophetic vision. We await it and with us the whole of creation which "has been groaning in travail" with us, awaiting for the sons of God to be revealed, for it, too, will one day "be set free from its bondage to decay and obtain the glorious liberty of the children of God" (Romans 8:19-22).

In all the intentions in which we can ask for God's kingdom to come, everywhere before our eyes arises God's work. It is also our good, for when we pray for our fellows, for the Church, we also pray for

120

ourselves. Unity in the Body of Christ, the bond which unites us all in one holy family, acts to make what is truly good common to all of us. Obviously then, the grace which sanctifies every soul individually is the good and salvation of the person whose soul it is; and yet, in some sense, it is also a common good. It would even seem that all virtues, all qualities, all good deeds of one person are also the good of his fellows. This is primarily because, by the very law of nature, there is a solidarity in humankind. It is on the basis of this law that Christ could suffer and die for us, and for us purchase God's grace.

Because of this solidarity all suffer when one suffers, because of it the effect of doing good deeds is mutually shared. Our prayers, always, even when we forget it, are prayers on behalf of all, they are a common good, for our heavenly Father is the Father of us all. Our good is the good of our fellow humans and, on the other hand, the good of another is also our good.

It seems that there would be no greater good fortune in life than to live among saints, to benefit by their good example, to gain through their prayers being heard. We would then have to do with those who are humble, good, gentle, merciful, patient. It would be a paradise on earth if all were good and holy.

Apart from this, God's gifts are often granted to a human community as such and then, in the narrowest sense of the word, become a common good. Thus the triumph of the fatherland and victory over enemies is the good of all. In the same way the triumph of the Church, our eternal fatherland, is a common good.

Regardless from what aspect we take this second petition of the Lord's Prayer, everywhere our good is at issue. That prayer leads us into, gives and reinforces in us, those concepts and feelings about our solidarity and union in God, our love for the family of which we are all a part, holy pride that we belong to it, holy love of its members. It teaches us to care more for the common good than for our own. The common good is more important than the individual good.

Finally, this second petition teaches us how to pray. To have the above concepts and aspirations as our own is the best prayer, the prayer of pure love for God and people. By being repeated that prayer very easily also instils in our heart the virtue of love, which in itself is already unceasing prayer. It must, however, be reinforced constantly, both by spoken and mental prayer.

121

It is a truth of the Faith that the act of loving God, of recognizing God's goodness for what it is -- that is, goodness higher than all goodness -- and responding with an act of will or desire commensurate with that recognition is sufficient to pour the supernatural virtue of God's love into the soul. That act suffices to secure the remission of sins, even the most onerous. The love of God must be united with a will to make amends before God for those sins by bringing them to judgment before the tribunal of the Holy Church.

How important are these truths of the Faith! They are capable of saving a great sinner even should he at dying desire to confess but without the possibility of making confession! If before death, recognizing God's goodness as the highest goodness, he should desire that goodness be shown him even in the form of eternal salvation, then by that very act of recognition is his soul cleansed and eternal salvation assured. Should it not then be stated that the Lord's Prayer can work miracles, that its every word brings salvation to those of good will?

Are they not a miracle-working school of prayer, those most holy words which we repeat after Christ and with Christ? They direct our intentions, turn our soul to heaven, weaken evil passions, strengthen virtues. Blessed are we that Jesus Christ has left us this treasure. Blessed are we that we have at our disposal such a sure way of pleasing the Most High, such a simple way to bring on ourselves His grace and blessings. Blessed are we that in our soul we carry that banner, that holy emblem, with which all of God's children are marked. That mark is borne by all the members of that holy lineage to which belong the Apostles and Evangelists, Martyrs and Confessors of the Faith. To it belong the Teachers of the Church, virgins, monks, hermits of the desert, and Christ's warriors. It is a sacred line which has produced great and outstanding heroes. It is a sacred house which has the Most Immaculate Virgin Mary as its Mother.

Blessed are we that we have our Brother, Christ, mediator between heaven and earth, who has left us such precious gifts, and daily gives us more through His holy grace!

THE THIRD PETITION: *THY WILL BE DONE*

It is not without emotion that I begin to write about this holy phrase. It has grown so close to the psyche of our people that, despite oneself, one thinks about those long generations of the poor, often wronged, so seldom happy, people who, working all their lives in the sweat of the brow, were notable for one valuable quality, one which Christ's Apostle calls "the patience of saints".

Often they did not know much about the Faith, heard few wise sermons, often could not even recite the words of the Lord's Prayer without error, often did not even understand what those words meant. That one phrase, however, "Thy will be done", they understood even amid the burdens and crosses of life they had to bear. These words could even be repeated by those among them who from force of bad habit were wont to use the Lord's holy Name disrespectfully, even use it in oaths to support falsehoods. When even greater pain gripped their hearts and life's burdens, like a cross, bore down on their shoulders, they were still capable of straining heavenwards with that simple phrase: "Thy will be done".

Sometimes you may have thought that you had before you a benighted drunkard, one who perhaps was incapable of observing the seventh commandment, and yet at some moment heroic feelings could still be roused in his heart.

It is difficult to suppress the upwelling of emotion at the thought of those long ranks of soldiers who with such yielding to God's will laid down their lives on fields of battle. Knowing our people and admiring their great qualities, although not blind to their great shortcomings, I believe that the greater part of those who died in battle -- so often without Holy Confession, without prayer, without even the possibility of making the sign of the Cross -- died with those words on their lips.

We can be serene about their eternal salvation. They had acted in that respect like the best of Christians. Even had the greatest theologian or saint been able to hear their confession before they perished they could not have given them better counsel or assured salvation to those dying with a more succinct formula. Those words contain the power to work miracles. They are a prayer from Heaven, still bearing the imprint of the angelic hands that carried them down to earth.

You who are orphans of those who died in battle, their brothers and sisters, parents, widows: cherish those words "Thy will be done" as a precious memento. They who died in foreign lands, far from their kin, could leave you no other keepsake. Could they have left you one phrase of comfort, of remembrance, like a testament, they would have told you nothing other than what I am saying now.

In serious illness, at the hour of death, repeat after Jesus Christ the words of His agony in the Garden of Gethsemane: "not my will, but Thine be done". Those words are not only adorned by the blood of our dear departed, they are also sanctified by the Blood of our Redeemer Himself. Remember these words in your suffering and before death. Remember that before He went to His death Jesus Christ underwent a terrible internal agony so great that His sweat fell to the ground like drops of blood. At the moment of dying repeat with Him and after Him: "Thy will be done".

Through the words, "may God's will be done", we first of all agree to and accept all of the dispositions of Providence concerning us. We agree to all the crosses we are to bear, all the suffering and sickness we are to undergo, and even to the death itself and its circumstances that Providence chooses to grant us. The prayer that teaches us to accept God's will is an excellent school of life.

The act of accepting death according to God's will and the time of death as given by the Lord God is an act of great value and merit before God. It can sanctify our last hour and earn God's blessing for that moment. To accept from God's hands out of love for God, our best Father, the suffering He sends on us out of love for us and for our salvation has great significance for God. It would be good to think deeply sometimes about this Christian act. Perhaps there is no need for a separate prayer to express complete surrender to God's will for it is found in the Lord's Prayer. Through this petition we ask for and merit that God's grace necessary for us to carry the crosses of our life like Christians, including that greatest cross -- death.

It is the Lord's Prayer which prepares us for this moment of suffering and teaches us to bear it Christianly and through God's grace gild, as it were, every cross we carry.

God's will is our sanctification. In both senses God wants our sanctity and we, by doing His will, achieve it. God has "no pleasure in the death of the wicked, but that the wicked turn from his way and live" (Ezekiel 33:11). This is why this petition relates directly to our own turning away from wickedness. Who of us is not a sinner? Who does not need to turn away from sin?

This petition also relates to the Christian life. In that life Providence guides us according to Its holy law and the inspiration of Its grace so that, following the Lord's way, we might day by day be sanctified. Our Father who is in Heaven is holy; let us, too, be holy.

"...Consecrate yourselves therefore, and be holy, for I am holy" God says in Leviticus 11:44, and this text is quoted by Peter: "You shall be holy, for I am holy" (1 Peter 1:16).

"Not every one who says to me, 'Lord, Lord' shall enter the kingdom of heaven, but he who does the will of my Father who is in heaven" (Matthew 7:21). This is the way to heaven, the road to sanctity. Sanctity is nothing other than the quality without which it is impossible to enter heaven. "...Nothing unclean shall enter it, nor anyone who practices abomination or falsehood, but only those who are written in the Lamb's book of life" (Revelation 21:27). Just as we are all called to eternal salvation, as it were invited by God into His kingdom, so we are all called to sanctity.

That sanctity obviously is not something that is our due, but is a gift from heaven that is poured into the soul of every child at the moment of Baptism. That sanctity is God's sanctifying grace. It grows in the soul with every good deed done, with every Sacrament worthily accepted, with every prayer devoutly said.

That sanctity is publicly acknowledged to every Christian by the Church in that every Christian has the right to Holy Communion and a priest cannot deny Communion to anyone, with the possible exception of a public sinner; that is, one who knowingly leads others into sin. That sanctity is recognized by the Church in giving unction to one who has lived a Christian life and, lying without consciousness at death's door, cannot confess. It is further recognized through the funeral of every Christian when the body is consigned to the earth amid prayers, smoke of the censer, sprinkling of holy water. In this way the Church also affirms the sanctity of the deceased's body.

That sanctity received by the child at Baptism should grow, and does grow through fulfilling of God's will and keeping His commandments.

Although God's commandments are not burdensome (1 John 5:3), and His yoke, as He Himself says, light; our weakness, our frailty, is so great that without God's grace we lack the strength to obey His will. We carry the immeasurable treasure of God's sanctifying grace and love in earthen vessels, as St. Paul puts it so powerfully (2 Corinthians 4:7). That is why we must yearn for help from God and express that yearning in prayer. Without that help, we can do nothing good.

The third petition of the Lord's Prayer reminds us of this daily and makes us ever aware of what those good deeds which should fill our life are. It teaches us to want God's grace and to ask for it. The petition is an excellent school of life and of prayer and is a daily reminder of the Apostle's admonition: "...Let anyone who thinks that he stands take heed lest he fall" (1 Corinthians 10:12). The petition teaches humility: that treasury of all virtues. It is a source of God's grace and truly a doorway to heaven.

In this way in every petition of the Lord's Prayer there open up distant vistas for the entire Christian life. In every word riches are concealed, in every word there is Paradise. They provide so fertile and worthwhile an opportunity for lengthy exposition that here I must perforce hold back and limit myself to a brief discussion of what comes to mind. There is no need to search far afield for a topic to discuss. The very first and most essential meaning of each word offers more than sufficient food for thought.

Let us sum up what the third petition points to so directly.

It indicates first of all submission to the will of God in suffering and in death. That submission grows to become that virtue of virtues -- love of the Cross and suffering, the desire for the Cross and suffering. Then it underscores the fulfilling of God's commandments, our weakness in this respect, the grace needed for its accomplishment. That weakness teaches humility and the need to act prudently. It teaches us to desire God's grace and to pray for it.

Clearly, each of these topics is of inestimable importance in Christian life and infinitely important for Christian preaching. In explaining the Lord's Prayer, only a little of what is most necessary and important can be said.

There is comfort in one thing, however, that the very nature of these topics is such that every word is a bottomless well of truth, every word is covered with treasure. It will be enough for the preacher in his human frailty to point to that well and those treasures if even from a distance. It will be enough to show even from afar how all of Christianity, all of revelation, all of heaven, are contained in every word.

Is not all of heaven also to be found in that word which should also be included in this summary: sanctity? It is because of sanctity that all who inhabit heaven are there, which makes them akin to God, which has always made the Saints such excellent teachers of the Gospel, mighty preachers of the Christian life, and examples for all humankind.

126

THE FOURTH PETITION:
GIVE US THIS DAY OUR DAILY BREAD

This can be understood in two ways. First of all in a, so-to-speak, material meaning. Through the word "bread" we express everything that is needed for daily life during our present time-limited existence. It is also possible, and even necessary, to understand "bread" as referring to the supra-natural bread of the Holy Eucharist which is our daily spiritual nourishment and which brings with it limitless benefits, unutterable good. And, beyond the Eucharist, there is the mystical bread -- God's grace -- which is bestowed through the Holy Sacraments. That is why the Greek word in Matthew rendered as "daily" bread in the sense that it is necessary to maintain life, is sometimes interpreted by another word, *supersubstantialis*, which almost corresponds to "supra-natural", that is, bread that comes from heaven.

Jesus Christ, through this petition, teaches us to ask for what is necessary, materially and spiritually, for our life and the life of our fellows. At the same time it teaches us to be satisfied with what is necessary, not to be greedy for what is unnecessary. It teaches us evangelical poverty in that station in life to which each of us is called.

Through that petition we further ask for the sacrament of the Holy Eucharist and for those sacraments that are necessary to us throughout life. We ask that we not die without those sacraments, that we confess worthily and well, that we not lose the grace of those sacraments given for the whole of our life: Baptism, Chrism, Priesthood; or for part of life: Marriage.

Further we also ask for that which in Scriptures is compared to nourishment for the soul, the word of God about which it is written: "Man shall not live by bread alone, but by every word that proceeds from the mouth of God" (Matthew 4:4). Through this petition we ask for everything that is necessary for the hearing and preaching of the word of God, whether for ourselves or for others; to direct the human will towards this, to sanctify it, elevate its aspirations, set it on the road that leads to ceaseless prayer; that is, school it in sanctity and prayer.

God does not forbid; on the contrary, He wants us to pray for our everyday needs. This is also simply necessary for the Christian life, for we should remember that our daily bread and everything necessary to sustain life are from God. They may be natural, material, gifts, but they are from God. We expect to receive them from His hand and we ask God for them. Being told to ask means being permitted to want because we are free to ask for what we are free to desire.

Prayer is nothing other than expressing our desires before God; all of our good and permissible desires, it might be said. A desire that cannot be expressed before God, desiring something that should not be asked for, is a desire we should not have. God permits us to care about bread, but does not permit us to care about bread alone, or care for it as do pagans. He does not, however, permit us to be anxious: "Do not be anxious, saying, 'What shall we eat?' or 'What shall we drink?' or 'What shall we wear?'. For the Gentiles seek all these things; and your heavenly Father knows that you need them all" (Matthew 6:31-2). And immediately He states almost as a law according to which Providence will satisfy all humanity's needs: "But seek first his kingdom and his righteousness, and all these things shall be yours as well" (6:33).

God assures the satisfaction of one's needs in proportion to how one first cares for God's concerns. But if one does not care, God does not in fact suspend His Providence, does not cease to tell His sun to "shine on the just and on the unjust". He does, however, exercise His right based on the law mentioned above (that God wants us to pray for our everyday needs) and through it by material insufficiency and poverty leads the human will to raise its eyes to heaven and to seek God's kingdom, and thus to set out on the road of Christian desire in which "all these things shall be yours as well".

Forcefully and repeatedly, Jesus Christ teaches people to put their hopes in God and to trust His Providence. "Look at the birds of the air"..."consider the lilies of the field"..."the grass of the field". "Therefore...do not be anxious about your life, what you shall eat or what you shall drink, not about your body what you shall put on" (Matthew 6:25). God who gave life and a soul, and these are the greater, will give what is the lesser, food. He who gave the body, which is more, will give what is less: clothing. God feeds the birds, adorns the lilies with raiment finer than anything Solomon wore. Are you not better than the birds, lilies, grass?

Replace your anxiety about what is temporary with a desire for the eternal good. Happy, blessed, are those who hunger and thirst not for temporary possessions, but for God's truth. "...They shall be satisfied" (Matthew 5:6) and all else shall be added to them. Those who are hungry and thirsty for earthly goods will, on the contrary, not only not be satisfied, but can even be punished for "you cannot serve God and mammon" (Matthew 6:24). "No one can serve two masters because; for either he will hate the one and love the other, or he will be devoted to the one and despise the other" (Matthew 6:24).

The Old Testament, too, in which earthly goods were considered a blessing and a reward for keeping the commandments, reproaches the greedy: "Woe to those who join house to house, and add field to field" (Isaiah 5:8). To an even greater extent is the New Testament filled with direct threats against the wealthy, those who are tied to and grasp after earthly goods. "Come now, you rich, weep and howl for the miseries that are coming to you. Your riches have rotted and your garments are moth-eaten. Your gold and silver have rusted and their rust will be evidence against you and will eat your flesh like fire.... Behold, the wages of the labourers who mowed your fields, which you kept back by fraud, cry out: and the cries of the harvesters have reached the ears of the Lord of host" (James 5:1-4). "Again I tell you, it is easier for a camel to go through the eye of a needle than for a rich man to enter the kingdom of God" (Matthew 19:24). "...Woe to you that are rich, for you have received your consolation. Woe to you that are full now, for you shall hunger. Woe to you that laugh now, for you shall mourn and weep" (Luke 6:24-26).

The goal of the New Testament is to turn the human heart away from being bound excessively to fellow creatures, to impermanent riches, but to raise it to value properly that good which is God. It is impossible to confuse these two categories: either God is valued above everything else, or something is valued more than God.

It can even be said that every sin is the valuing of something that is base and transitory above God, His mercies, His eternal good, even though there can be no comparison between them. Even a comparison is like a demeaning of God's infinite goodness. That is why the Gospels are so inaccessible and incomprehensible to a materialist. He carries in his soul a basic and deep obstacle that keeps him from turning to God: his god is the belly. He is not only incapable of loving God in heaven and even cannot turn to Him with real prayer. James' words apply to him, even when he prays: "You ask but do not receive, because you ask wrongly" (James 4:3). The words from Proverbs are also not inapplicable: "If one turns away his ear from hearing the law, even his prayer is an abomination" (28:9).

In asking for that bread that comes from heaven, which is the

129

Most Holy Body and Blood of Our Lord, we first of all ask for the hunger that is satisfied by that food, and the thirst that is assuaged by that cup. It is in proportion to that hunger and that thirst that the grace of that sacrament is given us. Through that prayer we ask for worthy preparation, plead to avoid the misfortune of a sacrilegious Communion. "Not unto judgment nor condemnation, nor like Judas" do we aspire to receive this divine, pure, immortal, heavenly, life-giving, awesome Mystery of Christ.

In this way the Lord's Prayer leads us into the Holy Eucharist, teaches us Eucharistic virtues: that is, virtues that are in keeping with the Eucharist. It lifts the sinful will to the level of a heavenly desire. This is why no human language can adequately express the depth of the mysteries of that hidden treasure that the fourth petition represents, cannot state the worth of that prayer, that school.

Finally, in asking for daily bread we also ask for that spiritual bread which is the Word of God. We ask for ourselves knowledge, understanding, for the capacity to hear, or if only to read, what will provide food for the soul.

For the faithful we ask for that good literature of which there is a lack, for devout Catholic books, for all the means of spreading that literature. We ask that the people may find those devout books appealing, that they bring the desired effect.

We ask that the spirit of preaching be given us, together with those qualities and gifts, and they are so numerous, that a good preacher should have. We ask that God's grace be on those who listen to our sermons.

The success of our pastoral work, it would seem, depends primarily -- if not exclusively -- on the fervour of our prayers. We are, after all, priests, men of prayer. We are, above all, mediators between God and the people. This is what our people need and this is what they value so highly.

For our people we need to be leaders in the many affairs of its life, true and agreed! We must be the people's advisors, also true. We have to be involved in all types of civic and social institutions, true again.

But a thousand times more important than this is what the people call "church services". In those services what is important is not the saying of "Lord, Lord" with a fine voice and in a fine vestment, but praying in such a way that the prayer will be heard. What is important is to have daring; to know how to use the power that prayer is.

And since, secondly, we are preachers of God's word, the Lord's Prayer is not only a school for us, one in which we are pupils, it is also a school into which we must of necessity also bring our faithful.

THE FIFTH PETITION: *AND FORGIVE US OUR DEBTS, AS WE ALSO HAVE FORGIVEN OUR DEBTORS*

In Luke 11 we find: "and forgive us our sins, for we ourselves forgive every one who is indebted to us". The meaning is the same whether we recite the Lord's Prayer according to the Gospel of St. Matthew, or that of St. Luke. The difference in expression is only one more evidence for what we have already mentioned, that Jesus Christ repeated the same teachings in different places and to different hearers, but not always in the same words.

These meanings are similar, for every sin is a debt, although the word "debt" covers much more. We are indebted not only through sin committed, but are also indebted by having omitted using God's gifts in praise of God to the extent we should have.

All that we have, all we have received: life and soul and all its faculties, every day of life, every act of every faculty of soul, the body and its qualities and powers, are all God's gift. For this the Almighty is due not only thanksgiving but, also above all, service.

In the first place we must use these gifts the way God wants them to be used: for His glory. " ...Whether you eat or drink, or whatever you do, do all for the glory of God" (1 Corinthians 10:31) that God may be glorified in all things. Our good deeds must be so done that people might glorify the heavenly Father. For this, above all, we must recognize and remember that everything which God gave us, He gave us, as it were, temporarily. Putting it in human terms, it is as if it were all borrowed, like the talents in the parable (Matthew 25:14-30), so that by good use of these talents, these gifts from God, we might earn for ourselves that which will always be ours: an eternal reward.

As also debts we owe, we should consider those remnants of sin which, after remission, are left as something still owing before God's justice. This can be paid through deeds of repentance, through prayer, fasting, and charity.

The whole Gospel, or even better, divine revelation, is a commentary on these words of the Lord's Prayer. All of divine revelation speaks of the fall of man, of the merciful forgiveness by the heavenly Father who loves us sinners so much that He sent His Son into the world for our salvation. Everything in divine revelation is in some way related to that act of redemption and salvation. Every Gospel parable explains this act of redemption: treating either a different aspect of it or treating it from a different perspective. But there are parables which explain this act of redemption in a more specific way: for example, the parable of the Prodigal Son or the parable of the Wicked Servant.

The first of these parables presents the infinite love of the merciful Father who waits only for the son's return and, when he does, runs out to meet him. His own goodness and mercy, already shown, anticipate the son's repentance. Christ died on the Cross for us while we were yet sinners. Through giving His life He came to meet us, anticipating that we would repent. It is as if His unceasing forgiveness is there even before we repent.

The second of these parables, about the Wicked Servant, shows a condition that must be met before we can be forgiven. In forgiving us, remitting our debts, God places on us a condition without which there is no forgiveness. Otherwise, as the parable says, payment of even those debts already forgiven will be demanded. "...If you forgive men their trespasses, your heavenly Father also will forgive you; but if you do not forgive men their trespasses, neither will your Father forgive your trespasses" (Matthew 6:14-15).

The Lord's Prayer as given in Matthew's Gospel permits us to ask for forgiveness of debts in the same measure that we forgive debts owed us: "forgive us...as we forgive". In Luke, Christ demands that we forgive our debtors before we pray. Only when that forgiveness has already been granted, does Christ allow us to ask for forgiveness. "Forgive us our sins, for we ourselves forgive every one who is indebted to us" (Luke 11:4).

This is exactly like another Gospel passage where Jesus Christ says: "...If you are offering your gift at the altar, and there remember that your brother has something against you, leave your gift before the altar and go; first be reconciled to your brother, and then come and offer your gift" (Matthew 5:23-4).

In one or another way, Christ has established parity between the way we treat our neighbour and the way God treats us. In one aspect, however, there is no comparison. Our dealings with our fellow humans involve minor matters. They are like small debts, 100 denarii, say. Our dealings with God have to do with an indescribably huge debt, 10,000 talents (Matthew 18:24).

Even when an injustice done against us by men seems very great to our way of thinking, it is small compared to what we owe God both for His gifts to us and for our sins against Him. In that analogy between our relations with our fellow humans and God's relations with us, mercy is shown us in that God's mercy is placed, as it were, into our hands. That principle, entirely just, is a magnificent gift from heaven to us from two points of view. First, it assures us of God's forgiveness of our debts; second, it is assurance of forgiveness by our fellows.

These words of the Lord's Prayer are a healing medicine to treat all malice, sense of having been wronged, or memory of injustice. They directly compel a person to that Christian, evangelical, and humane virtue which is mercy and gentleness. They compel, I say, because he who does not want to forgive his neighbour, who remembers injuries, who thirsts for vengeance would not dare to say the Lord's Prayer and by so doing call down upon himself from God an act of justice towards himself of the kind he has displayed towards others.

Through the Lord's Prayer, one who is vengeful calls down heaven's vengeance on himself. He who remembers and dwells on past wrongs done him cannot say the words which in Luke (11:4) are a pre-condition for forgiveness, "forgive us...for we ourselves forgive". By combining injustices done to us and by us in the same sentence, this unconditional imperative to forgive our neighbour creates a dilemma even while we are reciting the prayer. It is truly the judgment of Solomon being visited on us. Here the words of the righteous Simeon come true: "that the thoughts out of many hearts may be revealed" (Luke 2:35).

The Lord's Prayer indeed reveals and uncovers the very depths of the soul and the evil that may lie there. At least this is what happens when we understand the words of the prayer and apply them to ourselves. Then they penetrate the depths of the soul like a sword. Truly, "...the word of God is living and active, sharper than any two-edged sword, piercing to the division of soul and spirit, of joints and marrow, and discerning the thoughts and intentions of the heart" (Hebrews 4:12).

This petition of the Lord's Prayer is like a mark of authenticity on divine revelation. Only God's Wisdom could provide such a lesson, such a cure, teach such a prayer. Even at first glance, these words appear capable of working miracles, even to one who considers them very superficially and can understand only their immediate meaning.

But these heavenly words which Christ places on our lips have their own immeasurable depth. They reveal to the soul such infinite perspectives that again it needs to be said of them that they are a whole world, a heaven, which reveals the loftiest ideals of Christian life and sanctity to us. Forgiveness and remittance for which we ask have already been given, and we are allowed to draw as much as we want from this well of living water. We can seal up this well, we can turn away from it, we can even refuse to accept God's gifts, which is what we do when we keep remembering injuries done to us. God's mercy and forgiveness are already given, and the comparison of God's mercy with how we act is in itself another eloquent lesson. It is simply a repetition of: "I forgave you all that debt because you besought me; and should not you have had mercy on your fellow servant, as I had mercy on you?" (Matthew 18:32). In those words one hears, like the echo of thunder, "You wicked servant!" and, "in anger his lord delivered him to the jailers". In the same way the words, "I forgave you all that debt", evoke the image of Christ washing the feet of His disciples, and from afar is heard the echo of His most holy words: "you also must wash one another's feet".

Despite ourselves, we are reminded of the words of the Apostle who, too, had deeply offended God by denying Christ and who through his entire life tearfully reflected on this petition of the Lord's Prayer. "Since therefore Christ suffered in the flesh, arm yourselves with the same thought" (1 Peter 4:1). And again: "...to this you have been called, because Christ also suffered for you, leaving you an example, that you should follow in his steps" (1 Peter 2:21). To make sure we receive this teaching of Christ which is so hard to absorb, he reminds us: "...Love covers a multitude of sins" (1 Peter 4:8). With these words he encourages us to a sacrifice, great but certainly holy. Again: "If the righteous man is scarcely saved, where will the impious and wicked appear?" (1 Peter 4:18). Both through warnings of dire consequences and through encouragement, he shows the necessity of following the example of God's mercy, not just in any way, but even to the point of a complete self-sacrifice out of love for those who have offended us, to go even to Golgotha. That is how the chief Apostle understood the Savior's threefold question: "...Do you love Me...?" (John 21:15).

The beloved Apostle, who laid his head on Christ's bosom at the Last Supper, did not understand Christ's teaching differently: "By this we know love, that he laid down his life for us; and we ought to lay down our lives for the brethren" (1 John 3:16).

It is no wonder then, that the Saints, as we often read in their lives, were so used to repaying good for evil, and that the people who hurt or offended them could be sure to receive from them, sooner or later, an expression of their extraordinary love in return. Of many such examples, the one that comes to mind who always acted this way, was St. Francis de Sales. Did St. Paul not do the same? In order to share in the blessings of the Gospel, to be saved, he made himself: "a slave to all...all things to all men," including his enemies and those who persecuted him (1 Corinthians 9:19-23). Do the following words have any other meaning? -- "To the present hour we hunger and thirst, we are ill-clad and buffeted and homeless, and we labour, working with our own hands. When reviled, we bless; when persecuted, we endure; when slandered we try to conciliate; we have become, and are now, as the refuse of the world, the offscouring of all things" (1 Corinthians 4:11-13).

He not only practised this, offering himself for the souls of men (2 Corinthians 12:15), but also explained the reasons why it must be this way. Christ "died for all," he says, " that those who live might live no longer for themselves but for him who for their sake died and was raised" (2 Corinthians 5:15). St. Paul adds: "From now on, therefore, we regard no one from a human point of view" (2 Corinthians 5:16). This means that we owe it to Christ to see only Christ in human souls. This is a debt imposed by our love of Christ. Not to remember offenses against us, to erase them completely from our memories is, after all, a simple obligation of Christian love, for: "Love is patient and kind...bears all things...endures all things" (I Corinthians 13:4-8). You cannot limit love, cannot say: so far and no further.

He who through selfishness, for it cannot be through anything else, remembers an offense against himself, already does not love God above all else. He puts himself and his own affairs above God. With that he uproots all love from his heart because either love is without reservation above everything else, or it does not exist at all. That is how we must love our neighbour, because the love of a neighbour is one and the same virtue as the love of God. This is exactly what St. Paul means by "we regard no one from a human point of view" (2 Corinthians 5:16). Our relationship to our neighbour is regulated not by the flesh, but by faith and divine grace.

This teaching is affirmed and proven so many times in the Gospels and in all of Paul's and the universal epistles, that I have no doubts when I say that this is a doctrine of faith: a doctrine revealed by God. Obviously, only in some, perhaps rare, instance are we bound to this self-sacrificial love of neighbour. We are always, however, obligated not to remember offenses against us, we must repay evil with good, depending at times on our more specific obligations. Thus, a pastor must hear the confession of a dying man, even with risk to his own life, and even if that man is his greatest enemy.

AND LEAD US NOT INTO TEMPTATION

In the sixth petition we pleade: "And lead us into temptation".

Obviously, we are not asking that God keep us isolated from all temptations, because temptation is a test for the soul. Temptation in itself is not only not a sin but, on the contrary, an opportunity for good deeds.

Temptation develops virtue in the soul. It tempers the soul. That is why St. James says: "Count it all joy, my brethren, when you meet various trials" (James 1:2).

What we ask for is that temptation not overcome us, that we not yield to temptation and fall in the battle. It is the yielding that Christ calls being "led into temptation".

The whole of life is a struggle with an endless chain of temptations. From all directions we are put to the test: by the devil, the world, and ourselves. We ask for victory in all these trials, in the whole struggle. We ask for the grace to remain in God's grace to the end, which is equal to eternal salvation. The heavenly reward is represented in Holy Scriptures by many rich symbols and described in various words, but above all, it is a reward granted to one who overcomes. In many places the Book of Revelation refers to one who has achieved salvation as one who has conquered. St. Paul often compares the Christian life with that of a soldier in the service of Jesus Christ.

In pleading for victory over temptation, we ask for all the qualities which make a good soldier. They are all gifts from heaven: the virtue of bravery and that gift of the Holy Spirit which we call courage; as well as prudence, perseverance, patience, and so many others. Above all and in the first place here belong the virtue and gift of the fear of the

136

Lord.

Speaking in human terms, without regard to divine revelation, fear is not a quality, but rather a weakness in direct opposition to the virtue of courage. People who know little about and pay little attention to the teaching of Jesus Christ are inclined to think that fear is not a virtue and that an act which comes out of fear is not good. That is not the way it is. Only that fear is bad which is linked with to a desire to sin. One earnestly desires to sin but refrains from the act only because of fear of its consequences and punishment. This kind of servile fear has no value because it does not turn the soul away from sin. When one turns away from evil and, fearing God's punishment, turns away from sin and truly does not want to sin, that person does well even though the basis of his action, fear, may still be far from filial love.

When one boasts that he never feels fear of God's punishment or of hell, he can confidently be told to his face that doubtless he has many times in his life committed acts of which he is ashamed, acts contrary to his conscience, contrary to his convictions. It is not easy to act always out of a filial love for God; it is not easy to fear offending the Father more than to fear His punishment. This type of filial fear, full of love, is a virtue of persons spiritually well-developed and upright. Human weakness and the strength of the passions are such that a person indeed needs fear of divine punishment, fear of hell, as a motive for avoiding sin. When this motive, although undeniably lower than that of love for God, keeps a person from evil, it renders him a great service and is a true virtue.

Fear of the Lord corresponds to this, sixth, petition because through it we ask to avoid future or anticipated evil. We call these acts or perceptions of the will by which one turns away from evil, fear. Fear prepares us for victory over evil by teaching us to prepare for victory and carefully to avoid all that may lead to defeat. Fear teaches us to seek the means to victory and victory itself in Him who said: "I have conquered the world".

The seeking and struggle for all that leads to victory and to avoidance of defeat are the most necessary qualities of a warrior who desires to be always victorious in all aspects of life. Courage does not say that danger be ignored or underestimated. On the contrary, it demands that danger be looked squarely in the eye, that the whole situation be taken into account, that one's own weaknesses and needs be understood, and then that one arm oneself properly so that the enemy might be defeated.

The enemy is malign, tenacious, determined, persevering, powerful, like "a roaring lion". He advances continually, attacks from all directions. Vigilance in this struggle can never be relaxed, care must be taken not to overlook any thing, no matter how minor, that might aid in the fight.

Because the Lord's Prayer from its very first word is a plea for gifts necessary not only for ourselves but for all our brothers, and is a prayer of Christians generally, if not of all humanity, and since it is also a social prayer, the words "lead us not into temptation" have their own depth and far-reaching significance for Christ's triumph in His Holy Church. Those colossal, immeasurable, titanic struggles between good and evil in the whole world, in which all nations of all ages are involved and in which, as in the lives of individuals, there are waves of defeat and victory, decline and uplift, will end. They will end, and this we believe, with Christ's victory.

We are invited to take part in this struggle and victory by the supreme leader of this army, not only because our own personal victory is concerned here, but victory of good over evil in our life and our heart, victory of God's grace over the forces of darkness within us. This whole struggle is our struggle. It is ours also because it concerns us, our brothers, our people, the future of us all. It concerns our homeland in heaven, it concerns Christ and our God. This struggle and future victory will also be our triumph because we are invited to take part with all our life in the struggle and victory by the supreme leader Himself. This petition of the Lord's Prayer, "lead us not into temptation", repeats the call to this universal human struggle and victory.

Are broader horizons or loftier vistas needed? Is the human mind able "to comprehend with all the saints what is the breadth and length and height and depth" (Ephesians 3:18) of every word and concern of God? How can meagre words describe what the mind cannot grasp? Only he can be "filled with all the fullness of God" (Ephesians 3:19) in whom, as in St. Paul, Christ lives and in whose speech Christ, "in whom are hid all the treasures of wisdom and knowledge" (Colossians 2:3) speaks.

Only He, Christ, could explain fully what He had in mind when he taught us this prayer. Only He could tell us what the victory is for which we pray, and what are the hidden manna and the white stone (Revelation 2:17) and the rod of iron (Revelation 2:27) and the book of life (Revelation 3:5) and "What no eye has seen, nor ear heard, nor the heart of man conceived, what God has prepared" for the victor (1

Corinthians 2:9).

God will certainly respond with His grace to our prayer not to let us fall into temptation. He is only waiting for that prayer. Already now, even before that prayer, He is ready: "God is faithful, and he will not let you be tempted beyond your strength, but with the temptation will also provide the way of escape, that you may be able to endure it" (1 Corinthians 10:13).

The Lord's Prayer and that gift of grace for which we ask through the Lord's Prayer for help in times of temptation, are already that aid promised by St. Paul.

THE SEVENTH PETITION: ...*DELIVER US FROM EVIL*

In essence this is but an explanation or a supplement to the previous petition. We are delivered from the evil because God helps us not to fall into temptation. That is why St. Luke omits this last petition just as he omits the third ("Thy will be done") showing it is in fact only a repetition of the first and second petitions. Nevertheless, it is not without reason that the longer text of St. Matthew has been accepted in practice by the Church and not without reason do we voice this seventh petition.

Actually, it is indeed an explanation or a supplement of the sixth petition, but it places before the eyes of a Christian, more explicitly and clearly, the fundamental problem of all ethics, and especially of Christian ethics: the problem of evil.

What is evil? Where does it come from? How can we free ourselves from it? These are the questions to which an answer is so difficult to find outside Christian belief and Christian ethics. I need not remind you to what degree these two notions and their corresponding qualities are so closely and irrevocably bound to each other.

The concepts of good and evil are unchanging and clear in Christian faith and ethics. God is the highest good and, more specifically, the only good. "No one is good but God alone" (Mark 10:18). Generally, Christianity calls all that leads to God and brings one closer to God, a good. The absence of that good on the part of those who should, in whatever way, be expected to possess it -- that is evil. Thus the truest evil is sin. Evil can be all that which becomes a cause

139

of our sin, even if the cause comes through no fault of ours. Evil can be our ignorance of that which we should know. Fallacy and error are evil. The propensity of the will to sin and of the mind to error are evil. Asking to be delivered from evil encompasses all of these and others of its manifestations.

In Scripture the word "sin" is used to describe not only a sinful act, that is, willful and conscious transgression of God's commandments, but also sinful inclination and passion and all that is directly and most closely a cause of sin. It is in this light that St. Paul speaks of the dominion of sin, of service to sin, the reign of sin over us (Romans, Chapter 6). We also may speak of evil in this same wider sense when we look for what it is that the Lord's Prayer teaches us to avoid and for which things it tells us to pray, and how it paves the ways of the Lord in our heart, preparing and giving the proper direction to our will and our desires.

It might seem that this should not need to be repeated, because this thought returns in every petition, from various directions. By the ordering of our will and our heart, by placing in our life right desire and right prayer, the Lord's Prayer is God's continual school of Christian life and of prayer. It is self-evident that we will not only not exhaust, but will not even try to indicate, even superficially, the endless breadth, depth, and height of those teachings which converge around the concept of sin and consequently around the concept of repentance, even though in looking at the topic in this light we would not be straying far from a direct explication or analysis of the last petition of the Lord's Prayer. Through this petition we express a desire for repentance; and we pray for it and all that is necessary to achieve it.

But perhaps presenting the topic in this way would take us too far. It might be more useful, on the basis of Holy Scriptures, to present not so much the need or benefit of repentance, but rather the very essence of evil or sin, seeking in every detail uncovered by our analysis to prove the limitless perspective which every one of these elements may open before our eyes.

First, as a beginning: an observation necessary so that this limitless perspective may be created for us.

Our body's eye is constructed and transmits images in such a way that an object close to the eye seems large while an object far from the eye appears small. Size diminishes in proportion to distance. When considering that which is moral evil, this relation is exactly the inverse:

the closer we are to the matter, the smaller it seems; the farther we are, the larger it appears. We will return to this observation later and see that it is not only undeniable, but that it may be almost understood in the form of some mathematical law. Perhaps we will be able to find the reason for this strange phenomenon and to juxtapose this reason with the general principles of our ethical life or even of God's laws.

Even now, merely to observe this strange, indeed paradoxical and incredible, phenomenon will help us make an important point. From near, a moral evil may loom immensely large or endlessly deep in its evil; but we determine that the image of this colossus appears a million times smaller to our eyes than it actually itself is. From this we can infer what great depths of understanding would be opened to us if we were able to observe this evil not from near and therefore diminished, but to look at it from that vantage point from which it would appear undiminished. We must then necessarily say to ourselves: if this sin, seen from near, and therefore diminished, is still so great, then how huge it must seem when seen from that other point of view.

Let us now look at the concept of sin in Holy Scriptures and identify the elements which constitute it.

There sin is presented primarily as slavery. In the Gospel according to John, Christ says: "...Everyone who commits sin is a slave to sin" (John 8:34). Many other passages reflect this same thought. For example:

"Let no sin...reign in your mortal bodies. Do not yield your members to sin as an instrument of wickedness.... Sin will have no dominion over you...." (Romans 6:12-14). I will not cite many texts, but will only say that Jeremiah calls sin a "yoke...upon the neck" (Lamentations 1:14). In Lamentations 3:7 he calls it "heavy chains". Isaiah characterizes sin as "cords of falsehood" (Isaiah 5:18) and again, "transgression lies heavy" (Isaiah 24:20). St. John says: "He who commits sin is of the devil" (1 John 3:8), for sin is the work of the devil. The Book of Wisdom equates sin with the dominion of Hades on earth (Wisdom 1:14). Sirach calls it a "yoke of iron" and "fetters of bronze" (Sirach 28:20). For St. Paul, we were all "slaves of sin" (Romans 6:20).

All those ways of describing sin correspond to that truth of which we are convinced by our own experience every day of our lives. We know that a path which leads directly to slavery constantly opens up before our feet. Each of us knows the slavery of a bad habit, slavery of passion, the slavery of some demeaning relationship. In the Lord's

141

Prayer we ask for freedom from all which in our soul is a beginning, a danger, or already some bond or yoke to force us to go against our will where we do not want to go. After all, St. Paul himself testified to this: "I see...another law at war with the law of my mind.... I do not do the good I want, but the evil I do not want is what I do" (Romans 7:19-23). Even the classical author, Ovid, observed this: *Video meliora proboque, deteriora sequor* ("I see the better way, but follow the worse").

We ask for freedom, which begins with being freed from the minor, petty, everyday fetters which threaten the freedom of God's children. "...If the Son makes you free, you will be free indeed" (John 8:36). "The truth will make you free" (John 8:32).

This freedom begins here and must lead to freedom from death for death, too, is slavery. Desiring this freedom, desiring resurrection, we see in this petition not a symbol but a reality. We seek to grind death under foot through Him who by His death trampled death. This means all death, the one which puts us in the grave as well as the "second" death which is even worse, for it casts us into the abyss of Hell.

We ask for freedom from every burden, every yoke. Experience teaches us what a great burden the reproach of an impure conscience can be. A millstone around the neck would be lighter by far. And in the distant perspective we see the freedom with which a soul is lifted to heaven, freed from the burden not only of sin, but from sinful flesh and all the material nature which so greatly oppresses and holds us in such captivity.

Let us apply to the concept of slavery the law of inverse perspective of which we spoke earlier. Is not the worst kind of slavery one that binds the body and soul in chains to such a degree that the desire for freedom ceases, that the idea of freedom is lost, that the person in chains views himself as free?

To the sinner, the chains of sin seem completely tolerable. He feels comfortable in them. The farther from prison, however, the worse and more evil the prison seems.

In other places in Scriptures sin is described as darkness. "...The light has come into the world, and men loved darkness rather than light" (John 3:19). Christ came "to give light to those who sit in darkness and in the shadow of death" (Luke 1:79).

From the Old Testament it will suffice to refer to the Wisdom of

Solomon where sin is called "a chain of darkness", a "long night" (Wisdom 17:17,2). Elsewhere sin is referred to as "foolishness" (Ecclesiastes 10:1).

The seventh petition of the Lord's Prayer speaks of the desire for light in a progression from those weak rays which enter the darkness of our lives to the light of truth which makes us free (John 8:32). It is a desire for that "light into the world" (John 12:46) which Christ gives us, for that light of the world which is Christ, for that light with which "the righteous will shine like the sun in the kingdom of their Father" (Matthew 13:43), even for that "unapproachable light" (1 Timothy 6:16) in which the Almighty dwells and which is the Almighty (John 1:9) in Whose eyes the heavens themselves are not clean (Job 15:15).

Again, the opposite view. "...Who does evil hates the light, and does not come to the light, lest his deeds should be exposed" (John 3:20). To the degree that he recognizes the light and distances himself from the darkness, he becomes sensitive to the evil of darkness, ignorance, and error.

In the Scriptures sin is further described as sickness, corruption, pestilence, infection; like the bite of a serpent. "Your hurt is incurable," says God through Jeremiah, "and your wound is grievous" (Jeremiah 30:12).

Jesus Christ compares sin to wounds in the parable of the Good Samaritan (Luke 10:30-35) and generally refers to sinners as ill when He says: "Those who are well have no need of a physician" (Luke 5:31).

Sin is further presented in Scripture by terms related to physical ailments: leprosy, blindness, paralysis, and even death.

Therefore, in the Lord's Prayer we ask for health from the beginning of our earthly life, health that comes from the hope which a doctor inspires when he but visits the sick and particularly that God will give true health to the joy of all, for "he will wipe away every tear from their eyes, and death will be no more, neither shall there be mourning nor crying nor pain any more" (Revelation 21:4).

Finally, Holy Writ presents sin as that which is most loathsome, most repugnant, is lowest, meanest, most foul; that which is farthest from all that is noble, beautiful, holy, from what is goodness, and propriety. Sin is the betrayal of God (Jeremiah 3:11-12), open revolt (Jeremiah 2:20), an "abomination that makes desolate" (Daniel 11:31), dung and worms (1 Maccabees 2:62). In a word sin is the opposite of what St. Paul so succinctly states as being the ideal: "...Whatever is true, whatever is honourable, whatever is just, whatever is pure whatever is lovely, whatever is gracious, if there is any excellence, if there is anything worthy of praise, think about these things" (Philippians 4:8).

On the road toward God, the closer one is to the goal, the more the virtues, good deeds, and worthy qualities become as one. Similarly, on the road away from God, as we become more distant from Him, that which we call evil proliferates and multiplies into endless varieties of meanness, degradation, vileness, blood, and mud.

St. Paul, in many passages of his epistles, gives us long examples either of sins or the vile qualities of sinners. I will cite just one of these passages, for perhaps it is equally and particularly applicable to the situation today:

...Understand this, that in the last days there will come times of stress. For men will be lovers of self, lovers of money, proud, arrogant, abusive, disobedient to their parents, ungrateful, unholy, inhuman, implacable, slanderers, profligates, fierce haters of good, treacherous, reckless, swollen with conceit, lovers of pleasure rather than lovers of God, holding the form of religion but denying the power of it (2 Timothy 3:1-5).

Is it surprising that the Christian soul seeks to escape the serpents' nest, the reeking sewer that the world is more and more becoming; that it strains to freedom, to the light, to health and life, to heaven, to God? It aspires to achieve this liberation through prayer, and in the Lord's Prayer, in proportion to its sincerity and good will, it finds a remedy against all the evil in which the entire world lies.

THE LONGING FOR THE INFINITE

In giving thought to the words and petitions of the Lord's Prayer, we found in every one of them a perspective that led our mind and heart into an endless expanse. Each of God's words bear this mark of God's greatness: infinite loftiness, distance, depth, reflects, at least from afar, God's infinite essence (John 5:7).

In praying, due to the nature of prayer, we are predisposed to seek this infinity. Without it we feel helpless and completely weak in the full sense of the word. We feel like, we ought to feel like, the paralytic by the Sheep Gate who for years could not move because he had no one to carry him into the healing pool.

It would be easier for a caterpillar that is here in the grass at Pidliute to enter into relations with the Pope of Rome or Japan's Mikado, than for us insignificant worms to enter into relations with the Creator of the universe, the All-Highest Lord of heaven and earth. And yet, prayer by its nature is such an entering into relations, it is a conversation, the union of our spiritual essence with the spiritual essence of the Deity.

We need infinity to reach as far as God, to pray; and how much more so to find favor with Him, to be heard. We seek this infinity to find at least something of it in whatever form infinity might take. It is because of this, for example, that the Prophet David and following him all of the Holy Fathers of the Old and New Testament and the whole Church on earth, and perhaps in heaven, used the formula that so often occurs in the Psalms: " Praise him, all his angels, praise him, all his hosts!" (Psalms 148:2). There are hundreds of similar passages and so there is no need to cite them except perhaps to recall the song of the three young men in Babylon.

The Prophet's soul sought to establish a bond with the angels to extend if possible the action of his soul on to infinity. In that desire to extend the effects of his soul beyond himself, he calls on all creatures and even on inanimate manifestations of nature to praise God. Thus he addresses the sun, the moon, the stars, light, the heavens, clouds in the sky, fire, hail, night, frost, tempest, all animals, serpents, and birds in the sky. He turns to all the kings of the earth and all nations, to youths and maidens, to the old and to children, calling on them to praise God. In that uniting with all of those works of creation David seeks to extend his essence to the outermost limits on both the material and spiritual plane in all possible directions which would, at least in some small way and from afar, reflect God's infinity.

This same desire and this same need of the soul is to be found in that so-natural Christian practice of seeking in Holy Scriptures ways how to pray. This is done to learn from those, as Scripture records, whose prayers were heard in order to learn what is needed so that our prayer, too, would be heard. In this way our weakness would be bolstered by their strength, our grasp extend farther than the frailty of our human nature allows. Unable ourselves to reach the infinite with our hands, we reach out together with those who were able once to extend theirs to heaven itself. Thus the Christian, standing through his faith before the throne of God in the limitless expanse of the heavens, gladly uses the words of others he finds in the Gospels.

With the two blind men he will call in his soul: "Have mercy on us, Son of David" (Matthew 9:27). At other times he will say with Peter, "...Bid me come to you on the water" (Matthew 14:28), or ask with the disciple: "Lord, teach us to pray" (Luke 11:1). Or again he will repeat with the Canaanite woman: "Yes, Lord, yet even the dogs eat the crumbs that fall from their masters' table", and "Lord, help me" (Matthew 15:21-28). Christian feeling in its own lowliness and humility will readily seek God's help, like the Canaanite woman, knowing that God does not favour the proud, but extends His grace to the meek.

At other times the Christian will hope with the woman who had a flow of blood: "If I touch even his garments, I shall be made well" (Mark 5:28); or say of his soul what Jairus said of his daughter: "My little daughter is at the point of death. Come and lay your hands on her, so that she may be made well and live" (Mark 5:23). He will repeat with the tax collector who stood at the door of the temple, not daring to raise his eyes to heaven: "God, be merciful to me a sinner!" When one of the storms which are so frequent in life strikes he will cry out with the disciples; "Teacher, do you not care if we perish?" (Mark 4:38). But perhaps the Christian will most often turn to that, perhaps best, form of prayer which simply presents what is lacking, as did the Most Holy Virgin in Cana in Galilee: "They have no wine" (John 2:3).

The Christian soul everywhere seeks to extend itself into infinity as the greatness of God and the weakness of man demand. This same thought manifests itself in many of the ritual prayers used by the Church. What other meaning can the words, *"Now and ever and unto ages of ages"*, have? In every act of worship we seek to project that act into endless ages, or repeat it to infinity. Also it is as if we are not satisfied with the infinity that stretches into the future, but seek it in the past, *"Now and ever"*. This desire to extend infinity into the past is expressed strikingly by St. Jude in the closing lines of his epistle: "...To the only God, our Saviour through Jesus Christ our Lord, be glory, majesty, and dominion, and authority, before all time and now and for ever" (Jude 1:25).

This same thought is stated by St. Basil in his prayer, one so rich in content, which we priests repeat six times daily: "...Who is owed worship in all ages, in all of time...". This is the worship that seeks God before the beginning of existence and also through the eternal ages of ages that stretch before. The human soul, unsatisfied by the worship of

God in the one place where the body in which it resides finds itself, would like to do worship in every place in the whole universe, to make space as infinite for worship as time is. This is what St. Basil expresses in the words: "...Owed worship in heaven and on earth".

We, as if dissatisfied by the material vastness of earth and the universe, rise into the spiritual heaven, into the heaven of heavens, to worship Deity everywhere where Deity is to be sought.

A similar thought is found in some of the prayers of the Liturgy of St. John Chrysostom, as for, example, in the first prayer of the faithful we pray: "...At all times, and in every place". Also in the prayer during *"It is meet and right..."* we say: "To worship you in all places of your dominion". In this way we try to expand our thoughts and desires in all directions and into infinity -- and not without success. When it concerns the object of our desires and our pleas, our praying encompasses all of heaven, and truly even into the endless vastness of thought. It rises into those distant infinite worlds that are above or beyond the heavens reaching the very essence of Him WHO IS, embracing Him through an act of knowing, a desire to love.

As concerns the subjective inclination of our soul to rise to the object of our desire, we look and find the means for that in many practices which, though simple, are dear to the Christian heart. We look for and find what we desire not only in that object and that subjective inclination of our soul, but both in the subjective essence of our soul and the objective value of our prayers, in our fellowship with Christ.

In examining the meaning of the Lord's Prayer we have not yet turned our attention to what is most important. Most important is: that in saying the Lord's Prayer we are repeating His prayer after Christ and with Christ. The desires of our hearts are united with His desires, with the desires and intentions of His Heart.

If the Lord's Prayer, in each of its words bears the mark of heaven, if God's revelation can be discerned in each of the thoughts expressed there, if God's work and the salvation brought by Christ are shown there, then each of those words opens miraculous wells of healing waters to every soul desiring them. Repeating His Prayer after Christ and with Christ is something so unutterable, so heavenly, so more lofty than earthly matters, so much higher than anything that is flesh, that the experience cannot be expressed in other terms or called anything other than a second kind of Eucharist.

With every word of the prayer we receive Christ, become His communicants. Through the Lord's Prayer we partake of His intentions, His desires, His Heart, His prayer. Through the words of the Lord's Prayer we drink of His virtues, His pre-eternal wisdom, His boundless sanctity, His light. Through those words we touch His goodness, we touch His Heart, we abide in Him, live in Him, become Him, join our weak intellect to His wisdom, unite our will to His sanctity.

Christ gave us the Lord's Prayer, the prayer that we all say before Communion together, publicly, so that we might prepare properly to receive Communion and in order that in Communion we might unite with Him and afterwards pray with Him, using His words.

It is truly a Eucharistic prayer. Reciting it in Christ, through Christ, together with Christ, we in practice achieve the union with Him that is given us by the Holy Eucharist. By the words of the Lord's Prayer we render the Most High worship which rests entirely on the Eucharistic sacrifice and issues from it. All of the petitions of our prayer are pleas that are sustained by the Eucharistic sacrifice, bathed in the Blood of Christ.

Priests bring that sacrifice in a special way, but it is also brought by the faithful who are not priests. St. Peter calls, not the priests alone, but the whole Christian people "a royal priesthood", and "a holy nation" (I Peter 2:9). In another place he says that all of the faithful should "like living stones be...built into a spiritual house" on the rock that is Christ. That spiritual house based on Christ and built of all of us is "a holy priesthood, to offer spiritual sacrifices acceptable to God through Jesus Christ" (I Peter 2:5).

The words of the Lord's Prayer are those spiritual sacrifices acceptable to God which even those who are not priests can bring. The one who is nourished by the Eucharistic bread, who drinks from the cup of the Eucharistic wine, through the Lord's Prayer enters into a union with the Deity that is acceptable to God, and that possesses endless value, endless power, and is directly worthy of God.

It is with that intention and in Christ that we say the Lord's Prayer. To that intention we add the limitless qualities of our prayers and the endless desires of our heart. These rise above all expanses, above all transient time, into those spheres in which in God's eyes a thousand years are like yesterday that has passed on the far-off and lowly world. Then it is that through the Lord's Prayer we bring a Eucharistic Sacrifice to the All-Highest. It is not only that sacrifice that we bring now in the

Holy Liturgy as priests, or as the faithful present at the Holy Liturgy through the priest. It is also that Eucharistic Sacrifice that has been brought for almost twenty centuries now and will be brought for eternal ages to come, uniting humanity with God; bringing the Deity endless praise and worship, thanks and service; asking all heaven for all the earth for eternity.

That is the Eucharist of the ages in which we are united with the Apostles who brought the Eucharistic sacrifice in those first Holy Liturgies, and with the Most Pure Virgin Mary who was the first to receive Holy Communion. In it we are united with those long ranks of martyrs who added streams of their blood to the Eucharistic Cup that we hold in our hands, and with the sacrifice of the Saints and with all their prayers, placed by heaven's angels over long centuries before the Throne of God.

In that Most Holy Eucharist of the ages we are participants in the drama which began at the Last Supper and which will end when Christ's work has been fulfilled and the moment come, should such -- though unknown to us -- be the disposition of God's will, that the action of the Eucharistic Sacrifice cease.

THE ETERNAL EUCHARIST, EUCHARIST OF THE AGES

This is perhaps what we should call the Most Holy Eucharist celebrated and received by humanity from the first moment of its initiation and to the eternal ages. This is not the abstract Eucharist of which theologians speak, but a concrete one, as it exists in the real order of things. This Eucharist comprises all of those Holy Liturgies celebrated by all the priests "after the order of Melchizedek", beginning with that of Jesus Christ Himself at the Last Supper in which He yielded His Life to suffering, the way of the Cross, and crucifixion, and extending into the future to that last Holy Liturgy offered by the last priest.

Thus, the Eucharist encompasses in itself all the offerings of the Apostles, of all the holy martyrs, saints, teachers of the Church, monks, hermits, priests, and others, and others, without end. And not only the offerings of Holy Liturgies, but also all of the Holy Communions from that first Holy Communion received by the Most Holy Virgin after the Last Supper to the final Communion which is yet to be received in times eternal.

Also included is all of the sacrifice made by individuals, all of those drops of water added to the wine which is to become Christ's Blood, beginning with the sacrifice made by the Most Pure Virgin under the Cross for which she drew strength from that first Holy Communion. Included as well are the deaths of all of the martyrs, all the sufferings of all the saints, all of the exertions, labours, and self-sacrificing struggles of the Christian life, all the vows of men's and women's monastic orders, all the prayers that mankind has hitherto said and will say through the ages, all of those sacrifices and offerings, which derived their power and worth only from Christ's Sacrifice.

That is why to the Holy Eucharist of the ages belongs the work of sanctifying humankind from generation to generation. Every step in that work, every breathing of the human chest, every beat of the human heart, which in any way turned to God or sought to rise to God, all were bought at the price of Christ's Blood, all were made pure and sanctified by the Most Holy Eucharist. The Eucharist is the giving of thanks to the Most High for all of those favours already bestowed and for all of those which are yet to be bestowed and will be bestowed in endless ages of ages. This is the giving of thanks for all the glory of all the Saints and for all of their acts of praise and thanksgiving in Heaven.

The Most Holy Eucharist of the ages also encompasses the Old Testament and the sacrifice brought by Melchizedek, and of the prefigurements of Christ's Sacrifice and all of Christ's work from Adam to John the Baptist. It enfolds as well all of the future to the Second Coming and on into endless ages.

When we bring the sacrifice of the Divine Service either as priests, or as the faithful through the power of that royal priesthood by which those receiving Holy Communion participate in the sacrifice, we can celebrate not only that particular service of today and at this particular altar, but we can also offer the Eucharist of the ages, as well. Through it we can render worship, give thanks, please God we can, petition. Against our will and despite our weakness (or, rather, despite the fact of our *nothingness*) when we offer the Most High the Eucharist of the ages it is as if we have become contemporaries of Melchizedek and of those Apostles of the latter days who, with Enoch and Elijah, will yet wage battle against the Antichrist and his minions.

There is something unutterably uplifting and comforting in standing before God's altar with the Holy Apostles, not those who are now in the kingdom of Heaven and do not bring the bloodless sacrifice, but with those who -- I do not say at one time, because it is happening today -- in mortal bodies and with human frailties stood before God's altar. They bring this sacrifice together with us, and with them millions and millions of priests after the order of Melchizedek. This suffices to lead us to forget ourselves, to lose sight of ourselves and in that moment to be what we truly are -- nothing.

We are nothing both in the Holy Eucharist and in prayer, the everything in us is Christ. He is in our hearts, He who in our souls lives the inexpressible life of God's grace, He who brings Himself as a sacrifice for us and sheds His blood for many. In us He prays to the heavenly Father. He is the only power, the sole worth of our prayers. He is our Eucharist. With Him and in Him we are like that atom of water that perishes in the ocean, like that minuscule crystal of winter snow that joins with the sun in the sky -- not with its rays, but with the sun itself -- with the sun's heavenly body.

Our desire for the infinity of space and time does not suffice to make our prayers (which, like ourselves, are "nothing") to become something, to rise to God in heaven, be heard. For that we need the worthiness of Christ. Every word of our prayer must carry Christ. It must carry Christ as the priest carries Him when bearing in his hands the Lamb. Every word of our prayer must be such that at the bottom of its meaning is found the Eucharist -- Christ. Without this it is empty and futile. With it is holy and endless in sanctity. Without it, it is a transitory sound, a trembling, a vibration of air. With it, it has worth greater than all the treasures of the world, and power greater than any created power.

THE LORD'S PRAYER -- THE GREATEST PRAYER

Regardless of the prayer or the words we use in turning to God, if we are praying properly, in Christian fashion, we can say nothing other than that which is contained in the Lord's Prayer. We cannot desire anything better, or more lofty, or more in keeping with our needs than that which we express through the desires and petitions of the Lord's Prayer.

Because this prayer is above all of our comprehension, even then when we understand but little of what we ask for, if we have a good intention and if we continue to direct our attention to God as much as we are able, the Lord's Prayer always pours light and warmth from heaven onto our souls. Yet it is necessary according to our capacity that

151

we also understand what it is we are asking for, think about it, and desire it.

The Lord's Prayer recited consciously and with understanding, said by the intellect, the soul and heart, obviously has greater value. Then, and only then, it is a school of God's Wisdom in a double sense. It is a school in which God's Wisdom teaches us, and it is also a school in which we learn and gain God's Wisdom.

The Lord's Prayer is the last word in prayer, the ultimate prayer, the absolute prayer. Apart from that prayer, so to say, there is no prayer. Everything that is prayer is embodied in that prayer. A prayer will be prayer when it is an extension or replication of the Lord's Prayer.

For this reason I think that in the most solemn moments of life, when a family or a community is to pray, when prayer is needed in some special way, it will be most appropriate, to repeat the Lord's Prayer and not search for another.

Let a priest who has need to suggest final thoughts and the last words of prayer to one who is dying, not search far afield, but repeat the Lord's sacred words clearly, loudly, and unhurriedly to him who is slipping away. If it appears that he has lost consciousness, and if it is possible to do so, let one sing the words of the Lord's Prayer. Perhaps something of that prayer will penetrate to the awareness of him who is unconscious, as well.

In times of great need, of burdensome testing, in time of cataclysm, persecution or misfortune, let those gathered in the name of Christ pray using His words. .

Let those who, following the counsel of the Holy Apostle James, desire God's Wisdom -- the highest and most precious of Heaven's gifts -- seek it in that school of wisdom which is the Lord's Prayer...

THE GIFT OF PENTECOST

First Published
in
L'vivs'ki Arkhieparkhial'ni Vidomosty
(The Lviv Archeparchial Bulletin)
May - October 1937

With the Feast of the Descent of the Holy Spirit, that "post-festal and last feast" as the prayers of the *Triodion* express it, we bring to an end the series of feasts of the Lord that begin in December with Christ's Nativity and are included in this, [first], half of the Church year. After it, only as an exception, does some feast of the Lord occur and then only as connected to commemorations related to Church history, that is, of those who had found favour with God [the Saints]. Following Pentecost we have only the Feasts of the Eucharist and Co-Suffering (added by the Union [of Brest]) and *Spas* [or Transfiguration] which relate to the practice of Christian life, and the Feast of the Exaltation of the Precious Cross which calls to mind a historical event.

Thus the Church year is divided in two nearly equal halves. In the first half we mark the work of salvation by celebrating *the Savior*, in the second we mark that work by referring to those *who were saved*. The Feast of the Descent completes the circle of feasts in the same manner as the Descent of the Holy Spirit itself completes Christ's work. Through what and how *completes*? The answer to this question will be the subject of this writing.

What particularly impresses in the work of God's revelation is, to use the words of the Prophet Isaiah (54:13) quoted by Jesus Christ: "...They shall all be taught by God" (John 6:45). Within this teaching we can distinguish three different Teachers, three different Schools.

The first Teacher is Christ. He empowered the Church to be a Teacher. He promised and sent a Teacher -- the Holy Spirit. How are these three different Schools bound together into one organic whole? The very differentiation of three Teachers, because of human frailty and blindness could have, and indeed did, become the cause of divisions among Christians and differences in understanding the very School of God's revelation.

Why three Schools?

These are problems which even at first glance should impress and awe everyone who has reflected even partially upon Sacred Scriptures. Why is God's teaching divided among three Teachers of whom each one possesses methods that are innate to that Teacher and essentially different from that of the others; and even, so-to-say, with different fundamentals of teaching?

155

It must be asserted, first of all, that Divine Revelation, and therefore religion, and Christianity, and Sacred Scriptures, and the Church, are a School in which we are called to learn forever: from childhood and on into old age. Church ordinance places the responsibility on Christians to attend the Divine Liturgy and hear a spiritual homily on Sundays and feast days. Some who find it a burden to hear a sermon, or even those whose professions involve intellectual work, think that a sermon does not bring them any benefit. Instead, they replace it with reading from Sacred Scriptures or a religious book.

It, however, should not be so. Even those who have a teaching office or mission in the Church are not freed from this obligation. In a word, religion is an obligatory school for all, in which we must learn from childhood to old age. That is why it is important for us to know the system of this School of ours, and primarily to understand its threefold level or character. There must be no doubt about this difference. It is expressed very distinctly in Sacred Scriptures that, as we call it, code of Divine Revelation.

THE SCHOOL OF THE CHURCH

In the first place, the Church teaches, on the basis of Christ's very clear command, and with full authority, to teach. Christ said, "...Make disciples of all nations, baptizing them...teaching them to observe all that I have commanded you" (Matthew 28:19). These last words that Christ, according to Matthew, addressed to the Apostles, affirm completely the teaching office of the Church. Christ's next words affirm also the infallibility of that office: "...And lo, I am with you always, to the close of the age" (Matthew 28:20). "To the close of the age", these words refer not only to the Apostles alone, but to the Church. They promise infallibility because the presence of Divine Wisdom when the teaching office is being fulfilled is a sure defense against every error for the entire apostolic or teaching body of the Church.

This passage alone could suffice but there are many others in Scriptures that confirm what is self-evident. "...As the Father has sent me, even so I send you" (John 20:21). "Behold, I send you out as sheep in the midst of wolves" (Matthew 10:16). "...Go rather to the lost sheep...preach as you go, saying..." (Matthew 10:6-7). "He who receives you receives me, and he who receives me receives him who sent me" (10:40).

Judging from the way the Apostles applied Christ's words, we cannot doubt that from the very beginning they were possessed of the notion that they were teachers of the people and had authority from Jesus Christ to teach, an authority so exclusive to them, as if all of Christ's teachings were their monopoly.

The greatest of them, the great Apostle Paul, calls the Gospel outright as being *his own* ("...to strengthen you according to my gospel" -- Romans 16:25). The Gospel which he preaches to the people he had received directly from Jesus Christ. "...The gospel which was preached by me is not man's gospel. For I did not receive it from man, nor was I taught it, but it came through a revelation of Jesus Christ" (Galatians 1:11-12). That is why he pronounces an anathema against everyone who teaches otherwise. "But even if we, or an angel from heaven, should preach to you a gospel contrary to that which we preached to you, let him be accursed. As we have said before, so now I say again. If anyone is preaching to you a gospel contrary to that which you received, let him be accursed" (Galatians 1:8-9).

This certainty does not preclude St. Paul's submitting his gospel for review by Apostles senior to him, that is, to the Church. "...I laid before them (but privately before those who were of repute) the gospel which I preach among the Gentiles" (Galatians 2:2).

Although he was willing to anathemize even an angel, he submits his teaching to the Church, and this he does "through a revelation", that is, having been commanded to do so from on high. Thus he exercises his authority to teach the people with greater confidence. He demands "the obedience of faith" (Romans 1:5) and submission of self to the truth (Galatians 5:7). He does not spare but rather reprimands vigorously: "O foolish Galatians! Who has bewitched you?... Are you so foolish?" (Galatians 3:1-3). All in all, always where necessary, he knows how to impose his authority. But he is also quiet and gentle in his dealings with the newly-converted, "like a nurse taking care of children" (1 Thessalonians 2:7). He calls himself the least of the Apostles and more often beseeches "by the meekness and gentleness of Christ" (2 Corinthians 10:1). He is "humble when face to face with you" (10:2); "his bodily presence is weak, and his speech is of no account" (10:10). When necessary, however, he knows how to use his authority not only through "weighty and strong" words, but to be "severe in my use of the authority which the Lord has given me" (2 Corinthians 13:10). It happens that the faithful "may find me not what you wish" (2 Corinthians 12:20). It happens that in his ardor he asks with bitter irony the assembly which he himself had founded: "What do you wish? Shall

I come to you with a rod?..." (1 Corinthians 4:21).

The office of teacher that he has from Christ is such that he can convey it also to others. In order to see how notions concerning the pastoral and, particularly, the teaching office of the Church had already become set, two passages from the Apostle should be cited consecutively: one from his epistle to Timothy, the other to Titus. In these he sets laws, organizes, gives counsel and directives in individual cases, and informs about severe penalties stemming from his judgment. "Hymenaeus and Alexander, whom I have delivered to Satan that they may learn not to blaspheme" (1 Timothy 1:20). He repeats the teachings given long ago, admonishes, advises, and most of all teaches and recommends ways and methods of teaching.

We need not pursue Paul's thoughts further. We will not present the teachings and practices of the other Apostles or cite either what the Fathers of the Church or the Ecumenical Councils, those main organs of the Church's teaching, taught. We have only confirmed the teaching office which Christ has given the Church and which the Church exercises.

THE SCHOOL OF CHRIST

Obviously, the Church is only to impart, preach, preserve, and explain the Gospel. The Gospel here is not meant in the literal sense; that is, the books recorded by the four God-inspired evangelists. It is rather meant in the sense in which St. Paul understands it; in the sense in which Luke calls Philip, one of the first deacons, an evangelist; in the sense "of the whole of Christ's teaching", written and unwritten.

It follows from the fact that the Apostles and the Church preach Christ's Gospel, that the whole of the Church's teaching is the teaching of Jesus Christ, and thus it is self-evident that the chief, the only Teacher is Jesus Christ. Yet, we must take a closer look at the teaching of Sacred Scriptures on this matter in order to define in greatest detail what Christ's teaching in the context of the whole of His work is. Obviously, Christ is Teacher because He is Savior. He teaches in order to save.

As Savior, Christ unites in Himself so many attributes and is referred to by so many names in Sacred Scripture that, because of the sheer number of these, both the teaching office and the name of Teacher might appear almost secondary.

Christ is the Lamb of God who takes on Himself the sins of the world, as well as the High Priest who brings the sacrifice. He is a High Priest after the order of Melchizedek. He is the second Adam, the first-born of all creation, the Alpha and Omega, the beginning and the end. He is the King, and the Judge to whom "all authority in heaven and on earth has been given", the Immanuel, the Good Shepherd, the door of the sheep, and the Bread of Life.... Together with this He is also Teacher and as such He possesses the attribute of being the only one as He is in all His other tasks and work. Just as "no one comes to the Father, but by me" (John 14:6); just as there is "one God, and there is one mediator between God and man" (1 Timothy 2:5); and, just as "there is no other name under heaven given among men by which we must be saved" (Acts 4:12), in the same way He is the only Teacher.

In order to clearly illustrate in what relation the teaching office stands to all other offices of Christ, let us hear what Christ says about Himself, how He sets out His mission. Before Pilate, Christ thus describes His kingly office: "You say that I am a king. For this I was born, and for this I have come into the world, to bear witness to the truth. Every one who is of the truth hears my voice" (John 18:37). If with Pilate we ask, "What is truth?", and if we await Christ's reply with greater patience than did Pilate, or if we ourselves search for it, we shall find it in His hierarchical prayer: "Sanctify them in truth; thy word is truth. As thou didst send me into the world, so I have sent them into the world" (John 17:17). But before this He had said: "I have given them thy word" (17:14).

From this it clearly follows that Christ defined His mission by His teaching office. In another place Christ calls Himself, or says about Himself: "I am the way, and the truth, and the life" (John 14:6). If we ask: what life? -- we will get in reply: "And this is eternal life, that they know thee the only true God, and Jesus Christ whom thou has sent" (John 17:3).

Others, for example Nicodemus, called Christ a teacher: "Rabbi, we know that you are a teacher come from God" (John 3:2). And Christ Himself, after the washing of the feet, says to His apostles: "You call me Teacher and Lord; and you are right, for so I am" (John 13:13). He takes the appellation of Teacher to Himself to the extent of not permitting the disciples to apply it to anyone else. "But you are not to be called rabbi, for you have one teacher.... Neither be called masters, for you have one master, the Christ" (Matthew 23:8-10).

Christ refers to Himself by other names, too, but all of them

159

perhaps ultimately relate to His teaching office. For example, He says: "I am the light of the world; he who follows me will not walk in darkness, but will have the light of life" (John 8:12). Again, He says: "I came as light into the world, that whoever believes in me may not remain in darkness" (John 12:46). The nature of this light relates, obviously, to learning, perhaps learning as applied to life but, nonetheless, learning. This is also how what He says about Himself is to be understood: "The light is with you for a little longer. Walk while you have the light, lest the darkness overtake you; he who walks in the darkness does not know where he goes. While you have the light, believe in the light; that you may become sons of light" (John 12:35-36). Not differently does the Apostle John refer to Christ in that wonderful foreword to his Gospel where he describes the pre-eternal birth of the Son of God. "The true light that enlightens every man was coming into the world" (John 1:9). The Prophet Isaiah presented Christ in a similar manner: "... Those who dwelt in a land of deep darkness, on them has light shined" (Isaiah 9:2)... Nor did the Simeon, that prophet who stood on the threshold of both the Old and New Testaments, and who had held Christ in his arms, call Him: "a light for revelation to the Gentiles" (Luke 2:32).

Christ calls Himself the Bread of Life: "I am the bread of life" (John 6:48), and a little further on: "I am the living bread which came down from heaven" (6:51). That appellation, too, relates to the teaching office primarily because bread, being nourishment for the soul, is a symbol for learning. That is why it is said that "man does not live by bread alone, but by every word that proceeds from the mouth of God" (Deuteronomy 8:3 and Matthew 4:4). And also the Eucharist, to which Christ alludes in calling Himself the Bread of Life, is the main way in which Christ imparts His teaching. It becomes the nourishment of souls when Christ, present in the guise of bread, speaks to souls in the soft voice of His grace, and teaches them. In another sense, too, the Eucharist is learning or a School because it is an example and a lesson of humility, love, and sacrifice of unmeasured profundity.

Christ also calls Himself the Resurrection and the Life: "I am the resurrection and the life; he who believes in me, though he die, yet shall he live" (John 11:25). This name, as well, pertains to the teaching office since resurrection is seeing God. Knowing God is the sense of life in this and the next world, that is the knowledge that Christ's teaching gives.

Christ also calls Himself the Good Shepherd. But the office of a good shepherd includes the following, to use Christ's words: "The sheep hear his voice, and he calls his own sheep by name and leads them out. When he has brought out all his own, he goes before them, and the sheep follow him, for they know his name" (John 20:3-4). Both learning and example belong to the pastoral office which is also a living lesson in life.

Based on this it follows that Christ is that sole Teacher of humankind in concert with whom, only through the marvellous miracle of His Wisdom, can another Teacher, the Holy Church, also be an only Teacher.

We will see shortly how these two Schools are united by the wise hand of God into one organic whole and why Christ gave all His teaching to the Church, the true and sole Teacher of humankind. For the time being it is only necessary for us to affirm that divine revelation and Sacred Scripture know a third School, a third Teacher, who again is alone of His kind. That Teacher is the Holy Spirit.

THE SCHOOL OF THE HOLY SPIRIT

Already the Old Testament prophets spoke about the Holy Spirit as Teacher. The Prophet Joel, in a passage read as a *paroemia* on the Feast of the Descent of the Holy Spirit, wrote: "...I will pour out my spirit on all flesh; your sons and your daughters shall prophesy, your old men shall dream dreams, and your young men shall see visions. Even upon the menservants and maidservants in those days, I will pour out my spirit"(Joel 2:28-29). And in the Book of Ezekiel we read: "A new heart I will give you, and a new spirit I will put within you; and I will take out of your flesh the heart of stone and give you a heart of flesh. And I will put my spirit within you, and cause you to walk in my statutes and be careful to observe my ordinances. You shall dwell in the land which I gave to your fathers; and you shall be my people, and I will be your God" (36:26-28).

Promising to send His Spirit from heaven from the Father, Christ defines Him clearly as Teacher: "And I will pray the Father, and he will give you another Counsellor, to be with you for ever, even the Spirit of truth, whom the world cannot receive, because it neither sees him nor knows him; you know him, for he dwells with you, and will be in you" (John 14:16-17). Again: "...The Counsellor, the Holy Spirit, whom the Father will send in my name, he will teach you all things, and bring to your remembrance all that I have said to you" (14:26). In yet another place we find: "...It is to your advantage that I go away, for if I do not go away, the Counsellor will not come to you; but if I go, I will send him to you. And when he comes, he will convince the world concerning sin

161

and righteousness and judgment" (John 16:7-8). And once more: "I have yet many things to say to you, but you cannot bear them now. When the Spirit of truth comes, he will guide you into all the truth; for he will not speak on his own authority, but whatever he hears he will speak, and he will declare to you the things that are to come" (16:12-13).

When we review Church literature about the time just after the Descent of the Holy Spirit, we will observe that the Holy Spirit fulfils such a tremendous role of Teacher and Leader in the Christian community and in the Church that there truly is no better way of describing the teaching office of the Holy Spirit than as rendered in our prayer "*O Heavenly King....*".

Indeed, in the history of the Church and in revelation given through the Apostles, and in their work, the Holy Spirit "is everywhere and fills all things". He is the treasury of all spiritual goods; He is the giver of Life. It would appear that a Gentile or even Jew joining the Christian Church and hearing the apostolic teaching, was apt to ask immediately: "Where is this Leader and Teacher of whom you always speak? Show me the Holy Spirit!"

Let us take, for example, the first history of the Church, the Acts of the Apostles. They begin with an account of their baptism "with the Holy Spirit" (Acts 1:5). St. Luke, the first historian of the Church, whom we must thank for the invaluable accounts and the preservation of such an exceptional archive of primary documents from those times, gives an account of how the Holy Spirit descended upon the Apostles, how He filled the whole house in which they sat, how the tongues as of fire appeared and settled upon every one of them: "And they were all filled with the Holy Spirit and began to speak in other tongues, as the Spirit gave them utterance" (Acts 2:4).

The Apostles, above all St. Peter, explain the descent of the Holy Spirit to the people by means of Old Testament prophecies; they welcome them to baptism and distribute the gift of the Holy Spirit. "You shall receive the gift of the Holy Spirit" (Acts 2:38). We read the sermons of St. Peter who was "filled with the Holy Spirit" (Acts 4:8). From that moment, he who lies to the Church authorities lies "to the Holy Spirit...not...to men but to God" (Acts 5:3-4) and thus "tempts the Spirit of the Lord" (5:9).

Appearing before the Sanhedrin, Peter refers to his own testimony and the testimony of the Holy Spirit: "And we are witnesses to these

162

things, and so is the Holy Spirit whom God has given to those who obey him" (Acts 5:32). In the Christian community, people are "full of the Spirit and of wisdom...full of faith and of the Holy Spirit...full of grace and power" (Acts 6: 3,5,8). Some, like Stephen, being "full of the Holy Spirit, gazed into heaven and saw the glory of God, and Jesus standing at the right hand of God" (Acts 7:55).

The Apostles dispersed from Jerusalem to impart the Holy Spirit to the newly-converted through the laying-on of hands (Acts 8:15-17). In one instance the Spirit of the Lord seizes one of Christ's servants and moves him from one place to another (Acts 8:39). An inner voice, the Holy Spirit, speaks to the Apostles and bids them do what is necessary at a given moment (Acts 10:19). The gift of the Holy Spirit is given by the laying-on of apostolic hands, but it often happens that, even without that laying-on, the Holy Spirit descends from heaven on those who hear the sermon, and His grace "had been poured out even on the Gentiles" (Acts 10:45).

Righteous and godly people are described in a straightforward way: they are full of the Holy Spirit (Acts 11:24). The Holy Spirit guides a gathering of disciples and speaks directly to them: "The Holy Spirit said: 'Set apart for me Barnabas and Saul'" (Acts 13:2). The Holy Spirit sends the Apostles where they are needed, where they are to work, where they should preach (Acts 13:4). They, "filled with the Holy Spirit" (13:9), preach everywhere about Jesus Christ. During their first Council when the Apostles meet to consult, the Holy Spirit is so clearly Leader and Teacher that the decisions of that Council are couched in an interesting formula: "For it has seemed good to the Holy Spirit and to us" (Acts 15:28). The Holy Apostle Paul states in his missionary sermons that none other but the Holy Spirit chooses the disciples who are to be "overseers to care for the church of God which he has obtained with the blood of his own Son" (Acts 20:28).

This continual leadership, this teaching office of the Holy Spirit appears even more clearly in the Epistles. St. John the Apostle states simply to the faithful: "...You have been anointed by the Holy One, and you all know" (1 John 2:20). They have no need to be taught by anyone, for "...the anointing which you received from him abides in you, and you have no need that any one should teach you; as his anointing teaches you about everything, and is true, and is no lie, just as it has taught you, abide in him" (1 John 2:27).

According to the teaching of all the epistles, the Holy Spirit dwells in Christians: "He yearns jealously over the spirit which he has made to dwell in us" (James 4:5). St. Peter describes those among the faithful who are chosen as "sanctified by the Spirit" (1 Peter 1:2). The Gospel is preached "through the Holy Spirit sent from heaven" (1:12). It enables prophets to prophesy (1:11 and 2 Peter 1:21).

St. John talks of the "anointing by the Holy One...which teaches you about everything" (1 John 2:20,27). For him it is through the Holy Spirit, though how the Spirit expresses and manifests Himself, that we know that those who keep Christ's commandments "abide in him, and he in them" (1 John 3:24; 4:13). About Jesus Christ "the Spirit is the witness" (1 John 5:9).

Speaking about those who are worldly and follow "their own ungodly passions" (Jude 1:18), St. Jude Thaddaeus says simply that they are "devoid of the Spirit" (1:19). On the other hand the faithful are enjoined to "pray in the Holy Spirit" (1:20).

In his writings the Apostle Paul continually returns to speak of the Holy Spirit. From him we also learn about the wonderful manifestations of the Spirit in the original Corinthian community, to which we shall return later. According to the teaching of St. Paul, "God's love has been poured into our hearts through the Holy Spirit which has been given to us" (Romans 5:5). "...The Spirit of him who raised Jesus from the dead dwells in you" (8:11). "...The Spirit of God dwells in you" (8:9). "...All who are led by the Spirit of God are sons of God" (8:14). The Spirit of God in us is the spirit of sonship through whom we cry: "Abba! Father!" "It is the Spirit himself bearing witness with our spirit that we are children of God" (8:15-16).

"...The Spirit helps us in our weakness; for we do not know how to pray as we ought, but the Spirit himself intercedes for us with sighs too deep for words" (Romans 8:26). It is He who desires in our hearts (and gives us desires), "because the Spirit intercedes for the saints according to the will of God" (8:27). In general, the Kingdom of God is "righteousness and peace and joy in the Holy Spirit" (Romans 14:17).

It is the Apostle's wish that the faithful may be made better so that "by the power of the Holy Spirit you may abound in hope" (Romans 15:13). He himself has become a "minister of Jesus Christ to the Gentiles in the priestly service of the gospel of God so that the offering of the Gentiles may be acceptable, sanctified by the Holy Spirit" (15:16), filled "by the power of signs and wonders, by the power of the Holy Spirit" (15:19).

"For the Spirit searches everywhere, even the depths of God....
No one comprehends the thoughts of God except the Spirit of God....
Now we have received...the Spirit which is from God, that we might
understand the gifts bestowed on us by God" (1 Corinthians 2:11-12).
The Apostles teach "in words not taught by human wisdom but taught
by the Spirit, interpreting spiritual truths to those who possess the Spirit"
(2:13).

The Apostle repeats with emphasis that Christians are "God's
temple and that God's Spirit dwells in you" (1 Corinthians 3:16),
returning to this assertion several times. In his teaching it is a remedy
against unchastity: "Do you not know that your body is a temple of the
Holy Spirit within you, which you have from God ? You are not your
own; you were bought with a price. So glorify God [the Holy Spirit] in
your body" (1 Corinthians 6:19-20).

The Apostle, advising abstinence to the faithful, refers to the Holy
Spirit: "And I think that I have the Spirit of God". The Holy Spirit is so
much present in every deed of a Christian that "no one can say: 'Jesus is
the Lord' except by the Holy Spirit" (1 Corinthians 12:3). "...No one
speaking by the Spirit of God ever says 'Jesus be cursed!'" (12:3).
Christians "by one Spirit...were all baptized into one body...and all were
made to drink of one Spirit" (12:13).

WHY THE "SCHOOL OF THE CHURCH"?

The fact that the truths of divine revelation are imparted by three
different Teachers (and each one of them so independent that only by
invisible and hidden bonds are they united into one organic whole) has
become the reason why people, not perceiving that hidden connection,
have, in accepting divine revelation, emphasized one element at the cost
of another. That is the reason why large communities have become
divided, have fallen away from Christ's Church, or broken away from it.
They thought that without the Church they possessed truer teachings
directly from Christ or from the Holy Spirit.

Such were primarily the groups that formed at the time of the
Reformation that broke away from the Church. All of them rejected the
teaching office of the Church and accepted only the teaching authority
of Sacred Scriptures, that is, the teachership of Christ Himself, and of
the Holy Spirit. In rejecting the teaching of the Church, they threw away
at the same time that that part of Christ's teachings which was unwritten

165

and preserved only in Church tradition. From this so-called reform movement other movements came into being which exaggerated the teaching office of the Holy Spirit at the cost of Christ's revelation. They replaced it almost entirely by what they called the inspiration of the Holy Spirit but what was really only their own dreams or visions. This is the road followed by all the sects who wanted to see in the Holy Spirit the only Teacher and Leader in the Christian life.

Divine Providence permitted those erroneous conceptions in people. It must have had good reason to convey the teachings of revelation in that particular, and no other, way even though this ostensibly gave people an opportunity to accept and understand God's truths one-sidedly and thus erroneously.

No doubt human nature needed divine teaching to be presented in this way because without it people would have been incapable of receiving it. They would have been incapable of receiving it above all because divine teaching was intended for humankind, not for individuals; or it was designated for people such as they indeed are before God, that is, not as isolated beings, but as a people, as one body. Divine teaching was given to people to restore and rebuild the unity of humankind that had been corrupted by the fall. Therefore, the goal of the teaching of revelation already had within it the characteristic attribute of the revelation itself, that of having been given to humankind and not to separate individuals.

The fact that divine revelation is given to humankind as a whole, and not to individuals, is a truth revealed in Holy Scripture. It is so clear that it should be wondered at how the Protestants can entrust divine teaching to the personal interpretation of individual people. With this kind of personal interpretation, the very essence of revelation -- that it is given to humankind to renew its unity -- is lost.

Of the very many that could be chosen, only three passages from Holy Scripture clearly illustrating this essence, will be cited; most particularly Christ's arch-hierarchic prayer. Christ prays not only for the Apostles but "also for those who believe in me through their word, that they may all be one; even as thou, Father, art in me, and I in thee, that they also may be in us" (John 17:20-21). Here it is not a matter of spiritual unity alone, which is invisible, nor of that unity which at a future time will unite in heaven those who have believed in Christ. The unity for which Christ asks has as its goal that "the world may believe that thou hast sent me" (17:21). It is external unity which is to be proof of the Gospel's truth as evidenced by the love that the disciples have or

166

should have for one another. "By this all men will know that you are my disciples, if you have love for one another" (John 13:35).

This unity of all the disciples is external to such an extent that Christ calls it "glory", His glory and that of the disciples. "The glory which thou hast given me I have given to them, that they may be one even as we are one, I in them and thou in me, that they may become perfectly one, so that the world may know that thou hast sent me and hast loved them even as thou hast loved me" (John 17:22-23).

This societal goal of divine revelation is set out by St. John in his first epistle. Its object, like that of all the Gospel teachings, is "that you may have fellowship with us; and our fellowship is with the Father and with his Son Jesus Christ" (1 John 1:3-4). This is so because the whole of Christian life is such an interconnectedness and fellowship of all. "...If we walk in the light, as he is in the light, we have fellowship with one another, and the blood of Jesus his Son cleanses us from all sin" (1:7). This teaching is the subject of almost the whole of this epistle. God's Word "abides" (2:14) in "whoever keeps His word, in him truly love for God is perfected" (2:5). God's word cannot abide in those in whom there is no love.

The fellowship of the first Christian communities can be presented as proof of the social, or societal, aim of revelation. In Acts we read that when "with great power the apostles gave their testimony to the resurrection of the Lord Jesus, and great grace was upon them all" (Acts 4:33). The first consequence of that apostolic preaching was that "...the company of those who believed were of one heart and soul, and no one said that any of the things which he possessed was his own, but they had everything in common" (4:32) and "...there was not a needy person among them" (4:34).

If the aim of the preaching and, generally, of revealed teaching is unity among the faithful, then the teaching must be so presented that people be enabled not to divide on how it is presented and received but, on the contrary, that they be united in and through that preaching.

When revelation had been given to humankind, it had to have been given in a manner that people could become teachers of others, that they could help others in the understanding and acceptance of that teaching. From this came the need for a purely human school of God's revelation. From this, too, came the need for the School of the Church. That School could by its nature both arouse the trust of the people and succeed in persuading them, setting the pre-eternal and infinite truths of the Most High before them in a way in which the people could understand and accept.

Those, that is the Teaching Church, called to be teachers of their brethren must be the School sanctioned and created by God and which conveys that teaching in His Name. It must therefore be given such attributes by God as would assure it the completeness and inviolability of the teaching. God, giving humankind His teaching through the mediation of a human institution, had to assure that institution's infallibility. Demanding from humankind obedience to that institution, He had to create a condition necessary to ensure that obedience would not result in people wandering directionless into error and falsehood. The human institution which was to become the School of divine revelation was to be the intermediary between people and God, to be a Divine-human institution. In fact, such is God's Church, and not only as a School, that is, a Teaching Church, but as a gathering of all the faithful, as humanity led by God to sanctification and of which the Kingdom of God is to be built.

The task of this human -- and all the same, divine -- School in relation to God's teaching had to be external. It had to rest upon the external presentation and conveying to the people of the truths contained in divine revelation. The Church as a School truly fulfils this office. The Church draws divine teaching both from the treasury of revelation as recorded in Sacred Scripture and also from that not recorded there, but living in Church tradition, and presents it to people as matters of faith. The task of the Church's teaching office is to present God's truth in human language and to convey those succinct dogmatic formulas from which it would not be permitted, on pain of anathema, for the faithful to depart. Whoever wishes to belong to the Divine-human body of the Church and wishes to be a disciple in that School, must accept the Church's pronouncements as the authentic expression of divine revelation.

We have seen that Jesus Christ obligates people to this. We have seen that Christ gave full self-government and independence to His Church. Christ gave His Church laws but left it to the free will of the people whether to keep them or not. He forces no one to obey those laws or to accept His teachings. Only that person is a member of the Church who freely desires to be, who submits to her direction, and receives divine revelation from her hands.

Christ replaces coercion, without which no human institution can function, by arranging His Church in such a way that it leads people, often against their will, along the road set out by divine intention. The Church is so structured that with powerful force it leads people into the obedience of faith, helping them overcome the anarchic impulses of a corrupted human nature and rewarding every victory in this struggle with goodness and strength. A person, once dedicated to the work of building God's kingdom in which the Church is engaged, labours even more and with a better will.

The teaching aspect of the Church is based on conveying to the people statements or formulas of doctrine ranging from definitions related to dogma set by Ecumenical Councils to little catechisms for children. To present the teaching of revelation to the people, where possible to explain it, to confirm that *this* teaching is revealed teaching, but *that* teaching is perverse -- that is the work carried on by the School of the Church. That is the work of the Church Fathers, of the Scholastics, of schools of theology. That is the work of preachers and of the Teachers of the Church.

Everyone who participates in this work may accept or reject the teaching of the Church, everyone may preach or not preach. In not accepting what the Church teaches or preaching what is contrary to what the Church teaches, that person excludes himself from the community of the Church and exposes himself to the doctrinal censure of the Church's teaching office. Obviously, this being the case, there could be and have been times in which whole nations fell away from the Church and doctrines contrary to revealed teaching spread among the faithful and among Church teachers to an extent that it might have seemed that revealed teaching would be replaced by human teaching.

THE GIFT OF INFALLIBILITY

In its entirety the whole teaching body of the Church possesses the covenant, and therefore the gift, of infallibility. This gift of infallibility, promised particularly to Peter, abides in his successors: Christ's Vicars, the Roman Arch-Hierarchs. When they, in the name of the Church, as teachers, teach the Christian world about the truths revealed by God, they possess the help from above that does not allow them to fall into any doctrinal error. This external God-given privilege is necessary for the teaching body of the Church in all the cases where human frailty or near-sightedness or human passion, might substitute some kind of human teaching for truth revealed by God. Then it is necessary for the infallible entirety of the Church to express its teaching

169

and juxtapose divine teaching to the human. Since it is possible for the teaching Church in its entirety to gather into Ecumenical Councils only infrequently and with great effort, it is necessary that this privilege of infallibility, promised and given to the Universal Church as teacher of humankind, be placed in her highest organ, the Ecumenical Arch-Hierarch.

Through its independent and sovereign role as teacher, the Church represents the teaching office of Christ before humankind, but does not replace it. Christ, although He gave His teachings whole to His Church and granted her the mandate to proclaim them and to expound them with authority and infallibly, does not cease to be Teacher of humankind in general or of each individual soul in particular. He remains that Teacher primarily through the words which He spoke and which clearly remain beyond the authority of the Church. The Church can only explain those words, she can neither alter nor expunge them.

Everyone who reads the Gospel receives Christ's teaching directly from His lips and stands directly in the company of His disciples. Apart from this, Christ remains with the Church as He Himself promised (Matthew 28:20). Through His grace and sacrifice, and through the Most Holy Eucharist, He is joined to every individual soul directly. He talks with and teaches every soul.

But because it is so easy for humans to alter Christ's teachings of grace or the mystical life that are so deeply concealed in the heart, or to err about them, Christ does in relation to them what He did during His life on earth. Then He bade those who had been cleansed of leprosy -- and we all have been cleansed of spiritual leprosy -- to show themselves to the priests, that is sent them to the Synagogue which then served as the Church: "Go, show yourself to the priest" (Matthew 8:4).

Christ, as it were, binds His teaching office to that of the Church upon which it is dependent. This is right, overwhelmingly right! His teaching office is exercised in the depths of the human heart during prayer or during Communion. It deals with individuals singly and therefore must be made subject to those general norms that pertain to His teachings as given to all humankind. Thus, His personal inherence in the human heart must be subject to the limits on individualism that are set by divinely-sanctified humankind, that is, the Church.

After all, every individual must particularly have the opportunity at any time to test if he is correctly realizing Christ's teaching office as exercised in relation to him individually, or whether, perhaps, he is adding his own fantasies and illusions to it. That unerring standard to be applied to Christ's teachership, that sure test which identifies the place where Christ's voice ceases and human thought intrudes, always a human weakness, is Christ's Faith as conveyed by the infallible teaching office of the Church.

So long as the soul clings to the virtues of Faith and Church, Christ teaches and the soul receives its teaching from Him alone. Even if one were to add words from his imagination to Christ's discourse, still in faith he has the possibility to condemn the words arising from his egoism as being adverse to the words of Christ. Christian humility and faith will be the source of his obligation to subject that imagination of his to the external teaching office of the Church.

It was necessary to have been the builder of genius and the divine artist that Christ is to have conceived and brought about such a union of two teaching offices into one organic whole. Every believer can be a learner in both Schools, can listen to both Teachers and avoid all danger of understanding the teaching badly or falsely. Both Schools are needed by him for, beyond the external formulation of teachings, beyond the knowledge of catechises or theology, the devotee must immerse himself in the bottomless depths which are found in the teachings of the Faith.

Beyond the external affirmation or perception of teaching which God has revealed and the Church presents as what is to be believed, every soul must penetrate the depths of understanding the truths of faith. Only light from heaven can give this understanding. Without the help of divine grace which helps us to receive divine teaching as truth, we would not understand revealed teaching. Revealed teaching would seem impossible to us and we would be vulnerable to Christ's reproach to Nicodemus: "Are you a teacher of Israel, and yet you do not understand this ?" (John 3:10). We understand revealed truth from the moment we accept it, but it is the grace given by Christ that leads us into the depths of that understanding. Through this grace He speaks to human souls, through it He enlightens the mind and opens the hidden, divine mysteries of faith.

This is the everyday experience in the life of one who takes an interest in revealed truth and likes to listen to, and particularly read, the Word of God. Perhaps a ray of light from heaven will fall on some word in that Book of books that Holy Scripture is. Then the soul perceives in that word such bottomless depths of mysteries and truth, and sees such an extraordinary light which somewhere in the depths of the heart opens up the hidden treasures of God's truth and teachings, that it seems that heaven has opened above it! Such is the understanding of God's revelation that the School of Christ gives!

It may happen that Christ's teaching, although directed to an individual soul, is intended for the whole Church. Then, just as in the case of the leper, Christ bids (through words recorded in the Gospel, and the truths of Faith themselves) that the teaching received from Him be submitted to the judgment of the Church. Christ often speaks in this way through lowly and uneducated people. They, as chosen directly by Christ, become, as it were, apostles, perhaps only for a moment. Christ directs that soul as He did Mary Magdalene: "...Go to my brethren and say to them" (John 20:17). It is possible to select a host of instances from Church history where in this way Christ not only conveyed His teaching to individual souls but also spoke to the Church.

Granted that Christ's teaching received in this way can influence the Church's actions, it, regardless, does not become part of those teachings of divine revelation given by Christ during His life on earth and by the Apostles. Such teaching does not become part of the divine revelation that was given overtly, in the presence of many. Therefore, Christians do not have the obligation to receive such teaching as divine revelation. They are free, without sin against the Catholic faith, not to accept such teaching. They are free, for example, to think that such teaching is an invention of such-and-such, even though saintly, person. When these teachings or mandates from Christ imparted, not through the Church's mediation, but through the mediation of individuals, become generally accepted in the Church, and when the consequences of such general acceptance become significant and exhibit a wealth of divine blessing, then it can happen that Christians generally accept this private revelation. But they do so not with that faith that is called Catholic, that faith which relates to the whole of original revelation. They accept this private revelation with the faith with which Christ's contemporaries accepted John the Baptist's mission, or with the faith with which those of the Old Testament believed in the Prophets. Those, for example, who venerate the Heart of Jesus may believe that Jesus Christ Himself commends such veneration. Such belief, however, is not the Catholic belief that stems from the original revelation. It is a different kind of faith, although divine, nonetheless.

THE NEED FOR INSPIRATION OF THE HOLY SPIRIT

Above the teaching office of the Church and of Christ, there soars

172

a third School, a third Teacher: the Holy Spirit Who, in Christ's words, was to guide the disciples "into all the truth".   By what means the actions of the Holy Spirit are bound into one whole with the teaching office of the Church and of Christ, is an incomprehensible mystery to all those who justify disobedience to the Church, who consider only the very inspiration of the Holy Spirit to be decisive.   This temptation might affect not only sectarians/heretics but, at times, even devout Christians.

From Sacred Scripture, however, it is evident that Christ Himself, the Savior, the Son of God, "in whom are hid all the treasures of wisdom and knowledge" (Colossians 2:3), because in Him "the whole fullness of deity dwells bodily" (2:9), said about the Church: "He who hears you hears me" (Luke 10:16). About the Holy Spirit He said: "...The Spirit of truth...will guide you into all the truth" (John 16:13).   It was Christ who bade the Apostles to "make disciples of all nations...teaching them to observe all that I have commanded you" (Matthew 28:20).   Of the Holy Spirit He said: "he will not speak on his own authority, but whatever he hears he will speak...for he will take what is mine and declare it to you" (John 16:13-14).

From this it is plain that both the Church and the Holy Spirit do not teach other than what Jesus Christ taught.   All three Schools are only three different aspects or forms or methods of presenting one and the same divine revelation about which Sacred Scripture states: "In many and various ways God spoke of old to our fathers by the prophets, but in these last days he has spoken to us by a Son, whom he appointed the heir of all things" (Hebrews 1:1-2).

In addition to the teaching office of Christ the Savior, Christ who Himself remains with us "always, to the close of the age" (Matthew 28:20) and does not cease by His grace to speak to every believer separately, why was there also a need for the descent of the Holy Spirit as Teacher to teach the people every truth?

We have seen that this third Christian School could become, and indeed did become, a pretext for discord and for wandering away from the true path. What was the reason for Christ to ordain this state? Jesus Christ explains the reason:

...It is to your advantage that I go away, for if I do not go away, the Counsellor will not come to you; but if I go, I will send him to you....I have yet many things to say to you, but you cannot bear them now. When the Spirit of truth comes, he will guide you into all the truth (John 16: 7, 12-13).

173

The presence of Christ in the flesh was an obstacle for the Apostles in understanding Christ's teaching properly. Christ "emptied himself, taking the form of a servant, being born in the likeness of men" (Philippians 2:7). The form of a servant was the reason that the Apostles thought about Christ in terms that were determined by what they saw with their eyes. Therefore, it was necessary for that outward form, which held the Apostles to a superficial understanding of Christ's teachings, to be taken away. That is why "...It is to your advantage that I go away".

In *On the Holy Trinity*, St. Augustine asks whether Christ could not have sent the Apostles the Holy Spirit while still in the body. Why did He say: "...If I do not go away, the Comforter will not come"? It is because they cannot receive the Spirit so long as they continue to know Christ in the flesh. When Christ is no longer in the body, not only the Holy Spirit but also the Father and the Son will be with them spiritually. In another place (*On Our Lord's Sermon*) he explains that it is only after the Ascension and the descent of the Holy Spirit that the Apostles can fully comprehend that Christ was always God, equal with the Father, even while He was with them in the flesh.

The Holy Spirit was to inspire, to elevate the teachings of Christ given to the Apostles and received by them in their fleshly state, at the same time purifying and sanctifying their souls and minds. It might be said that the Holy Spirit was to grant Christ's teaching, as it were, the final sanction, approval, and confirmation. He had to give witness to Christ: "And the Spirit is the witness, because the Spirit is the truth. There are three witnesses, the Spirit, the water, and the blood; and these three agree. If we receive the testimony of men, the testimony of God is greater; for this is the testimony of God that he has borne witness to his Son" (1 John 5:7-9). Also "...by this we know that he abides in us, by the Spirit which he has given us" (1 John 3:24).

But what is this: the Spirit, water and blood; and these three are one? In possibly a very daring application to our subject, we will put this in other words. These are -- the School of the Holy Spirit, and the School of the Church which administers the Sacrament, and the School of Christ who has shed His Blood; and they are all one and the same, one Truth in three Schools.

This witness to Christ perhaps does not exhaust the meaning of the gift of Pentecost. Both in Old Testament prophecies and in the first preaching by St. Peter, the gift of the Holy Spirit is presented explicitly and quite distinctly as the gift of prophecy: "...In those days I will pour

174

out my Spirit; and they shall prophesy" (Acts 2:18). St. Peter's inspired preaching and the workings of the Holy Spirit on the day of Pentecost and in the entire first era of Church history plainly indicate that through the gift of Pentecost the Spirit of foreknowledge and prophecy was given humankind. Although God's Spirit is poured out "on all flesh", to inspire people supra-naturally cannot cease to be His task.

In relation to Christianity the Holy Spirit must be analogous to what, when applied to human nature, is called "the inspiration of genius". It is generally the case among people that this element cannot be captured either in formulas or enclosed in any norms or boundaries. The inspiration of persons who possess genius evades all attempts to impose forms, principles, and patterns upon it. It cannot be calculated or directed into the stream of shareable human experience, of formulas, and observations. It is to some degree limitless and unknowable.

To what degree exactly is that higher element of inspiration present in the School of the Holy Spirit? How is it bound into one whole with Christ's teaching, with faith in that teaching, and with understanding of that faith according to the dogmatic formulas set by the Church? How can the foreknowing Spirit be joined to dogmatic formulas?

How can unlimited freedom be given to the Spirit whom Christ Himself compares with the unfettered wind which "blows where it wills, and you hear the sound of it, but you do not know whence it comes or whither it goes" (John 3:8)? How can that freedom be left to "every one who is born of the Spirit" (John 3:8) and yet ensure that all upon whom the Spirit is poured -- and it is poured "on all flesh" -- remain faithful to the dogmatic formulas and the interpretations of the Church? This is indeed a wonder of wonders, one possible only through the work of God's hands. That work is the organization, the ordering, of Christ's Church.

The infinite freedom of the Holy Spirit's inspiration is constrained by faith in the teachings of Jesus Christ, and the authority of the Church's teaching office. It is constrained in an incomprehensibly simple manner: the inspirations of people of genius are subject to the judgment of and obedience to the Church. These, the judgment and obedience, are necessary so that the inspiration, given to individuals, might serve the whole; that the individual not come into conflict with the community. That individual must remember that only through being a member of the Christian body does he receive inspiration and then only to strengthen the unity of that body. The judgment and obedience are also needed so that people might learn from the experience of everyday life

175

that what appears to be inspiration but does not lead toward the unity of the whole body in Christ is spurious inspiration. This is because the whole of divine revelation, in all its details, has but one goal: the salvation of humankind, and the renewing of the unity that was once lost.

The inspiration of geniuses must be subject to the authority of the Church for the same reason that should a contrary gospel be preached, even by an angel from heaven, "let him be accursed" (Galatians 1:8). Obviously, that angel is no longer an angel, but a demon who assumes the form of a radiant angel (2 Corinthians 11:14). Likewise, it should be obvious to Christians that inspiration seemingly from heaven that opposes obedience to authority or contradicts the understanding of the Christian faith is not truly from heaven. It is wisdom not from above, but rather "earthly, unspiritual, devilish" (James 3:15).

The constraining of inspiration, or rather the attempt to constrain it, is also necessary for the people. Without it, it is all too easy for them to err. All too readily does self-love suggest the thought that they are above the whole, above society. And yet the foundation of all Christian virtues -- humility -- teaches every Christian that he is nothing compared to humanity, that in himself he is fallible. Easily does he take a demon for an angel of light, and easily does he err about the most fundamental truths of life, taking evil to be good, and falsehood to be the truth. As the Prophet says: "Woe to those...who put darkness for light, and light for darkness" (Isaiah 5:20).

Humility alone is not enough for the Christian. It is by far too difficult a virtue and corrupted human nature is too prone to falsehood and evil. Too often the assertion that "every man is false" (Romans 3:4) is confirmed, every day and everywhere.

The most-wise ordering of the Church and its structure, which makes one of many, averts the possibility that inspiration from heaven be too great a danger to the individual. Despite this, inspiration will be so a great a danger for humankind that under its banner millions will fall away from the truth, millions will be lost. Only those will be saved who yield to the truth (Galatians 5:7) and not trust inspiration without first submitting it to the test of truth. They will not fully trust even themselves, even not trust their own spirit. They will put their own spirit to the test to determine whether it is from God.

How can the true nature of their spirit be determined? "By this you know the Spirit of God: every spirit which confesses that Jesus Christ

176

has come in the flesh is of God" (1 John 4:2). This is the touchstone by which inspiration is to be tested: faith in Jesus Christ. And yet a second touchstone: "Whoever knows God listens to us, and he who is not of God does not listen to us [the Apostles, the Church]. By this we know the spirit of truth and the spirit of error" (1 John 4:6).

But then, what now remains of unlimited freedom, where is the creativity of inspiration? In what does the prophetic Spirit reside? How will the prophecy of Joel and the promise of Peter be fulfilled? How then are we who have, following the Apostles' counsel or command, also "received the gift of the Holy Spirit" (Acts 2:38) to "give portents" (Joel 2:30)? Let this be the subject of our further search. For the moment, in Christian humility, faith, and obedience to the Church, we have the union of three Schools of divine revelation.

It is on such foundations of a structure reflecting God's wisdom that the truth of God's revelation rests in humankind. Humankind, to be "all taught by God" (John 6:45; Isaiah 54:13), must pass through these three levels of God's School in order to receive the whole of divine revelation without harm.

The question is: does the system of the three Schools and three Teachers for one and the same teaching correspond to the natural way by which the human intellect in general comes to the truth? Does Christ's structure, necessary to receive God's Word, correspond to the basic principles of human understanding?

THEOLOGY, AND PRINCIPLES OF HUMAN UNDERSTANDING

All human knowledge and, consequently, all human learning, and indeed all the discipline of human scholarship, are composed of three elements, one rising above the other. All three, however, mutually complement each other. A person first observes; then understands; finally thinks. It is obvious that there is no observing without some kind of subsequent understanding and thought. The whole of understanding is founded upon what has been observed, and provides the material for thought.

If this differentiation be applied to learning, we must assert that the first task of every branch of learning is to observe, let us say: historical facts, phenomena of nature, texts of law. To understand all of the facts, phenomena, or texts that have been observed is another

177

matter, and involves a higher school.

Unquestionably, observing facts or phenomena in a new field of study may involve the life's work of countless scholarly researchers and necessitate immeasurable intellectual effort of all humankind. But all the same, those who understand and explain these facts and phenomena fulfil a function which stands on a higher level in the evolution of the human intellect. Observation and understanding, the two lower functions, are vastly helped by the third element of human knowledge: thought, reasoning. In the scholarly disciplines this might take the form of intuition, genius, that rise to the level of inspiration. Rising above millions of observations already explained, the human intellect through a leap of genial hypotheses paves a road that leads to as-yet-unknown areas of truth about what had been studied. Those hypotheses are the guiding light for a more complete and better understanding, for new research, for new findings.

Is this not the basis for all learning, for all evolution of human knowledge, for the activity of the human intellect? We will also find this same type of evolution in theology, in the study of God's revelation.

If we differentiate between the fields of study that are ancillary to theology from theology itself, it is clear that these ancillary disciplines are scholarly disciplines similar to all other scholarly disciplines. They are nothing other than the disciplines of history, geography, archaeology, linguistics, etc.

On the other hand, if we define theology proper as the study of God's divine revelation, then we will find that the predictive element of prophecy or foreknowledge must have a broader -- and therefore different -- application than in other scholarly disciplines. The subject studied by theology is God's revelation and for this reason the study of this revelation must be prophetic, inspired, marked by foreknowledge, all of which the Holy Apostle Peter ascribes to the Holy Spirit. "...No prophecy ever came by the impulse of man, but men moved by the Holy Spirit spoke from God" (2 Peter 1:21). After all, this is teaching so grounded in divine revelation that it was included in the Symbol of Faith [The Creed], and was determined and proclaimed by the Church (possibly in the first century) to be revealed teaching. In the Symbol we say: "And in the Holy Spirit,...Who spoke through the prophets".

This inspired character of the subject studied by theology demands, one might say, that all those who are engaged in the study of God's teaching reflect, if but at a distance, the light of the prophetic

178

Spirit. This is particularly made necessary by the fact that in all study the intellect must be adequate to the subject studied (*adaequatio mentis cum re*). Without this the study itself will always be alien to the mind, and no common language will be found.

To us it appears that in many passages from Holy Writ we can find at least indications, although very clear and definitive, that this is what true theology must have. For example, Christ says: "He who is of God hears the words of God; the reason why you do not hear them is that you are not of God" (John 8:47). Or: "If any man's will is to do his [God's] will, he shall know whether the teaching is from God or whether I am speaking on my own authority" (John 7:17). To be "*of God*": that is the pre-condition without which we cannot hear the word of God or understand that Christ's teaching is from God. That to be "*of God*" is like prophetic light reflected onto the soul; in every instance it is an attribute of the mind, an attribute given from above.

Assuredly, even without that light or even without faith the natural intellect is able to achieve something in theology. It can gather texts, compare them, count them, and state what so-and-so thought about them. Even without any prophetic spirit much can be said about the words recorded in Sacred Scripture, and about the opinions of people about those words, about those teachings. But I think that all that is still not theology. It is but preparation for theology, or an auxiliary discipline.

If being "*of God*" is a prerequisite for those who study true theology, then this applies more broadly and is more true in relation to that higher theology which is not study *about* God's revelation, but is study *of* God's revelation itself; it is divine learning, God's learning.

PROPHETIC THEOLOGY

It is in this prophetic sense that the Eastern Church calls the holy Apostle John and a few exceptional Fathers or divines -- Theologians; for example, Gregory of Nazianzus and Symeon the New Theologian, a great mystic of the Eastern Church. In this sense theology requires a prophetic spirit. Every theologian must, to some degree, be a prophet, as well; and he becomes one through the study of theology itself. Perhaps it is in this sense that Jesus Christ says: "No longer do I call you servants, for the servant does not know what his master is doing; but I have called you friends, for all that I have heard from my Father I have made known to

179

you" (John 15:15).

Thus, Christ, having already "made known" to the Apostles what He had heard from His Father, has raised them to the level of His "friends", endows them with a character, above all, obviously an intellectual one, that in some degree raises them to His level. The same is expressed by Christ in the following words: "My mother and my brothers are those who hear the word of God and do it" (Luke 8:21). To hear Christ's teaching (meaning obviously to fulfil that teaching gladly and with faith) develops in the human soul a spiritual affinity to Christ. This is reflected primarily in the intellect and makes it, as it were, close, akin, or similar to the prophetic Spirit of the Teacher.

Let us look now at how this element of inspiration has from the outset influenced theology in practice.

Divine revelation is given humankind in Sacred Scriptures and in Church tradition. The human mind must first of all identify, must observe, perceive, the teachings revealed by God that are in Sacred Scripture. As if from some infinite treasury, it must extract from Sacred Scripture those truths that are to become the subject matter of Church teaching.

One can even trace the evolution of human theological study chronologically. For example, one can postulate that the age of the Fathers was occupied most of all with perceiving God's teaching by confirming facts, texts, and events. The Scholastic Age was already focused entirely on understanding the truths of revelation. All the same, in the studies of the Fathers and of the later Scholastics, that is both in the observation and in the understanding of God's revelation, intuition was necessary: that "anointing which you received from him" and which "teaches you about everything" (1 John 2:27). This is why both in the age of the Fathers and in the age of the Scholastics the first witnesses to revelation were the Saints who, more than others, represent this prophetic element. We see that at that time such geniuses as Basil, Gregory of Nazianzus, or Augustine, through their work laid the foundations for what the Church was to teach. Later the Ecumenical Councils were to clothe that revealed teaching in dogmatic definitions which would be conveyed to Christians as articles of faith.

Even more did both the Fathers and the Scholastics need that Spirit of Christ, that mind of Christ, as St. Paul says (1 Corinthians 2:16), to recover the truths of divine revelation from the boundless treasury of tradition.

180

God's divine revelation was given to humankind in the following way:

The Apostles and disciples of Christ, having received the Holy Spirit and being full of that Spirit, as, for example, Stephen was, preached Christ's teaching without recording it. The original divine revelation was given, not only directly by Christ and the Apostles, but also by the disciples, as when St. Luke and St. Mark received the prophetic Spirit in order to write their Gospels. It was perhaps more than likely that Christ's disciples possessed the prophetic and infallible Spirit in the preaching of the Gospel, as the Acts of the Apostles attest.

Of the eighty-two or eighty-four of Christ's disciples, scarcely seven recorded in writing what they preached, although all of their preaching was done in the Holy Spirit. Their unrecorded teaching passed to their successors and became that treasury of divine revelation which is safeguarded in the Church. Throughout the ages the Church has not ceased to draw out new truths from this treasury even though they belong to that original, first, authentic divine revelation. But they become obligatory theses of God's teaching only when through the work of the Church they are explained and defined and given by the Church to her faithful to believe.

In this way the work of those who labour to extract the revealed truths from the treasury of revelation resembles the work of extracting metal out of a mine. The metal is there, but it is in the form of an ore or other mixture or chemical compound. Just as in those mines some infallible indicators are necessary which would show the presence of valuable metal, so did theologians need that instinct which confirms the presence of the gold of God's teaching in the mines of Christian literature and Christian spirit. They needed that Spirit of God which has been poured out on the Christian community.

In this way does humankind labour in the field of divine teaching to determine what is contained in revelation and to give an external, human, form to what is found in the Gospel. This is the subject matter of the Church's teaching. But to achieve this, the teaching of the Holy Spirit is also necessary, for without Him it would be difficult, and perhaps simply impossible, to determine what truths are contained in Sacred Scripture and what in divine tradition is indeed the truth of God's revelation. Only "...by this we know that he [Christ and His teaching] abides in us, by the Spirit which he has given us" (1 John 3:24).

Even to a greater degree do theologians need the prophetic Spirit to understand divine revelation. For, God has revealed to us through the Spirit. For the Spirit searches everything, even the depths of God. For what person knows a man's thoughts except the spirit of the man which is in him? So also no one comprehends the thoughts of God except the Spirit of God. Now we have received not the spirit of the world, but the Spirit which is from God, that we might understand the gifts bestowed on us by God (1 Corinthians 2:10-13).

PROPHETIC CHRISTIANITY

Indeed, faith itself grants us the power to recognize as true that which God has revealed, and the very recognition of what is true cannot exist without some kind of understanding. It would be enough for the understanding that is necessary for faith to be something like that found among children. Without faith, however, people would not be able to understand even that much. Without the help of faith these people would ask with Nicodemus: "How can this be?" (John 3:9). What Christ said to Martha applies to them: "...If you would believe you would see the glory of God" (John 11:40). Without this faith, a person will see nothing, understand nothing.. But even if such a person were to believe, it would still be far from the faith that is as a grain of mustard seed (Matthew 17:20).

To the beginners, those who are just now approaching understanding, to those who until now have only observed and affirmed what they have observed, the words of the Apostle Paul will apply. Of these he said: "I fed you with milk, not solid food; for you were not ready for it; and even yet you are not ready, for you are still of the flesh" (1 Corinthians 3:2). Here the Apostle speaks to those who believe but do not as yet understand, to those whom also Christ addressed: "I have yet many things to say to you, but you cannot bear them now" (John 16:12), those who believed but would not admit their belief for fear of the Pharisees, that they not be excluded from the synagogue, "...for they loved the praise of men more than the praise of God" (John 12:43).

It is enough for that faith, however weak, to be alive, for "...as the body apart from the spirit is dead, so faith apart from works is dead" (James 2:26). Faith, which works through love, even though it may be only little educated, is sufficient for a person to abide in Christ, and Christ to abide in that person. Christ is the vine and people are the branches. "He who abides in me, and I in him, he it is that bears much fruit, for apart from me you can do nothing" (John 15:5). Faith refined

182

through education is not necessary for Christ in His grace to abide in a person. An active faith, a faith which reveals itself through love for others is sufficient. "He who loves his brother abides in the light, and in it there is no cause for stumbling" (1 John 2:10) because he who loves his neighbour keeps the whole law. "No one who abides in him [Christ] sins; no one who sins has either seen him or known him" (1 John 3:6).

Faith, even when not highly educated, gives sufficient understanding of Jesus Christ to keep a person from sin.

And by this we may be sure that we know him, if we keep his commandments. He who says 'I know him' but disobeys his commandments is a liar, and the truth is not in him; but whoever keeps his word, in him truly love for God is perfected. By this we may be sure that we are in him: he who says he abides in him ought to walk in the same way in which he walked (1 John 2:3-6).

To achieve a fuller understanding of the truths of faith one ought first to rid oneself of all the things for which the Apostle Paul reproached the faithful: "for you are still of the flesh" (1 Corinthians 3:2).

The Apostle does not say how far that state of being "of the flesh", which is an obstacle to a knowledge of God's truths, might extend. It appears though that it must be far-reaching when the very presence of Christ in human flesh was an obstacle to the Apostles' fuller understanding of His teachings. Seeing Him in "the form of a servant", that is, seeing the human nature of Christ, they were as if hampered from attaining a higher understanding of Christ's teaching. "You cannot bear them now...it is to your advantage that I go away" (John 16:12; 16:7). The food which beginners cannot bear is the "teaching of the Spirit" (1 Corinthians 2:13). It is given only to those who have become spiritual, it makes them spiritual. As long as people do not understand the "teaching of the Spirit" they remain "babes in Christ" and "of the flesh" even though they may be believers. For the Apostle these two designations have one meaning (1 Corinthians 3:1).

CREATIVE THEOLOGY

Thus it is that the prophetic element is indeed needed for a fuller understanding of the truth of revealed teaching. Thus it is, in the full sense of the word, that the anointing by the Holy Spirit "teaches you about everything" (1 John 2:27). Thus it is that "the Spirit of truth...will guide you into all the truth" (John 16:13).

It seems to me that the need for the School of the Holy Spirit is fully explained by the inner laws of the human mind and its operation. One thing only remains to be explained, but it is a weighty matter and of extreme significance.

We have spoken thus far about theology and its levels or stages of development. We have compared the School of the Church, that is -- theology, to the function of observing and establishing what is true. We have compared the School of Christ's faith and grace to the function of understanding established truth; and we have compared the School of the Holy Spirit to the function of thinking.

This third comparison might require further explanation.

It seems to me that the act of thinking, which soars above the acts of observation and comprehension, is similar to the comparison which Christ Himself had made in relation to the action of the Holy Spirit. It is also like the wind which "blows where it wills, and you hear the sound of it, but you do not know whence it comes or whither it goes; so it is with every one who is born of the Spirit" (John 3:8).

Only thought, which rises above the object observed and comprehended can, as if by prophetic intuition, conquer unknown territories and illuminate incomprehensible phenomena. Therefore, out of all the operations of the human intellect, thought best corresponds to the teaching of the Holy Spirit and, accordingly, best states and explains its needs. Within the range of operations of the human intellect, unfettered thought marked by genius or prophecy is also creative thought. It gives birth equally-well to masterpieces of art, as well as to inventions marked by genius and discoveries of hitherto-unknown laws of nature.

Thought gives birth to ideas which are something more real than reality. Ideas are norms into which reality is poured like some formless material poured into a mould. Ideas are the norms that give form to existence; they are what is most compelling and most real in existence itself.

Let us clarify this abstraction by a concrete example. The thought of a genius begets an idea which over many generations imposes itself so forcefully on people that all their efforts are directed to the executing or fulfilling it. Take, as an example, the idea of Germany's

184

unification, born in the thought of Bismarck. Take the idea of communism born in the thought of Marx.

An idea, child of thought, is something so very real, either angel or demon, that millions of people devote the course of their entire life and thought exclusively to its fulfilment, to pour soulless and formless matter into its mould. This is why demonic bolshevism is something that is real, that is compelling, that has form -- born out of the thought of Marx's genial, although demonic, thought. Here I call a lie something demonic. As is well known, there is nothing more that is of the devil than a lie (compare John 8:44).

Is there something in the gift of Pentecost that also corresponds to the creative power of human thought? When considering what the Holy Spirit, as given to humankind, fulfils, we have noted what Christ said about the Comforter: that He guides people into all truth. We have seen that at least in some sense the prophetic Spirit is necessary to make the formulas of faith and the very understanding of faith complete. We have, however, as yet not affirmed any creative function of that prophetic Spirit.

Is human thought, with the prophetic intuition and natural inspiration that are both accessible to any person without supra-natural help from heaven, to be something more creative than the prophetic inspiration of the Holy Spirit? Or is perhaps this comparison not well-chosen? Is perhaps, too, the thought of the human mind not an image that would provide an analogy with which to explain the action of the Holy Spirit?

Let us assume this to be the case! The analogy may be badly chosen. But then, how is the marvellous paradox possible that the human mind, without supra-natural help from heaven, could be more creative than that same human mind inspired by the Holy Spirit? This is what would happen if we did not find creative power in the Holy Spirit; and we have not yet found it. "To teach" every truth is not yet creative power, it does not yet create anything. So, if the function of the Holy Spirit is to fulfil, complete, and deepen the teaching of the Church and of Christ, where is the creativity in the teaching of the Holy Spirit?

It can be said that even the expounding of revealed teaching is something creative. Whether this expounding lies in formulating and defining that teaching as the Fathers did in the Councils, or whether it consists of a profound elucidation and comprehension of the teaching: everything that is done through the prophetic and supra-natural divine

185

Spirit is creative.

Without a doubt, a work of Christian literature embodying the utterance of wisdom of which St. Paul speaks, or "of knowledge according to the same Spirit" (1 Corinthians 12:8), will be a masterpiece. A Father or Teacher of the Church, and no less a Scholastic, when he writes words that utter the wisdom or knowledge bestowed on him by the Holy Spirit, with the aid of the Holy Spirit becomes a truly creative individual. It can be said without fear of contradiction, that such words of wisdom could in effect become a creative idea for future generations, this is the analogy we sought in the working of the natural human mind.

For example, the notion of a congregation or an order is a kind of creative idea. Let us take, for example, the congregation of Redemptorists, Jesuits, or Salesians. The idea of those congregations or orders initiated by their legislators or born out of their spirit, is a statement full of genius which will require the work of future generations to be realized. All in all, it makes no difference if this idea is one word or an entire string of words, a discourse granted by the Holy Spirit. There is perhaps no need to recall that the whole history of the Church is a stream of such creativity.

I must, however, admit that this creativity seems to me to be still insufficient. The analogy of the natural mind which also begets ideas appears to me to be complete. But one aspect disturbs me.

If the School of the Holy Spirit is to lead into only that kind of creativity, then what are those persons to say who have never had a genial thought and have never uttered a word containing wisdom or knowledge? Were they, too, not learners in that School? Did not they, too, try to be assistants to the Teacher in that School, if only from afar? I say assistants, for hardly would any mortal dare call himself a teacher in the School in which the Comforter is the Teacher.

We have affirmed that because the subject of the teaching of the Church, of Christ, and of the Holy Spirit, is in itself replete with inspiration, and with anointing, and is in itself complete; it can, through the action of the Holy Spirit, search and examine even the depths of God (1 Corinthians 2:11). The prophetic Spirit must be more broad, it must flow in more abundant streams onto humankind than the prophetic spirit which we called the natural intuition of a genius.

If God has given flashes of genius to His creatures through their nature alone so that in every scholarly discipline almost every generation can boast of genial thoughts, and simply of geniuses even though one-sided; then it does not appear likely that what the Prophet Joel foretold would come to pass. In the Book of Joel (2:28) God speaks: "And it shall come to pass afterward, that I will pour out my spirit on all flesh; your sons and your daughters shall prophesy...and your young men shall see visions". It would be a gift no greater than the gift of genius or genial intuitions as distributed by nature.

The Apostle Paul confirmed the fulfilment of Joel's prophecy already on the first day of Pentecost. Can it be that the pouring-out of God's Spirit onto humankind could call forth only creative ideas analogous to those ideas of genius which we mentioned above?

On the other hand it should be admitted that the genial and creative ideas revealed by the history of the Church are always, after all, a facsimile of Christ's creative ideas, an adaptation of the Gospel. Naturally, this circumstance does not take away either creativity or genius from those ideas, but it does all the same in large measure sublimate their creativity and genius to the genius and the words spoken by the God-Logos Himself.

Let this be at least a justification for our seeking the prophetic and creative Holy Spirit not only in the works of Church literature that are wise with the wisdom of God, and not only in the genial creative words of Church life, but seeking it as broadly as God's Spirit is poured out on humankind.

In that search we will probably have to pass from the sphere of the theology of our theological schools and from the sphere of that theology which is God's revelation -- to that theology which is the Christian life.

CHARISMS

In his first Epistle to the Corinthians, the Apostle Paul speaks of spiritual gifts, that is, those gifts of the Holy Spirit that later Christian tradition first called *pneumatika*, and afterwards *charismata*, gifts which the Scholastics defined as "graces given as a gift", in other words, "those only given as a gift but not at the same time sanctifying the soul".

The following distinction is made: 1) graces given freely as a gift for the benefit of the Church; 2) the grace which sanctifies the soul. Paul speaks about these gifts primarily as manifestation of the Holy Spirit for the common good (1 Corinthians 12:7). He distinguishes the following spiritual gifts:

To one is given through the Spirit the utterance of wisdom, and to another the utterance of knowledge according to the same Spirit, to another faith by the same Spirit, to another gifts of healing by the one Spirit, to another the working of miracles, to another prophecy, to another the ability to distinguish between spirits, to another various kinds of tongues, to another the interpretation of tongues (1 Corinthians 12:8-10).

In his Epistle to the Corinthians Paul differentiates between the types of service rendered within the Church as follows: "And God has appointed in the church first apostles, second prophets, third teachers, then workers of miracles, then healers, helpers, administrators, speakers in various kinds of tongues" (12:28). When writing to the Ephesians he lists the different kinds of services provided for by God thus: "And his gifts were that some should be apostles, some prophets, some evangelists, some pastors and teachers" (Ephesians 4:11).

When we search for the reason in these apostolic texts why these charisms were granted, we discover the same reason in both: "to equip the saints for the work of ministry, for building up the body of Christ, until we all attain to the unity of the faith and of the knowledge of the Son of God, to mature manhood, to the measure of the stature of the fullness of Christ" (Ephesians 4:12-13). To the Corinthians Paul says the same, although in a more concentrated form: "To each is given the manifestation of the Spirit for the common good" (1 Corinthians 12:7).

If we examine the spiritual gifts of the Holy Spirit, we will understand how all contribute to the building of the Body of Christ. The greatest part is related to proclaiming the divine teaching. To this part belong the utterance of wisdom, the utterance of knowledge, and that special gift of faith that is in the Holy Spirit, as well as those spiritual gifts that Church teaching numbers among the graces freely given, although it does not name charisms. Here should be included the service rendered by the Apostles, prophets, teachers, Evangelists, and perhaps to a great degree, pastors.

Other charisms which are also service, or under one name embrace both charisms and service, also relate, though indirectly, to the preaching of the Gospel. Such are the gift of working miracles, glossolalia -- the gift of speaking in tongues, the interpretation of those tongues, the gift of discerning spirits, and the grace of healing. Of these the gift of working miracles corresponds to a "higher gift" as the Apostle calls it, but the grace of healing and different tongues is numbered among charisms and services. All these gifts relate to the teaching of the Gospel, as evidence of its truthfulness.

Thus we confirm by referring to the teaching of St. Paul to which we turned our attention above: the gifts of the Holy Spirit, the charisms, are granted as inspired by the Holy Spirit either to proclaim Christ's teaching and to expound it; or, to strengthen among the people conviction as to its truth.

If we distinguish between what these spiritual gifts and services are in the person possessing them, and what they cause in those persons for whom the teaching is intended, it will be easy to perceive that all of their creative power depends on the building of the Body of Christ; that is, on the purpose for which they were granted and on the effects they produce on those who hear and see them.

In so far as they relate specifically to the teaching of Christ or of the Church, their prophetic role is not a creative one. They help to formulate the teaching and to understand it. To the teaching itself they add nothing.

That divine revelation originally imparted by Christ and the Apostles is so complete that in no way is it possible to add anything to their teaching. It is possible only to confirm or observe what is contained in the original revelation (the teaching of the Church rests on this), and to understand and expound the teaching of God's revelation (and this is granted through Christ's grace, particularly through faith).

The prophetic element in inspiration can help both by formulating the Church's revealed teaching, and by expounding the teaching on which faith depends through preaching. Neither through one nor the other does the inspiration of the Holy Spirit add anything that is new to the original divine revelation, to the teaching of the Church and God's grace. In this sense it is not a creative force.

It becomes both creative and necessary in the building of the Body of Christ for which it is intended. Here it does not add theoretical truths to the original revelation, but acts to adapt the truths of revelation to, and implement them in life.

THE THEOLOGY OF THE CHRISTIAN LIFE

To understand properly what the Holy Spirit in His School adds to the School of the Church and to the School of Jesus Christ, we must turn our attention to the circumstance that the whole teaching of divine revelation was intended by Our Lord Jesus Christ to be not theory, but practice.

In conveying His teaching to the disciples -- to the Church -- Jesus Christ states clearly that people are to be taught, and to observe everything they have been taught. That is why He calls His teaching not so much teaching, but rather a commandment. "...Make disciples of all nations...teaching them to observe all that I have commanded you...." (Matthew 28:19).

From the very beginning divine revelation was first of all a commandment, a law, and its perfection would be realized only after the fulfilment of that law. Every law, although in itself it might be most perfect, remains mere theory if it has not yet been realized in practice and in the experience of life. Similarly, the whole of the teaching of divine revelation although in itself fulfilled and complete, attains its true realization only in being practised in life, being applied to life. Only in the practice of life does the teaching become that manifestation of God's glory and God's wisdom which it was intended both to be and to bring about. This manifestation is "...building up the body of Christ, until we all attain to the unity of faith and of the knowledge of the Son of God, to mature manhood, to the measure of the stature of the fullness of Christ" (Ephesians 4:12-13).

To the extent that the teaching revealed by God relates to the Kingdom of God, it has the nature of a plan that only upon completion will show the grandeur and beauty of the structure in its entirety. The whole power of the action of the Holy Spirit lies in the building of God's kingdom. In the course of that building His creative inspiration also develops.

Can we in any way call that creativity also a theology, and speak about a third -- the highest -- theology: the theology of the Christian life?

To answer this question we delve into Church teaching of the time when theology itself was evolving, and with it the concept of what the study of theology actually is. Among the theologians of the fourth century we find expressions which lead us to a wider or deeper understanding of theology rather than the specific concept of a scholarly discipline that theology assumes in our schools. For example, St. Athanasius speaks about the Holy Trinity as being *theologoumeni*; and about the heavenly Father, *Patir en Huio theologeite*. In Gregory of Nyssa we find the expression *theologein Christon*; in Gregory Nazianzen, *to Pneuma theologoumenon*. In John Chrysostom there is a juxtaposition of theology to economy. The first refers to the divine nature of Christ, the second to His human nature: *"Hoi men estrapsan tin ekonomiam, ho de (Ioannis) bronta tin theologian."*

If we define theology as the revelation and manifestation of God, then we must concede that God, responding to human recognition of Him, reveals Himself more in His works than in His words. The words of divine revelation, that is, the words which God has spoken, what He has said about Himself and what He teaches, are only a small part of what God tells humankind about Himself through His works. Divine revelation itself is just as simple.

When we look into the books of both the Old and New Testament, into that old and new theology as Theodoret put it, we recognize God more from His works than from His words. Men who are inspired by the Holy Spirit tell us most of all about the works of God; that is, the Holy Spirit grants us to know God through His works: those manifestations of His nature. In other words, the Holy Spirit presents to us the building of God's kingdom which began with the Creation.

As concerns the building of Christ's kingdom in that perhaps more specific sense in which the Apostle Paul speaks of the building of the Body of Christ, it must be concluded that the books of the New Testament, aside from teaching doctrine and theory, also tell of that building. That work of building was Christ's whole life. Even after His Resurrection those of His acts which were recorded as well as those that remain unrecorded, again relate to that building.

Divine Providence so willed that both the books of the New Testament and New Testament revelation itself, also not end with the earthly life or even the Resurrection of Christ. The New Testament tells us about how the Apostles and disciples set about that work of building and how they carried it out.

A marvellous conjunction of very rare and interesting

circumstances have as a result that the books, inspired by the Holy Spirit, give us a striking picture of what the building of Christ's kingdom was for one of the greatest, if not the greatest, Apostles -- St. Paul. In this way the example of a living person is drawn into the sphere of God's revealed teaching. That person amid difficult struggles builds Christ's kingdom both in his soul and in his body, or if we prefer to put it more specifically, prepares one brick, or rather "a stone" for that edifice (1 Peter 2:5-6).

The first, the original, revelation ended with the death of the last of the Apostles. We should rather say here, not with the last of the Twelve but the last of the seventy or seventy-two [apostles]. Then the well of that, so to speak, official Church -- because given to the Church -- "divine revelation" in which was gathered everything that God had declared through His Son (Hebrews 1:2) and through the Son's Apostles was emptied. The work of building which the Apostles had just undertaken obviously did not end with the termination or closing off of that particular revelation. After all, that work consisted, and still consists, in preparing and dressing those stones, "...like living stones be yourselves built into a spiritual house" (1 Peter 2:5), which will be completed only with the Second Coming, the *parousia*, of Christ will consist.

It is self-evident that the revelation of God's glory is to be evident not only at the beginning of this task, but throughout the whole task to its very completion. Therefore it is equally self-evident that, although necessarily maintaining the difference between original revelation and the fulfilment of that revelation in the Church, only the whole taken together will be that theology which presents everything about Himself that God has imparted or will impart to His creation.

Then, without a doubt, it is right to differentiate between the three theologies; of which one is more complete than another, where one rises above another to found the great teaching about God.

The first theology is that of our own theological schools. The second is the theology of divine revelation in the stricter sense of the word; that is, of the Holy-Spirit-inspired books of the Old and New Testament and of Christian Tradition. The third is the theology that envelops the whole of what God reveals about Himself to His creatures, conveying revelation through the Prophets and His Son, and fulfilling this revelation through the action of the Holy Spirit.

In the first theology we, the people, are called only to

confirmation of the fact and content of original revelation.

In the second theology, through a marvellous and almost incomprehensible imperative of the Divine will, we are called to be God's helpers in making known the teaching, in proclaiming and conveying to the people the divine truths through God's name.

In the third theology, all of us (not as in the preceding ones -- where some are chosen by divine Providence), inspired by the Holy Spirit are called upon to erect altars to Him, first of all in ourselves and then in our fellows.

The first theology corresponds to the intellectual acts of observing and confirming; the second, to the act understanding; and, the third, to the act of creative and independent thinking.

THE THEOLOGY OF LOVE

In the twelfth chapter of his First Epistle to the Corinthians, the Apostle Paul presents his teaching on the spiritual gifts granted for the good of the Church. He awakens the faithful to the desire of God's incomprehensible and heavenly gifts: among them the gift of prophecy, the gift of wisdom, and the gift of working miracles. Then he veers off into another direction so suddenly that, surpassing all expectation, it cannot but create astonishment in us.

It is as if, above his readers, he has opened heaven, and has made them direct participants of the Holy Spirit. Suddenly he begins a new mighty melody more lofty by a whole heaven than everything that hitherto was to be found in his song. Now in an inspiration which puts into his mouth poetic images and forms and even a heavenly rhythm, which can be discerned despite the most inept translation, he intones a song of praise.

This is the most majestic passage, or one of the most majestic, in all of the New Testament. This is the Apostle's song of love, a New Testament *Song of Songs*. Its words are so arranged that the discernible poetic inspiration reveals the spiritual ecstasy in which St. Paul wrote those words. They represent the peak of Christian ethics, "the fulfilling of the law" (Romans 13:10) and a binding together of "everything in perfect harmony" (Colossians 3:14).

All is presented in such a wonderful and magnificent form that this passage simply shines with heavenly light and of all the passages in the Holy Scriptures calls most attention to itself. The Apostle spoke justly when he said of himself that Christ spoke in him. The words of that song are distinctly the words of Christ, Christ glorified -- words spoken from heaven after the resurrection for the comfort, lifting up, and joy of humankind.

Those words of Christ are as high as heaven, as wide as all the worlds, as profound as the greatest of God's mysteries. Having those words as something to be repeated, even without attempting to explain them, one is seized with the urge to kneel and through intense prayer to receive God's wisdom so that we "may have the power to comprehend with all the saints what is the breadth and length and height and depth, and to know the love of Christ which surpasses knowledge" (Ephesians 3:18-19).

When we speak of love it is obviously the love of Christ of which we speak.

Faced with such words of Christ in His glory, it becomes evident how necessary the guidance of the Holy Spirit is so that the words inspired by the Holy Spirit might at least in part, at least superficially, at least a little, be understood. Who after all has comprehended the limitless depths of God's teaching if not the Holy Spirit alone who knows that "which is of God" and "searches everything, even the depths of God" (1 Corinthians 2:10)?!

That song is as follows:

If I speak in the tongues of men and of angels, but have not love, I am a noisy gong or a clanging cymbal. And if I have prophetic powers, and understand all mysteries and all knowledge, and if I have all faith, so as to remove mountains, but have not love, I am nothing. If I give away all I have, and if I deliver my body to be burned, but have not love, I gain nothing.

Love is patient and kind; love is not jealous or boastful; it is not arrogant or rude. Love does not insist on its own way; it is not irritable or resentful; it does not rejoice at wrong, but rejoices in the right.

Love bears all things, believes all things, hopes all things, endures all things. Love never ends; as for prophecies, they will pass

194

away; as for tongues, they will cease; as for knowledge, it will pass away...

So faith, hope, love abide, these three: but the greatest of these is love (1 Corinthians 13:1-9, 13).

"Make love your aim" (1 Corinthians 14:1) is the path which the Apostle has shown to the faithful, a path higher than the gift of miracles and the gift of prophecies, higher than all wisdom and knowledge. In what is it higher? It is obviously higher in that it builds the Body of Christ *more* than do prophecy or the gift of miracles the whole of whose creative power is bound up with building the Body of Christ. All of revelation, all of Christ's teaching, and the entire Church have only one fundamental goal: to build the Body of Christ.

If the prophetic inspiration of the Holy Spirit produces the most lofty radiance in both human and divine theology, then inspiration from heaven is itself the creative power of that loftiest theology which is the most immediate preparation for the happiness of seeing God.

That *peak of theology*, that peak of all knowledge of divine revelation, given in Sacred Scripture or apart from Sacred Scripture -- by Christ and the Apostles -- and given in many centuries by the Holy Spirit through the confirming, expounding, and most of all the fulfilling of divine revelation is -- ***love of God and of others***. Of all the wonderful miracles of the song of Christ, which Paul repeats, this love is the most marvellous miracle of miracles. St. John expresses these two virtues with the one and same word because before God they are the one and same virtue. "God is love, and he who abides in love [for others] abides in God, and God abides in him" (1 John 4:16).

We would perhaps be led too far if we thought to present the whole power of that love which builds the Body of Christ. To show it we would possibly have to speak of the participation of love in the whole of spiritual life as well as about what spiritual life is both in the work itself and in the history of humankind's salvation.

When lecturing in courses dealing with the spiritual life, usually called ascetic or mystic theology, because one suitable term that would cover both was lacking, I searched with difficulty for a condensed brief designation of the spiritual life and for the study of that life. I found it in the phrase: *theology in souls*.

In order to exhaust this subject it would probably be necessary to present the whole of theology and all of its history and evolution from early times. However, so that this theology in souls, this creative theology of the Holy Spirit, might be presented only partly, I will compare three aspects or three stages in the workings of the Holy Spirit.

THE CREATIVE,
THE PROPHETIC THEOLOGY OF THE HOLY SPIRIT

When in the beginning God created heaven and earth, and darkness covered the deep, God's Spirit moved over the face of the waters. Thus did God manifest His intention regarding the whole of creation. God's Spirit was to animate the darkness of matter, illuminate it with a supra-natural light and draw it into the sphere of God's life. Matter was to be not only a manifestation of the "eternal power and deity" for "...since the creation of the world his invisible nature...has been clearly perceived in the things that have been made" (Romans 1:20), but also to serve to manifest or reveal the supra-natural creativity of the Holy Spirit. This is why the creative word said over the waters "Let there be light" (Genesis 1:3) is a direct act of God's Spirit. That light, external and material, is only a prefiguring, a symbol and outer image of that light of the Spirit of God which was to illumine matter.

The grand plan of the Creator surpasses the understanding of the created. To put it in human language, the intended task is a whole heaven higher, more perfect, and more complex than this act of creation. The body, by its very own nature, is incapable either of understanding or receiving the Spirit. This truth is evident from the very beginning.

Creation, even when endowed with a mind and a free will, even when already enlightened by the supra-natural light of the Spirit, by the life grace, is still alien and weak in relation to the Holy Spirit. It falls away from Him almost immediately, becomes only a soul in a body with no understanding of the Spirit of God. From that moment in every way to "set the mind on the flesh is death" and "hostile to God" (Romans 8:6-7). "...It does not submit to God's law, indeed it cannot; and those who are in the flesh cannot please God" (8:7-8). This is the reason why humankind can say, together with Paul: "...I do not do the good I want, but the evil I do not want is what I do" because "...it is no longer I that do it, but sin which dwells within me" (Romans 7:19-20).

Many centuries of humankind's struggle and effort were needed,

196

supported by that Spirit which intends to gain for itself what has been created, before finally there could be found a creature sufficiently pure and holy to be able to fulfil God's intention. Then, as in the beginning, God's Spirit again moves over the one from among all humankind, and there sounds from heaven: "The Holy Spirit will come upon you, and the power of the Most High will overshadow you" (Luke 1:35). And through the working of the Holy Spirit, the measureless miracle of God's mercy and wisdom occurs; "and the Word became flesh" (John 1:14) so that in one Person of God the nature of God is inextricably bound with human nature. As once in the beginning "there was light" (Genesis 1:3), so now into the world comes "the true light that enlightens every man" (John 1:9). It enlightens every man because "God is light and in him is no darkness at all" (1 John 1:5).

Coming into the world, it seeks to enlighten every man so that every man "who follows me will not walk in darkness, but will have the light of life" (John 8:12). This, however, renders a judgment against humankind. "And this is the judgement, that the light has come into the world, and men loved darkness rather than light, because their deeds were evil" (John 3:19). "He was in the world, and the world was made through him, yet the world knew him not. He came to his own home, and his own people received him not" (John 1:10-11).

It had to be that the Son of God, sent into the world by God, should through arduous efforts and struggle ... grapple with darkness and in that battle "I lay down my life for the sheep" (John 10:15). The Son of God was bound, scourged, He was crowned with a crown of thorns, He was crucified on a cross. It might seem to people that darkness had conquered. But it had not triumphed, for God "raised Jesus Christ from the dead" and will perform an even greater miracle: He "will give life to your mortal bodies also through his Spirit" (John 8:11).

Once again, as "in the beginning" and in Nazareth, God's Spirit soars above humankind and in the form of fiery tongues descends upon the Apostles, "resting on each of them" (Acts 2:3). A new and the most laborious task is left for the Holy Spirit to fulfil. He must make spiritual the whole of humankind, a fleshly humankind, possessed of a soul, rebellious, a humankind which revels in darkness, torn by mutual jealousy, fratricidal struggle and wars, a humankind wallowing in a swamp of blood and filth. All of humankind must be made spiritual by God's Spirit.

There in Nazareth, through the miracle of divine wisdom and omnipotence, in Mary's pure and holy virginal womb was fulfilled the work of union of the human and divine nature in the divine Person of the Word. There, amid the mud and mire, amid the blood and darkness, must God's Spirit fulfil that miracle so that divine nature might be united with the human in the unity of the human person. It must repeat that miracle as many millions of times as there are millions of individuals who are to become stones in the building of Christ's kingdom, or members of Christ's mystical Body.

There in Nazareth, God's Spirit causes the Incarnation of the Son of God to take place, there the task of incarnation must be fulfilled and the incarnation of God's Word spread to all humankind. There through His action is to arise the mystical body of the man-God, Christ, whose soul is the Spirit of Christ. There the Most Pure Virgin becomes a communicant of the Holy Spirit, giving of Her flesh the substance of human flesh to the Word of God, in co-participation with the Holy Spirit, its creative inspiration, bearing the Son of God. There humankind, inspired by the Holy Spirit, becoming a communicant of that Spirit, gives of itself and together with the Holy Spirit creates or gives birth to the mystic body of God's Wisdom. Only through this is fulfilled the task intended "in the beginning", begun in Nazareth, and completely fulfilled in the new, heavenly, Jerusalem.

This account of the creative workings of the Holy Spirit in a vastly abbreviated form presents the majesty of God's work weakly and from an infinite distance. This work is being fulfilled in the course of long centuries, and we are the witnesses or beholders of that work. But we are more than witnesses. Being participants in the Holy Spirit which abides in us we are joint-creators in the work of the Holy Spirit and, inspired by Him, we are His helpers. We are helpers in the work of building the external structure of apostolic or pastoral labour or even in the work itself of love of others, helpers and participants in the work of building Christ's kingdom in the life of each of us separately.

Thus, even inspiration by the Holy Spirit is the creative prophetic work of the Spirit. The theology of the Holy Spirit is a privilege not reserved to exceptional geniuses, but open to the participation of all who love the Lord Jesus. This is because God's love, "poured into our hearts through the Holy Spirit which has been given to us" (Romans 5:5), is the highest and fullest means, the most perfect measure, of any inspiration of the Holy Spirit to perform the simple, everyday, humble good works of the Christian life.

Let no one think that because good deeds of Christian life consists of ordinary, simple, humble everyday matters, and because they may

198

often be performed by one who is little-educated, unsophisticated, and intellectually-undeveloped, that they are therefore not manifestations of God, more majestic and lofty than all prophesying, as long as they arise out of the inspiration of the Holy Spirit, which is also granted to the poor as well as the rich for humble tasks. Those simple tasks of Christian life, which the Holy Spirit inspires people to do, are always a manifestation of God and can be, or rather always are, a new manifestation, as yet unseen and unwitnessed; otherwise they would not have been the work of the Holy Spirit. If even only for their completion these tasks require the creative power of the Holy Spirit, then once they have been completed they must bear the imprint of that creative power. How can this be?

The teaching given by Christ -- the Holy Gospel -- possesses an infinite depth (otherwise it would not have been the work of the Word of God) which also reveals itself in the circumstance that one and the same teaching of the Holy Gospel can be a practice adapted to life in an infinite variety of ways.

The theory of the doctrine is divine but it has been translated into human speech and copied by humans, it can be replicated in millions of forms, each one of them different and new. All of them taken together not only do not exhaust the prototype but unceasingly assert its immeasurable depth. This must first of all be stated concerning the imitation of Christ.

People through a Christian life and by the inspiration of the Holy Spirit, greater or less depending on the degree of humility in each individual, limn an icon of Christ on their soul. Those who are in pastoral work and who preach the Gospel, that is they give birth to spiritual children, render such an icon also on the hearts of the faithful; for Christian life is an icon of Christ. Every icon is the work of a man-God; that is, a human in whom God abides as a life-creating, vivifying, animating, guiding force in life.

Every icon is in some respect similar to the prototype, but no single icon exhausts the prototype. In His endless qualities, divine and human, Christ exceeds infinitely every human concept no matter to what extent it might be inspired by the Holy Spirit. That is why every icon can be so different, why it must be such a manifestation of infinity, why each icon is a true inspired theology in every sense of the word.

The slightest humble act of virtue done by the simplest of persons, but done because of God's love which has been poured into our

199

hearts by the Holy Spirit, is a loftier and a more complete theology than an entire most learned theological treatise. That is to say, the treatise in itself, leaving aside the merits of the one who wrote it and regardless of the influence of what is written there on human souls.

A treatise such as this, presented and understood as such, is not in itself the Spirit's creative inspiration. On the other hand, however, an act of love in the soul of a person, no matter how uneducated that person might be, is indeed the creative and inspired work of the Holy Spirit.

ACKNOWLEDGEMENT

The Publisher gratefully acknowledge the financial support, without which the Project could not have been brought to fruition, of the following:

W.W. Hrynyk Foundation, Toronto

A. Sheptytsky Council 5079, Knights of Columbus, Toronto

Ukrainian Catholic Church of Christ the King, London

Ukrainian Catholic Church of St. Mary's Dormition, Mississauga

St. Mary's (Toronto) Credit Union Limited

Ukrainian Catholic Brotherhood of Canada
        National Executive, Winnipeg
        Holy Spirit Branch, Hamilton
        St. Mary's Dormition Branch, Mississauga
        St. Nicholas Branch, Toronto

Ukrainian Catholic Women's League of Canada
        St. Basil the Great Branch, Toronto
        St. Josaphat Branch, Toronto
        St. Nicholas Branch, Toronto

Zenia & Omelan Chabursky, Toronto

Eugene Chorostil, Woodstock

Daria & Myroslaw Diakowsky, Toronto

Petro Jacyk, Mississauga

Kateryna & Hryhorij Swerhun, Toronto

Metropolitan Andrei Sheptytsky returning from Russian imprisonment, Railway Station Vienna, July 26, 1917.

**Metropolitan Andrei Sheptytsky
with Ukrainian scouts, Pidliute, 1928.**

Metropolitan Andrei Sheptytsky with children, Lviv, 1933.

Metropolitan Andrei Sheptytsky durin his visit to Canada, Basilian Fathers monastery, Mundare, Alberta, October 1921.

Bishop Nykyta Budka and Metropolitan Sheptytsky
in Canada, 1922.